Hurt

The publisher and the University of California Press Foundation gratefully acknowledge the generous support of the Barbara S. Isgur Endowment Fund in Public Affairs.

Hurt

CHRONICLES OF THE DRUG
WAR GENERATION

Miriam Boeri

UNIVERSITY OF CALIFORNIA PRESS

University of California Press, one of the most distinguished university presses in the United States, enriches lives around the world by advancing scholarship in the humanities, social sciences, and natural sciences. Its activities are supported by the UC Press Foundation and by philanthropic contributions from individuals and institutions. For more information, visit www.ucpress.edu.

University of California Press
Oakland, California

© 2018 Miriam Boeri

Library of Congress Cataloging-in-Publication Data

Names: Boeri, Miriam, author.
Title: Hurt : chronicles of the drug war generation / Miriam Boeri.
Description: Oakland, California : University of California Press, [2017] |
    Includes bibliographical references and index.
Identifiers: LCCN 2017026656| ISBN 9780520293465 (cloth : alk. paper) |
    ISBN 9780520293472 (pbk. : alk. paper) | ISBN 9780520966710 (e-edition)
Subjects: LCSH: Drug abuse—Social aspects—United States. | Baby boom
    generation—United States.
Classification: LCC HV5825 .B615 2017 | DDC 362.2092/273—dc23
LC record available at https://lccn.loc.gov/2017026656

To all who work to end the war on drugs
and start social recovery

CONTENTS

ACKNOWLEDGMENTS

This book would not have been written if it were not for my brother, Harry Stephen Williams. I want to thank him for protecting me when I was young, teaching me how to fight and not be afraid in tough situations, and giving me the empathy and insight needed for the kind of ethnographic research I do and love.

Next I must thank Thor Whalen, the mathematician and data scientist who took time to work with a sociologist as a co-investigator, and with patient collaboration and ingenuity created an innovative mixed methodology of data collection that allowed the incredible life stories of 100 baby boomers to be collected with such veracity, intimacy, and depth.

It would have been difficult if not impossible to have conducted this study without grant support from the National Institute of Drug Abuse (NIDA), an agency in the National Institutes of Health (NIH), which funded the Older Drug User Study (ODUS). I thank the Program Official, Jeffrey D. Schulden, for suggesting our proposal for funding from the American Recovery and Reinvestment Act of 2009. Without the additional money provided by this act after the Recession of 2008, the many people temporarily employed during this study might have remained jobless.

I thank all the members of the research team, starting with the core research assistants, Ben Tyndall (now Dr. Tyndall), David Gibson, and Craig Rafuse, who spent three years working day and night to ensure the stories were collected, transcribed, and analyzed respectfully, ethically, and honestly. Other consultants, students, and former students who helped at different times throughout the study period include Paul Boshears, Terry Carmon, James Costen, Mark Flanagan, Verna Gaines, Sarah Ghoeler, Jan Morian, and Denise Woodall—I thank you all and appreciate the time we worked together.

Two people deserve special thanks and credit for assuming the role of my academic parents: Claire Sterk and Kirk Elifson believed in my ability to conduct street-level fieldwork among marginalized drug users and became my role models and mentors. I am forever indebted to their skillful training and will always value their friendship.

My academic career started late in my life, and without the help, guidance, and support of the faculty at Georgia State University's Sociology Department while I was in graduate school as a single mother on food stamps, I would have never have finished my PhD. In retrospect, they were kinder to me than I deserved. Thank you Dawn Baunach, Elizabeth Burgess, Phil Davis, Denise Donnelly, Charles Jaret, Toshi Kii, Donald Reitzes, Wendy Simonds, Frank J. Whittington, and an inspirational pioneer of women in academia, the unforgettable Jackie Boles.

Also contributing to my understanding of sociological, historical, and public health issues that made this study successful were my colleagues at Kennesaw State University, including Sam Abaidoo, Judy Brown-Allen, Melvyn Fein, Darina Lepadatu, Tanja Link, Jennifer MacMahon-Howard, Rebecca Petersen, and Linda Treiber in the Sociology and Criminal Justice Department; Annette Bairan and Barbara Blake from the Nursing School; Mark Patterson and Nancy Pullen in the Geography and Anthropology Department; and David Jones and Tom Pynn in the Philosophy Department. I am enormously appreciative of the Vice President of Research, Charles Amlaner, and his devoted staff, who worked tirelessly on grant-making processes.

Tim Anderson, Tony Buono, Gary David, Angela Garcia, Anne Warfield Rawls, and Jonathan White welcomed me to the Sociology Department at Bentley University in the cold northeastern state of Massachusetts, and I want to thank them and the Dean of Arts and Sciences, Daniel L. Everett, for their continued support. I also thank Susan Starr Sered, at Suffolk University, who shared her insights on the homeless situation in Massachusetts. The Boston area, with its elite academic status, is a hard place to land as a lonely researcher, and other than Susan, my collaborators in Massachusetts have been mainly nonacademics activists working toward ending the War on Drugs, whose names I will not list for anonymity reasons. They know who they are, and I hope they understand how much I appreciate their warm embrace as the newcomer on the scene.

My list of academics to thank for contributing to my success as a scholar would not be complete without mentioning those who encouraged me personally or who befriended me at academic conferences where I sometimes felt like an outsider, especially Ellen Benoit, Philippe Bourgois, David Broad, Melissa Fry, Andy Golub, Michael Hodge, Charles Kaplan, Mansa King, Janja Lalich, Aukje Lamonica, Karen McElrath, J. Bryan Page, Polly Radcliffe, Craig Reinarman, Rashi Shukla, Merrill Singer, Rebecca Tiger, Avelardo Valdez (Lalo), Anne Whittaker, and Tony Zschau. I also thank my fellow sociologists who are bridging the academic/practitioner divide by supporting the Association for Applied and Clinical Sociology, including Anthony Troy Adams, Karen Albright, Gina Castillo, Augusto Diano, Marilyn Dyck, Michael Fleischer, Michael Hirsch, Robert Kettlitz, Megan Klohr, James Lee, Melodye Lehnerer, Alison Marganski, Sonji Nicholas, Lubo Popov, Jammie Price, Stephen Steele, Kathy Stolley, Jim Weist, Norma Winston, Newman Wong, and all members of this organization who are applying sociological insights to help make society a kinder and better place.

The devoted fieldworkers at the Atlanta Harm Reduction Center who allowed me to use their humble home for interviews, particularly Mona, will forever have my gratitude and admiration for the care they provide every day to the most neglected of the drug user population.

I am appreciative of Maura Roessner, Senior Editor at the University of California Press, for her enthusiastic support of my manuscript, and the promotional and editorial staff for their help. I also thank the anonymous reviewers for their brilliant suggestions and encouraging comments on earlier drafts.

I want to acknowledge my daughter, Atlanta Boeri, for writing the prologue and epilogue in a captivating style with a crime-story flair that makes the beginning and ending of this book memorable. My husband, Michael Brooks, and my five children and their partners deserve appreciation for answering my eccentric requests for their opinions and views on offbeat topics related to this book. Thank you for being so kind and so smart. And without mentioning her name, I enthusiastically thank the mother of an opioid-addicted son "on the run" for reading the first drafts of this book and alerting me that if I want people like those I interviewed to benefit from these stories, I need to make the book more readable and jargon-free. Academic writing sometimes veils authentic existence with dense abstract intellectualism, which ethnographic writing strives to avoid. After her honest comments, I rewrote the chapters while keeping the faces of the people I interviewed in mind. I hope they approve of the manner in which I presented their precious life stories.

PROLOGUE

1989, LANCASTER COUNTY JAIL

*They gave me 30 years. Over a quarter century. How did this happen? I didn't
have a weapon. I never used a weapon. All the bank tellers said I treated them
with respect except for one. I wouldn't call her a liar, but she misunderstood or
was coerced into saying she felt threatened. I don't even blame my friend who
snitched on me. She was scared on the witness stand. I could see it in her face.
She wouldn't even look at me. Who knows what they said to scare her—what
lies and intimidation.*

"Harry, Harry!"

*My eyes refocused in the dim room. My cigarette lay smoking on a can of
Coke. Their way of appeasing me since I had something they wanted. I enjoyed
the cig. The Coke, not really, but they wouldn't give me a beer.*

*"So . . . where is it?" the ranking officer said between clenched teeth. It was
not his normal demeanor to "say" anything. He usually barked orders and
growled questions. I called him Sergeant Gruff. I had something they wanted.*

*They gave me 30 years. That was already set in stone—three strikes and you're
out! I appealed of course, but I wasn't holding my breath. I would take any excuse
to be on the outside even for a day, as long as it did not involve snitching.*

*They were interested in the thousands of dollars still at large from my last
bank robbery. And I knew where it was hidden.*

*The next day I found myself tightly locked and chained in the back of a cop
car with Sergeant Gruff and another cop driving. My mind enjoyed the hum of
the tires on asphalt, a sound I could hear only outside the walls of the jail. I tried
to block the thought of the years of silent and lonely prison nights ahead of me,
and savor the sights and sound of relative freedom as we rolled out of town.*

"Turn left up here at the next road," I said, when I saw we were in Pequea. The cabin where we lived as kids for a few months was off the beaten track. It could hardly be called a cabin—it was more of a hunter's shack even when we lived there, with limited indoor plumbing and spotty electricity. Gruff believed me when I said it's where I hid my stash of money—the money they were after.

After a half hour of driving down a winding dirt and graveled road, we finally crunched to a stop. The cabin was where I remembered it. A shadow of itself—faded siding, peeling roof, and broken windows. It was up on the side of a gorge, slightly sloped on our side, but acutely steep on the backside. A small muddy creek cut down the side. Usually it flowed, but with the drought it was almost empty. I knew the pond where I was taking them would be muddy, if it was still there.

I unfolded my tall, lanky body from the back of the car. My joints cracked as I stretched. I pondered how much more they would crack the next time I would be getting out of a car many years from now.

"I have to take you up that hill to the pond," I said, pointing in the direction I remembered. "I can't do that with these cuffs." They took the cuffs off my legs but refused to unlock the handcuffs.

Ten minutes later we were out of the view of the street below. The pond was exactly where I thought it would be, reeking with sulfur-smelling mud. "It's in a metal box in there somewhere, on the left bank. You're lucky the water is low again." I could tell from their crinkled noses and furrowed brows they didn't feel too lucky.

"I guess you're gonna get a bit dirty," I said with a slight smile. "I'd love to help but . . ." I held up my cuffed hands. I knew they wouldn't free me. Fuck them.

They removed their shoes and socks, rolled up their pants, and gingerly stepped in. I watched as they sloshed around reacting to my intentionally terrible directions.

"No, to the left. Now around the root of that tree. Wait, try to the right. You don't feel a big rock?"

I couldn't help but crack a small smile watching them slosh through the smelly mud. Why? 'Cause the money wasn't there. It was never there. Yeah, at some point it was hidden in the cabin, but that particular stash was long gone for dope and debts.

Sergeant Gruff was watching me closely. As soon as he turned his eyes, I took the opportunity and started to run down the gorge. I struggled to stay upright. The slope was steeper than I remembered. Being cuffed didn't help. The trees were almost bare, offering little concealment. I turned my head to see how far away they were and slam—I ran into a tree trunk and lost consciousness.

I awoke cuffed and chained on the ground, blood from where I hit my head
still streaming down my face. Sargent Gruff was standing above me, muddy,
sweaty and stinking. I could feel his anger.
  "So . . . want to try again tomorrow?" I asked.
  "Enjoy the Hole, motherfucker!"

2009, PHILADELPHIA COMMUNITY COLLEGE

The Hole

When first given this assignment I knew that I had a plethora of experiences to choose from. Crimes, overdoses, deaths, poverty, anger, despair. I chose to relate the story that I have often told, an especially traumatic event in my life that ranged over a period of six years. The reason that I picked this story was to raise awareness of the draconian measures that the state is willing to take to enforce its anti-drug policies.

It was the mid-90s. I was in prison in Huntingdon, PA. The political climate at the time was such that the punishment for a dirty urine for marijuana had just been downgraded to cell restriction. That meant that if a prisoner was detected with marijuana in his system, he could stay in his cell in population, as opposed to going to the much more oppressive RHU, or restrictive housing unit, or, in layman's terms, "the hole."

That changed abruptly in 1995 when Tom Ridge took office as governor of PA. One of his first appointments was Martin Horn, a former head of the New York Parole Board. Governor Ridge appointed Horn as Director of Corrections, which made him the final arbiter of all state prison policy in Pennsylvania.

Horn immediately implemented a zero tolerance policy for drugs in PA state prisons. This policy, and the vigor with which it was enforced, actually had an eventual effect on drug trafficking and use across the state. Within one year, many had stopped or curtailed their use significantly. This was due partly to the much more severe consequences of dirty urines and partly because of the lowered availability. The lowered availability was partly a result of new laws, which made introduction of drugs into a PA prison a felony, and which mandated jail time for a first-time conviction.

The more severe consequences for the dirty urines went basically like this. A first dirty urine: sixty days in the hole, loss of contact visits for six months, a bottom-level clearance for jobs, programs, and housing, six months of weekly urine testing, followed by six months of monthly urine tests. A second dirty urine: ninety days in the hole, urine testing, and loss of contact visits for one year. A third and all future dirty urines: ninety days in the hole, urine tests, and loss of contact visits forever. This last seemed a particularly cruel sanction.

There are thousands of lifers in PA prisons. In PA, life means life. You get out when you die. Many of these lifers are teenagers who are more prone to drug use and the resulting sanctions. As a result, these teens, after their third dirty, became people who would never be able to touch a loved one again.

My situation was somewhat different. I had light at the end of the tunnel. I reached my third dirty fairly quickly. I was an avid drug user and sanctions had little effect on me, especially since I often had the opportunity to use while I was in the hole.

For the next five years I never managed to spend more than two weeks at a time in general population. I ended up spending the next five years in the hole, mostly for pot, before being transferred to a Special Management Unit in Camp Hill where I spent another year. Upon my release to general population in Camp Hill I found that there were seldom any drugs available and I managed to stay clean long enough to eventually make parole. The extreme sanctions that I endured for smoking pot had the effect of creating a lot of resentment, which I suspect I will always have.

Harry

Introduction

AFTER RELEASE FROM PRISON, Ted stopped all drugs but alcohol and became an alcoholic. When his third DUI landed him more time in jail, he and his wife lost their house. He began to use heroin again. When he stopped "cold turkey," the pain in his stomach came back. It was an unbearable pain, but doctors could not find a cause or a cure. Ted tried to drink it away.

> I tried to keep alcohol down as much as I could. That was the only thing that would help my stomach from hurting. Finally, I told my wife, "You better call 911." I took a steak knife and pushed it right where the pain was. The reason I did it was because I didn't want the pain in my stomach anymore. I wanted it to go away. If it didn't kill me then I was praying when I got to the hospital they could figure out what the hell was wrong with me. Somebody could fix something so I wouldn't have the pain anymore.

Ted is just one of the many baby boomers I interviewed who used drugs illegally to address physical, psychological, or emotional suffering while living under increasingly more punitive responses to drug use.

This book chronicles the lives of baby boomers who lived through a 45-year-long drug war while using what are considered "hard drugs" (heroin / opioids, methamphetamine, cocaine / crack).[1] They come from all socioeconomic classes and walks in life. They are diverse racially and ethnically and reveal different patterns of drug use behaviors. Some started using drugs early; others are late-onset. Most show discontinuous trajectories of using, stopping, and starting use again. Ages ranged from 45 to 65. All used hard drugs in the last 10 years and over half were still using hard drugs at the time they were interviewed. The in-depth examination of their individual drug use trajectories shows how the social environment contributed to their drug behaviors, and the life course analysis reveals the devastating result of drug policy that incarcerates while ignoring social conditions.

For example, Ingrid, orphaned by her parents, ran away from her abusive foster family and was introduced to heroin by a group of petty criminals who accepted her in their circle. Her first sexual experience was with a police officer: "He picked me up on the corner and made me believe that he was taking me to jail . . . I've been in jail more than I can count." Most of her arrests were for drug charges.

Likewise, Alicia, growing up in an inner-city community known for its open drug market, exchanged sex for drugs: "I done been in and out of jail a hundred times . . . I went to prison four times, because those are like an eighteen-month sentence, a nine-year sentence, then a two-year sentence, then an eleven-month sentence."

The demand for more prisoners to support a rapidly enlarging prison industrial complex led to a widespread increase in ethically questionable policing norms, such as the use of informants who snitched on friends to have their own charges dropped or a lighter sentence.[2] Solitary confinement, once reserved for the most dangerous criminals, became a commonly used strategy for exerting control over even the most benign prisoners.[3]

Elijah was caught in a sting operation that used his best friend as an informant: "I stopped dealing myself—but I didn't understand about informants. I thought friends was friends."

Similarly, Harry was first incarcerated as a juvenile for robbing a pharmacy for drugs based on the testimony of an adult informant who was an accomplice in the robbery. His last conviction, in which a 10-year sentence was added to a 20-year sentence, was set up by two informants. Harry spent most of his last five years of prison in solitary confinement.

Abel spent only four days in solitary confinement for marijuana possession, remembering the experience bitterly: "I can't believe in America that you can go from some crap-hole misdemeanor to being put in solitary confinement . . . Some people might not be as strong mentally and could suffer significantly from enduring something like." Solitary confinement in some prisons lasted for years.[4]

Informants and solitary confinement (the hole) became normal tactics used by the criminal justice system as the drug war escalated, fulfilling a chilling statement made in 1996 by General Barry R. McCaffrey, director of the Office of National Drug Control Policy (ONDCP): "We must have law enforcement authorities address the issue because if we do not, prevention, education, and treatment messages will not work very well. But having said that, I also believe that we have created an American gulag."[5]

People convicted for drug-related charges now make up the largest portion of the US prison population.[6] Moreover, due to international treaties, countries around the world enacted similar punitive policies.[7] Recently, some countries began experimenting with more humane responses, providing evidence that prevention, education, and treatment can work *without* incarceration.[8] Nevertheless, US drug policy has not changed, even while the number of US citizens with drug problems continues to increase.

The broad goal of this book is to understand drug use problems by examining drug users' lives at the intersection of race, gender, class, and age.[9] The life histories of baby boomer drug users help to unravel the dynamics of control and call attention to structural constraints implemented over time by US drug policies. Their drug trajectories set in social and historical context show that problematic drug use is dependent on time and place. The lives discussed in this book expose how the War on Drugs prolonged drug use at the individual level and expanded the drug problem at the national level.[10] We know that US drug policy failed to stop or decrease drug use.[11] The life stories of baby boomers provide critical insights on the impact of drug policy and support the argument that it is time to end this civil war and begin social reconstruction.

BABY BOOMER DRUG USERS AND THE MATURING OUT THESIS

The first baby boomers were born in 1946 and the last were born in 1964.[12] All of the people who are discussed in this book are baby boomers who continued to use hard drugs after age 35, which is the age when they should have matured out of drug use. This is important because the "maturing out thesis" proposed that users of narcotic drugs typically ceased taking drugs around age 35 or 36 when they learned to cope with the problems that caused drug use, became involved with families and careers, or simply tired of the drug-using lifestyle.[13] The "maturing out" thesis is based on research conducted in the 1960s.[14] The population studied at that time was the generation that *preceded* the baby boomers.

In 2000, the youngest baby boomers turned 36 years of age, which means they were now past the age when they should have matured out of drug use.

Although knowing the actual number of drug users is never possible, since they are a largely hidden population, data collected in longitudinal studies show trends in drug use and changes over time.[15] National trend data reveal that the baby boomer age group of drug users increased since 1979 as baby boomers aged, even while other age groups decreased in numbers during the same time period.[16] For example, longitudinal data collected by national surveys from 1979 to 2000 show that drug use for all age groups declined steadily *except* for the age group 35 and older.[17] As baby boomers aged, drug use among older adults continued to increase and older adults seeking treatment for drug use surged.[18]

It is now clear that many baby boomers did not follow the maturing out pattern of previous generations. We know that some individuals "matured in" drug use (never stopped using), while others "matured into" drug use (started late in life).[19] It is less obvious why.

THE IMPORTANCE OF SOCIAL AND HISTORICAL CONTEXT

The date that is most important for understanding baby boomer drug-using patterns is 1971—the year the War on Drugs was officially declared by President Nixon. By "War on Drugs" I am referring to the historical as well as the conceptual development of what has become the most influential force shaping drug policy *and* drug treatment in contemporary society.[20] Much like the prohibition of alcohol in the 1920s, the prohibition of drugs has been a disastrous failure.[21] The prohibition on alcohol lasted only 13 years before it was repealed. The War on Drugs has lasted 45 years and counting.

Baby boomers grew up and came of age during the start of the War on Drugs, making them the drug war generation. In 1971, the oldest boomers were 25 years old and the youngest were seven. The life stories of those who continued to use drugs during this time illustrate how drug war policy (not drug use) was the major cause for their pain, sorrow, social failures, and personal despair. I argue it was also the reason for their continued drug use past the age of maturing out.

We know that the War on Drugs drove incarceration rates in the United States to the highest in the world and contributed to the decline of the working class, the increase of single-parent families, and the devastation of minority communities.[22] Proof that the War on Drugs has failed to decrease drug use is shown by the increasing numbers of people arrested for drug possession over time,[23] and the expansion of drug trafficking globally, fueling crime and violence.[24] After years of punitive drug policy, drug overdose has become the leading cause of unintentional deaths.[25] Obviously, our current policies are not working toward controlling drug use.[26] In this book the voices of the people who suffered under the drug war policy provide contextualized evidence of a US landscape devastated by a civil war.[27]

MY STANDPOINT POSITION

Standpoint epistemology recognizes that all researchers have bias depending on their standpoint position, and that their beliefs or views are influenced by their race, gender, and class experience.[28] I am a White female. I have a PhD in Sociology, and I have studied drug users for over 20 years. As a sociologist, I believe my standpoint position is important. However, my current status in life provides little evidence of the background that led to my research interests.

I am the sister of Harry, whose story was introduced in the prologue. My older brother was a heroin addict and convicted felon who suffered under punitive drug laws. I consulted him often during the time I collected and analyzed the data for this study, incorporating his perspective to more accurately portray the lived reality of those in similar situations. My training and experience as an academic prepared me for conducting scientific research studies on drug users, but my insider knowledge as the sister of an incarcerated heroin user was critical to my understanding of the complex impact of the War on Drugs.

A BRIEF NOTE ON METHODOLOGY

The people discussed in this book were drawn from a study examining the life stories of 100 baby boomers.[29] One hundred lives were too unwieldly to include for a narrative portrayal of the findings, but the 38 lives discussed in this book illustrate the themes found in the experiences of all. They lived in Atlanta, Georgia, and its suburbs at the time of the interview.[30] They were diverse in terms of race, gender, and socioeconomic status. Educational attainment ranged from advanced college degrees to less than a high school education. Some owned their own houses, many lived in precarious housing situations, and a few were homeless. Although none lived in residential treatment when interviewed, all had been in drug treatment multiple times—most relapsed repeatedly. Except for my brother, all names are pseudonyms.[31]

I used ethnographic methods to find the people interviewed for this study and to learn more about their environment.[32] This involved hanging out with the people I interviewed and engaging with their lives, such as driving them on errands or to appointments, helping them find needed resources, and answering their calls in the middle of the night.[33] As a qualitative researcher, I was trying to make sense of the world from their perspectives and not impose my views on them.[34] The narrative approach used in this book does not hide the hopes and anguish they expressed.[35] My analytical self-reflection does not conceal my compassion.

Focused on the everyday details of people's lives, I incorporated a life course perspective to examine their *entire* life histories within the social, cultural, and political landscapes of the period, while noting individual situational changes over time and place.[36] Their stories are filled with personal problems, and it is easy to blame the individual. But the analysis of their lives over time reveals how policy, culture, and social context intersect at every period of their lives, sometimes creating their problems, at other times shaping how the problems are viewed and addressed.[37]

ORGANIZATION OF BOOK

Each chapter introduces a new life story with richly detailed description to illustrate themes that are discussed and evolve in subsequent chapters. As these themes are developed, they are supported with snapshots of other life stories drawn from the sample. Many of the people introduced in one chapter are referenced in later chapters, illuminating different themes and reflecting the reality of multifaceted lives.

Harry's story is revisited in each chapter with a more detailed and intimate account of his life, providing contextual depth and continuity beyond the main narratives. I was in contact with Harry almost daily throughout the three years that I conducted the research on baby boomers. When I talked with the respondents, or read their interviews, I was constantly reminded of a piece of Harry's story, a recent event in his life, or the challenges that Harry was facing. Sometimes this brought a smile to my face, as I realized their life story was similar to my brother's; sometimes it spurred me to action when

I felt morally obligated to help them in the ways that I was helping my brother. More than a few times I cried when I understood the hopelessness of their situation, their limited opportunities, and the consequences they would suffer for using drugs to cope with pain, boredom, or despair. But I stubbornly (and perhaps selfishly) insisted that this would not be the fate of my brother.

Chapter 1 focuses on the social, political, and historical context of baby boomer lives. Drug use did not happen in a social vacuum. Divorce was on the rise, yet no structures were in place to help single-parent households. Working-class jobs with livable wages virtually disappeared with the deindustrialization of American work and rising restrictions on unions. The American dream of achieving middle-class status was vanishing. This chapter begins to examine how changes in the social landscape impacted drug trajectories.

Chapter 2 discusses life course theory, a framework used to view lives over time in historical context, with a focus on transitions and turning points in drug user trajectories. A life course analysis of drug users from the baby boomer generation shows that drug trajectories were not developmental but instead discontinuous (interrupted) phases that were dependent on social context and situations that changed over time. It questions the belief that problematic drug use stems from a lack of individual self-control, and suggests instead that informal social control mechanisms are more important for controlling drug use behaviors.

Chapter 3 covers the domain of family and personal relationships, which are the emotional foundation of a meaningful social life. Social capital theory is introduced to highlight the importance of relationships that generate trust and provide access to needed resources. Incarceration, unemployment, and social stigma weaken bonds with family, partners, and other relations, and limit opportunities to connect to mainstream society. While focused on micro-level relationships, the analysis includes the impact of macro-level relations between social institutions. The stories in this chapter show the need to examine the social situations of problematic drug users in terms of their social ties and access to resources, as well as social structures that can provide opportunities or constrain their choices.

Chapter 4 delves deeper into the epic impact of the War on Drugs on the baby boomer generation, including mass incarceration and the disappearance of eligible and legally employed young men, which particularly impacted minority communities. The chapter provides examples of ethically questionable strategies used by law enforcement, such as the confidential informant (CI) to ensnare the most vulnerable, and solitary confinement for the management of an overcrowded prison population of drug users. It shows how drug policies turned experimenting adolescents and functional adult users into lifelong drug users, hardened criminals, and an underclass of disenfranchised citizens who faced barriers to housing, employment, education, job training, or any means of legally supporting themselves.

Chapter 5 examines race and ethnicity embedded in the social, economic, and political landscapes of baby boomers from birth to older age. The link between the War on Drugs and the "New Jim Crow" is illustrated in the narratives of baby boomers of color.[38] The stories of baby boomers who used crack contextualize historical phenomena, such as the so-called crack epidemic and its impact on Black communities.[39] Their life stories provide evidence of entrenched structural racism and discrimination, even among agencies designed to address these disparities. The focus on their everyday reality reveals themes of adaptation to the structural constraints and situational context of their lives over time by creating strategies to survive and meaning to believe in.

Chapter 6 discusses women who use drugs and their stigmatization in both mainstream society and drug-using networks. All of the women in this sample suffered rape, molestation, violent abuse, or other traumatic experiences. While their social roles, such as partner or mother, were sources of strength, they could also be sources of stigma and shame when they were not able to fulfill these roles to the standards of conventional society. The influence of relationships, pregnancy, motherhood, and aging on drug use trajectories, when viewed in situational context, exposes gendered barriers to recovery.

Chapter 7 focuses on baby boomers as they age through periods of deindustrialization, suburbanization, recurrent recessions, and increasingly punitive drug policies. Already socially isolated from mainstream society due to their drug use, aging increases their marginalization and feelings of hopelessness. As baby boomers near retirement, more resources are needed to address the social and health problems of aging incarcerated drug users and those who have spent many years of their lives behind bars, unable to work toward Social Security benefits. This chapter reviews the varied routes to controlling drug use as they aged, achieved abstinence, and relapsed, supporting the view that maturing out of drug use was hindered by the War on Drugs.

Chapter 8 discusses the expansion of the prison industrial complex during the lifetime of baby boomers and critically examines the emergence of alternatives to incarceration that include drug courts and coerced drug treatment. As the prison industrial complex lost popular support, the criminal justice system began merging with a new "treatment industrial complex," keeping the control of drug users within the ambit of law enforcement.[40] The discussion of treatment philosophies in this chapter reveals that while the social environment is recognized as an influential factor of problematic drug use, it is rarely addressed in treatment models that continue to focus primarily on changing the individual.

Chapter 9 discusses the implications of the previous chapters and provides insights on new approaches to drug use and workable solutions for drug use problems outside the criminal justice system. Political decisions made by powerful special interest groups destroyed the lives of those with less power, creating a bleak social landscape of desolate communities, broken families, and ruined lives, and transforming the American dream into the American nightmare. A reconstruction of this landscape needs more focused attention on social context and community resources. "Social Recovery" is suggested as a conceptual alternative to "abstinence only" treatment models and a needed component of treatment for problem drug use.[41]

The Epilogue ends the book by bringing Harry's story up-to-date. The in-depth personal details of his life provide a fuller understanding of the impact of social context and the ultimate consequences of punitive responses to drug use. The similarities between Harry's experiences and those of other baby boomers discussed in this book highlight the urgent need for a paradigm shift.

The Appendix includes the details of the Older Drug User Study (ODUS), the research study that provided the data for this book. It describes the mixed methods design used in the study, the strategies developed to assess trajectory discontinuity, and the data visualization images created to illustrate dynamic relations between drug use and social variables. The potential of these novel methods to distinguish between problematic and nonproblematic drug use, to identify influences on drug use behaviors at the individual level, and to target treatment where needed is proposed as a promising area for future research.

ONE

The Historical and Social Context

TED

Ted was 56 years old when I interviewed him in his home. He lived in a working-class suburban neighborhood in a crowded townhouse that he shared with his wife, adult children, and a boarder. Ted was on a methadone program, and although his life was relatively stable at this time, his thin, gaunt, and worry-lined face hinted that stability was a recent situation. His sunken cheeks were one indicator of long-term heroin use, and his sad, suffering eyes suggested someone who had returned from hell.

We conducted the interview in a converted basement room furnished with a sofa bed and overstuffed chairs. The furniture was too large for the space and our knees touched when I sat down on one of the chairs. I took out my study materials—a consent form, a small digital recorder, and a timeline tool to help Ted remember the exact years of the events he was about to recount.[1] While I was explaining the timeline to Ted, I noticed the fairly distinguishable lines of a tattoo on his arm where the old ink had bled together. The past and present became blurred like the tattoo ink as Ted revealed the historical details that still impacted him today.

He had been married to his wife for over 28 years. They were both using heroin when their children were taken by social services. Both were in a methadone program now. Ted's married life was not completely encompassed by drug use. Like many baby boomers who started using drugs at a young age, his drug trajectory showed more discontinuity than continuity—a pattern that did not support a developmental model of drug use.[2]

Ted started huffing glue and smoking cigarettes at age 10; in a few years he added alcohol, marijuana, heroin, and pharmaceuticals. His problematic drug use started with prescription medication. Convincing a doctor to pre-scribe pills was easy in the 1960s. In his early teens, a doctor gave Ted Desoxyn for energy, which Ted described as "pure meth." The doctor added a pain medication, Percodan, to help Ted with withdrawals from Desoxyn. At age 13, Ted was legally using and abusing two strong opioid prescription medications. He added heroin to his drug repertoire when a friend bought a bag of heroin for seven dollars and they shared it. His first experience with heroin was by injecting; he explained, " 'Cause that's what everybody else was doing." With his friends, Ted also started burglarizing to get money for drugs and robbing drugstores for more pharmaceuticals.

Ted's father left the family about the time Ted started hanging out with an older and rougher crowd in the neighborhood. His parents divorced that year, and in Ted's words, his father was "done with us, with my brother and I. He's definitely done with us." In a few years, Ted was sent to a juvenile reformatory, where he learned everything but how to reform. He also had someone to protect him:

> My brother was already there; my cousin was already there . . . a bunch of guys I knew from school were already there. Even though, at that age I was prime meat for the older guys. I was cute. I was young. But the only blessing I had was my brother and all the people that had already been there. I just got right into their clique. I was never violated or sexually anything done to me.

Ted's most traumatic turning point happened soon after he got out of the juvenile reform home.[3] He was describing how he was hanging out at home with a buddy he met in the reformatory, planning a robbery together, when he paused and looked down at his hands. I waited. After a prolonged silence, I was about to ask if he wanted to stop when he continued:

> We got a couple of shotguns, which we sawed off. We were going to start robbing drugstores and stuff like that. One thing led to another and I ended up killing my mother with the shotgun, accidentally . . . I blew her head clean off. I didn't even know she was in the house. I had the gun in my hand and I guess I was drunk and all doped up . . . My mother comes in right behind the chair. I didn't see her 'cause it was late, in December, December 7. How can you miss at Pearl Harbor, right? I had the shotgun here like this, and I felt somebody tug on it and when I tugged back, it went off and then that was it.

Ted paused as he looked down at his hands again while recalling the scene:

I stayed there for a little while trying to put her head back on, trying to get it straight. Oh God, I was—then I ran, I ran to one neighbor saying what I did, ran to another neighbor saying what I did, ran to a third neighbor because we were in a condominium. Finally, I set the shotgun on the floor at the neighbor's mailbox and said what I did. Then I got in the car and I ran. I got about half a mile away and then turned around and came back. By that time, the police were all there, and I got out of the car and said I'm the one that did it.[4]

Ted was first taken to a state mental health hospital, where they administered a variety of prescription drugs to treat his suicidal depression. He was charged with negligent homicide and possession of a sawed-off shotgun and received a 3- to 10-year sentence. By this point in the interview, we were only at age 19 on his timeline and I suggested a break. He looked up at me and said with a cheerless grin, "We haven't even touched the tip of the iceberg yet."

At the mental hospital, Ted was given Thorazine (chlorpromazine) for withdrawal from the opiates a doctor had prescribed previously. Then he was sent to prison. He said he never had any counseling or other treatment in his four years in the prison system, although it was mandatory when he left prison that he see a mental health counselor. The therapy he received at the time seemed to offer little more than being subjected to the dehumanizing clinical gaze of medical students. He explained:

She [the therapist] would set up a time and a date. I would go in there, I would be sitting at the head of the table and there would be maybe thirteen or fourteen psychologists sitting around the table and they would ask different questions on how, what, why? I think somehow I just blocked it out. I knew what I did. I know what I did. It took a long time.

Ted's pathway led through a revolving door of mental health facilities, jail, and treatment programs, with intermittent use of heroin, prescription pills, and alcohol. He experienced recurring and excruciating pain in his stomach that neither medical doctors nor mental health professionals were able to diagnose or effectively treat. Ted eventually found a drug that worked. "It's just nerves," he said. "I take Xanax and it goes right away." He does not have a prescription so he buys Xanax from street dealers. He occasionally drinks alcohol. Although he is in a methadone program, his face revealed signs that he is still hurting.

Ted said his parents divorced sometime in the 1960s, but missing from his story was insight into the historical and cultural context of what this meant in terms of how his family was viewed and how this might have affected him.

Divorce rates remained relatively static from 1950 to the late 1960s, when divorce began to increase steadily every year.[5] When Ted's parents split, divorce was not yet the norm, and social structures were not in place to help single-parent households. To many mainstream Americans, divorced parents were viewed as immoral, and split families were viewed as dysfunctional. The economic strain put on single parents did not get much relief from anyone outside the immediate family. Lingering cultural norms from the 1950s pictured the ideal family as a working father and a stay-at-home mother, and other family types were often looked upon with suspicion unless one of the parents had died. This may have put a strain on Ted's mother, who had to raise pre-adolescent boys without the help of a father figure and without the extra income a father who stayed connected might have provided.

Ted's narrative did not include the cultural influence of why heroin use was common among working-class White males in his neighborhood and why society's response was punishment. Missing from Ted's account was any mention of the Vietnam War and its impact on the psyche of young men at the time, such as the anxiety of being drafted among boys of Ted's age, and the shame felt by many after the disgrace of losing the Vietnam War.

The dramatic increase in drug use by people of Ted's age was largely due to the increasing numbers of young people who entered their teens from 1960 to 1970. The baby boomers grew up with greater material wealth than preceding generations, and arguably more relative freedom during their teen years than generations before them or after them.

Historians describe the 1950s to 1973 as the "Golden Years" due to rapid growth in economic security, growth of trade unions, rising wage levels, progressive taxation, mass production, and consumerism.[6] This time began a period of weakening moral authority and greater freedom for youth. It fostered a sense of optimism and radicalism that ushered in the excesses of the "sex, drugs n' rock n' roll" of the later 1960s. According to David Garland, the 1970s were a watershed decade for the growing middle class, who were "anxious about their hard won success and feared rising social issues such as worsening race relations, family breakdown, growing welfare, increased taxes, [and] decline of traditional values," ushering in reactionary politics.[7] After the freedom of the 1960s, drug users in the 1970s were targets of a new culture of crime control, with particular focus on the working class and poor.

The political dynamics that impacted Ted and other baby boomer drug users was missing from his narrative. Ted did not mention that he was born into a working-class family and that when he reached adulthood, the deindustrialization of the US economic system doomed respectable jobs that paid a living wage to working-class men and women.[8] He also did not acknowledge the disappearance of social clubs that previously provided a setting and means for young men and women to gain social capital, social bonds, and social identity.[9] Ted did not articulate his hopelessness as a state of anomie, which is when people live with a lack of purpose and social identity that can lead to emptiness and despair.[10] No—Ted, like most of the men and women in this study, blamed his troubles on his own actions and choices in life. He never insinuated that his choices were constrained by structural barriers or limited by his place in our system of social stratification.

Due to his incarceration, Ted missed much of the culture of the late 1960s, which proved to be a major influence on baby boomers of his age. He never enjoyed the "Summer of Love" because he was in juvenile reformatory.[11] Military service was not an option for Ted, so he missed the training and camaraderie that helped previous generations of delinquents turn toward conventionality.[12] In 1972, at age 19, when he might have been drafted, Ted was in prison.[13] Being incarcerated meant he also missed the benefits enjoyed by baby boomers, such as increased education, improved economic opportunities, and the culture of intellectual and hedonistic pursuit that filled the lives of many in his cohort. While other baby boomers were protesting civil rights injustices and the Vietnam War, political protest had no place in his life. Disconnected physically from mainstream society by prolonged imprisonment, Ted was also disengaged from changing cultural norms. While the more educated young people of his age were blaming society for their problems, Ted blamed himself for every bad action and unfortunate event in his life.

Ted's life story reflects the cultural, social, and political influences of the tumultuous US landscape, but how he perceived his situation was interpreted only with the tools he had available. Ted did not know that he was living through an historical cycle when drug use was perceived as a moral failure, rehabilitation ideals were on the decline, and an increasingly punitive response to drug use would continue throughout his adult life. After the 1960s, there was never again a lenient culture for drug users.[14] While Ted was incarcerated, millions of baby boomers were learning how to manage newfound social freedoms as young adults. Ted was learning inside a juvenile reformatory where he became part of a gang to survive, and with other delinquents as his only role models.[15] After leaving the reformatory, Ted used the skills he had acquired. He continued to engage in burglary—this time armed with a sawed-off shotgun, a technique he had learned while incarcerated.

Incarceration does not prepare young men well for a life in mainstream society—it does the opposite.[16]

Although Ted missed many of the material excesses enjoyed by baby boomers while he was growing up, he participated in the popular pastime of consuming drugs. Drug use is highest during adolescence, and when the baby boomers became teens, there were more adolescents using drugs than at any other time in history.[17] Drug use by youth peaked when the last of the baby boomers were in high school, and this instigated a backlash and more stringent drug policy. Ted was one of its casualties.

Widespread drug use was a cohort trend influenced by cultural changes and historical events, but Ted's drug behavior was viewed as an individual choice and not part of a cohort behavior.[18] When Ted continued drug use into adulthood, his drug use behavior was medicalized as an addiction, and he became a patient under the control of treatment services.[19] Treatment services produce the kind of patients they want to treat, and Ted was very compliant.[20] He accepted his label as an addict and tried to be a good patient by practicing total abstinence. He attended 12-step groups to stop drinking. Whenever he relapsed, he blamed himself. It became obvious that treatment was not working, but it was all that was offered.

As a sociologist familiar with critical academic literature, I understood it was not individual choices that led to drug-related social problems but instead the political and social situations constructed by society.[21] The problems of drug addiction are socially constructed problems that generate socially constructed solutions.[22] Although solutions range from punitive repercussions to treatment options, they all focus primarily on changing the individual while virtually ignoring the social situations of drug users and structural barriers to change. When Ted described the reformatory, I was reminded of when I visited my brother inside the walls of the juvenile reformatory in New Jersey. I remembered the lost, weary, fearful look in his eyes as only a preteen—cast off as a criminal.[23] At least Ted had some protection.

HARRY: THE SOCIAL CONTEXT OF CHILDHOOD

The first born of our family of six children, Harry was also the only boy. Our father, an alcoholic, could never keep a job, so our family moved a lot. Harry never finished one complete year in the same elementary school. By the time he was in junior high school, he was incarcerated.

Before he started to use drugs, Harry and the three oldest girls in our family were sent to a Christian orphanage after we were evicted from our home for not paying rent. Our mother, a devout Christian, trusted the advice of the pastor who suggested the orphanage while she tried to find a more permanent situation. She kept her youngest, a baby, and promised she would visit whenever she could find someone to drive her to the orphanage from the city. It was never often enough.

The children's home consisted of one large mansion-like building, where the girls stayed, and a farmhouse, where the boys lived and worked on the farm. "Aunts" and "Uncles" oversaw the childcare. Our two younger sisters, ages four and six at the time, wet their beds every night. The Aunt who took care of them made them get out of bed and stand all night with the wet sheets wrapped around them. She said it would teach them not to wet the bed. One of our sisters refused to eat. Her punishment was not being able to see our mother the first time she came to visit. This was the Christian home. I wondered at the time what non-Christian orphanages would be like, and thought I should be thankful. We all would have rather stayed with our mother—no matter where she was living.

Harry never saw his sisters except when we ate together in the big dining hall in the mansion. Even here the boys and girls were separated, so Harry could only wave, until an Uncle hit him hard on the head with a metal spoon for waving. After that he only made eye contact. I don't remember talking to Harry the entire time he was there.

When summer came, Harry spent most of the time with the other boys working on the farm. They ate breakfast before us, took lunch on the farm, and we only saw their tired bodies in the evening, hands barely holding up their heads.

One hot day, the Uncles and Aunts took all the children to a local swimming pool. Harry stood around the billiard tables watching boys who were not connected with the children's home play pool, a game he often watched when he accompanied our father to bars. When one of the boys invited him to join, indicating he would pay for the game, Harry picked up a cue stick. I was watching, hoping Harry would win, but before the game was over one of the Uncles came by, picked up a cue stick, and hit Harry on the back forcefully as Harry was bent over the pool table, unaware of impending pain. He returned to the children's home in a separate vehicle, and I never saw him again at the orphanage. At age 10, Harry ran away from the orphanage and found my mother in Philadelphia. Soon afterwards, we were reunited as a family. Dad, mom, and the kids all lived in one motel room, with the kids sleeping on the floor next to each other and rolling up our beds during the day. We did not care as long as we were together.

Two years and a few changes of residences later, we were living in a two-room apartment on the bottom floor of a converted Philadelphia brownstone. Once the home of a wealthy family, the apartments were now housing six families. Harry began to hang out with the neighborhood kids, smoking cigarettes on the large front cement steps and drinking beer and wine in the alleyways. He also picked up his preference for prescription pills. The local school was rough, and somehow my father got enough money to send the girls to a Catholic school. Harry, the boy, was sent to tough it out in the public school. Our father disappeared into skid row after school started and resurfaced a few months later with a job in New Jersey.

When the family moved to New Jersey, Harry spent a lot of time at the bowling alley. Similar to Ted, Harry hung out with older boys. Also like Ted, Harry began to rob pharmacies to get pharmaceutical drugs, and when he was caught, he was sent to the reformatory. I remember my best friend's parents would no longer let their daughter play with me when they heard about my brother—small-town people know all the gossip and are often unforgiving. My family, already stigmatized by an alcoholic parent, was now scandalized by having a family member incarcerated. Harry, as the oldest child, already understood the shame of our family situation, and as the only son, hid his pain.

The lack of a father figure was prominent in both Ted's story and my brother's life, and they both were free to choose their friends—something not unusual for working-class boys at the time. However, whereas Ted's father left the family and was gone from his life, my alcoholic father kept disappearing and reappearing throughout our childhood.

The social context of their lives in reformatories is dissimilar as well. Having lived in the same town as a youth, Ted joined his brother and friends in the reformatory. In contrast, Harry, the new kid on the block, was sent to the local state reformatory where he knew no one and had no one to protect him. Their lives were eerily the same but with very different outcomes.

The general theory of crime used by many criminologists suggests that Ted and Harry never learned self-control as children and their situations were due to choices they made as adults; however, others argue that the general theory of crime does not adequately capture the influence of complex life situations.[24] As Harry's sister, I knew him well, and I did not believe self-control theory captured the historical and social context of his life that influenced his behavior and the behavior of many baby boomers in this study.

HISTORICAL CONTEXT

The lives of baby boomer drug users provide extraordinary insights into the complex relations surrounding the construction of contemporary drug problems, exposing the power interests that constrained and constructed their social realities.[25] Their stories add a grounded understanding to abstract theoretical discussions.

Many academic arguments regarding deviant or criminal behavior involve a debate over the relative strength of structure (social systems that constrain action) versus agency (action controlled by choice).[26] Contemporary theorists often attempt to disentangle agency from structure or identify the matrix of influences interacting in each situation.[27] Based on this literature, structure is the more influential force, constructing drug use into problems that constrain and guide individual choice.[28]

Drug use was not always illegal in the United States. Before the Pure Food and Drug Act of 1906, there was little regulation of drugs, and morphine and cocaine were bought and sold liberally.[29] The Harrison Act of 1914 regulated and taxed opiate and cocaine sales and required doctors and pharmacists who sold drugs to register and record sales, which ended the period when these substances were sold as over-the-counter medicine. Overuse of opiates eventually became viewed as a medical problem, resulting in the proliferation of clinics where people with addiction were treated with legal opiates as pharmaceutical substitutes for illegal opiates.[30] People dependent on opiates were viewed differently depending on their social status and context. The nineteenth-century matron and the twentieth-century socially marginalized laborer both used opiates, but their experiences were different because of the social context and their social identity.[31]

The Eighteenth Amendment (the Volstead Act), passed in 1919, established alcohol prohibition, and intoxication by any substance was seen as a moral failing. A rapid increase in crime, gangs, police corruption, and widespread community violence directly linked to prohibition prompted the

Twenty-first Amendment to be ratified in 1933 and ended the prohibition of alcohol. Almost immediately, drugs replaced alcohol as the focus of moral entrepreneurs.[32]

The Federal Bureau of Narcotics (FBN) was founded in 1930 as the agency in the US Department of Treasury with a mandate to enforce tax and trade laws concerning drugs. The FBN's first commissioner, Harry J. Anslinger, who held this position for 32 years, mounted a zealous campaign to criminalize drugs, which some historians viewed as a mechanism to elevate Anslinger and give greater power to the FBN.[33] The most famous of his campaigns was the successful plan to place marijuana under the control of the federal government, which became official with the Marihuana Tax Act of 1937. During Anslinger's tenure as FBN commissioner, society's response to drug use became more unforgiving.

Anslinger's reign was ending when baby boomers were children. When the boomers were adolescents in the 1960s, the stigmatization of drug users was temporarily alleviated during a brief interlude in strict drug prohibition. It returned with renewed force in reaction to the excesses of the early cohort of baby boomers, who experimented with a variety of drugs in their youth.[34] Worried parents called for intervention, which resulted in a two-tiered system of treatment for upper and middle classes, and incarceration for poor and minority groups.[35]

In 1962, the Supreme Court declared addiction a disease and not a crime; nevertheless, people addicted to opioids were still incarcerated, especially the poor. Methadone maintenance was introduced in 1964, but not for all. While upper- and middle-class people dependent on opiates had access to legal methadone as treatment for heroin, it would be decades before methadone was more accessible, and only recently has it been used in some correctional institutions. Most of the baby boomers in this book experienced opiate or heroin withdrawal in jail without any medical help.

As more baby boomers became teenagers, experimentation with drugs became a rite of passage among their peers, and public outcry against drug use increased. In 1971, the "War on Drugs" was officially declared, and the punitive response to drug use has increased ever since.[36] The drug war received renewed attention and funding in the 1980s under the Reagan administration. Boomers were now adults, and many were still using drugs.

Concurrent with the increase in drug use was a rise in crime that started in 1960 and peaked in 1980.[37] While social scientists attribute this temporary increase in crime statistics to many factors, baby boomers were reaching adolescence and young adulthood during this period, a stage in life with few informal social controls such as a family or job, which was certainly one of those factors.[38]

The return of soldiers from Vietnam fueled an increase in heroin users in the 1960s.[39] The Drug Enforcement Agency (DEA) was created in 1973, and marijuana was made a Schedule 1 drug along with heroin.

Trends in drug popularity impacted the drug trajectories of baby boomers. Cocaine was a trendy drug of choice during the nightclub era of the mid-1970s to early 1980s when smoking cocaine (called freebase) became more popular than sniffing or injecting.[40] Crack cocaine use increased from the late 1980s to mid-1990s.[41] Various "drug epidemics" were publicized through the media, often with the intent to scare the public.[42]

The methamphetamine epidemic started on the West Coast of the United States in the 1990s and migrated across the country to the Midwest and Southeast, particularly in rural areas where methamphetamine labs proliferated.[43] Heroin replaced crack as the trending drug in urban areas in the mid-1990s.[44] Legally prescribed prescription pill abuse has been the driving force behind what has been called an "opioid epidemic" of prescription pills and heroin that has spread to every geographic area in the United States since 2000.[45]

The events in this historical period influenced boomers like Ted and Harry, who were juveniles around the time when drug use was increasing among their cohort. They were poor and did not have access to the treatment response that adolescents with more affluent parents could afford. Both boys resorted to crime as a way to obtain drugs once they became physically addicted. Both were sent to juvenile reformatories as a result. Efforts to rehabilitate delinquents were on the decline. Ted received some mental health attention after accidently killing his mother, but the treatment focused on immediate suicide prevention and did not appear to be effective over the long term.

Harry was incarcerated for 30 years of his life and missed trends in the popularity and accessibility of one drug over another. He always preferred heroin or prescription opiates.[46] Although like Harry, Ted started with opiates, he avoided illegal drugs after leaving prison at age 24, using only tobacco and alcohol for more than 10 years. In the mid-1980s, when crack was popular, he smoked it a few times. In 2000, while in his late forties, he returned to regular use of heroin and opiates with his wife, Teresa, who was more susceptible to drug trends.

I interviewed Teresa a few days after I had interviewed her husband, Ted. A tall and strong-looking woman with a striking combination of angular bone structure and rounded features, Teresa had the healthy skin and teeth one would expect to see on a model rather than a drug user. Dressed in fashionable clothes and a stylish haircut, she looked years younger than her age of 53. Commenting on her fleshy face, Teresa said her "fat cheeks" kept her from being drug tested while she was on probation. Teresa's childhood story was quite different than Ted's, but they traveled much of their adult life together and experienced similar consequences due to their drug use.

Teresa had been raised in a middle-class family by both parents; she was well taken care of, and there was no childhood trauma. Feeling a sense of belonging in her small hometown in New York, she married her high school sweetheart at 19. Like many of the youth at this time, she participated in social use of marijuana, LSD, cocaine, and "speed pills," which were trendy. She took the pills to lose weight and stay awake, since they were easy to find in her social network, but she stopped using them when she thought the pills were causing a ringing in her ears. During her first marriage, she stopped using all drugs except alcohol, marijuana, and occasional hallucinogens. She divorced her husband after five years, which appeared to be due to boredom. A year later she met the man who would be her next husband, Ted, in a bar, and they hitchhiked to Mississippi together. During this time, she engaged "mostly in drinking and partying. I went off the pill and I didn't drink or smoke or anything when I was pregnant with my son. Not cigarettes, no alcohol, no drugs."

Sometime after her first child was born, she and Ted moved to a small town in Florida. The year was 1987; Florida was experiencing a crack epidemic. Teresa did not appear to be a likely crack cocaine smoker. As a White woman in her thirties she did not fit the commonly held demographic of a "crackhead." She was employed in a hospital clinic and later opened her own home healthcare business. Yet she found that using crack did not interfere with her work or raising her children. The picture of a rarely described "functional" crack user emerged.

> I'd have it in the kitchen and the kids would be in the living room playing. I'd take a hit, whatever; I'd make their breakfast. It didn't affect me at all in any way where I was weird, like running downtown to buy more. It just perked me up. It made me perky.

Teresa was introduced to crack by friends of her husband, but Ted rarely used crack and did not seem to enjoy it as much. I asked how she maintained her supply.

I'm really a wild person anyway, so I don't let anything stop me. If I want to do something, I'm just gonna to do it. I wasn't really afraid of anything. I'd go into all these crack houses where these kingpin men were that were selling the drugs. I'd go up to them and sit down at the table and pretend like I had known them for years. Usually you didn't do that. It was very taboo. But they liked me. I was easy to talk to and they enjoyed my company . . . I was actually talking to them instead of "she's just over there getting crazy and smokin' crack." I would take a hit and talk and enjoy it, more than most of the people who were addicted to it, obviously. I wasn't addicted to it yet, I guess.

Ted and Teresa used various drugs together, but whereas Ted's preference was for heroin and opiates, Teresa liked to experiment on "anything that came up." Fearless and gregarious, Teresa was the one who generally discovered a new drug popular in the neighborhood and brought it home to Ted.

Soon after moving to a suburban town in Georgia, Teresa started using methamphetamine, another indicator that she was influenced by trends in drug use. Methamphetamine use in Georgia moved outward from the city and inward from rural areas into suburban communities. Teresa was introduced to methamphetamine by a suburban neighbor; she used it in a controlled way whenever friends gave it to her.

Crack was still the major drug problem in the city at this time, and when Teresa met a neighbor who used heroin, she accompanied him to the street drug market in the city to buy crack.

I went with him a couple of times to pick up some heroin. Remember I like crack. We'd go down, I'd buy a little bit of crack, he'd buy heroin, and I'd get a little bit of his heroin, he'd get a little bit of my crack, we'd trade off. Anyway, we'd trade off and then it got heavily, I didn't want the crack anymore and then I started doing the heroin. I started snorting it.

Teresa used drugs recreationally and did not appear to become addicted in the sense that drug use did not interfere with other social functions. She stopped and started at will. She ceased methamphetamine after six years of occasional use: "I didn't do anything for those few years. I was a good housewife, a good mother."

At the turn of the new millennium, Teresa and Ted started another drug gaining popularity—prescription opioid pills.

My husband hurt himself and got a lot of it [opioids] somehow. He had hurt his leg or something, I don't really remember. He just kept going to different doctors. They would give him stuff. Then he would say he spilled it in the trash and he'd get more. We did quite a bit but I never actually did more than two or three at a time. He was really into it more than I was. I liked 'em. Pain medication made you feel perky and nice.

Teresa's physical reaction to prescription opioids was not typical. "Perky" was an unusual word to describe how these pills made one feel. As neuroscientists have confirmed, the physical (biological) and psychological effects of drugs vary from individual to individual, and some people, like Teresa, were able to maintain control over even addictive drugs like opioids.[47]

SOCIAL CONTEXT

The trajectory of drug use cannot be fully understood without knowing the social context of the drug-using time and place. Historical cues provide one kind of context by drawing attention to what is going on in society in terms of laws, norms, and cultural events. However, the social context varies by individual, situations, and demographics.[48] Teresa's life story provides a fitting illustration of this variation when compared to the life of Ted or Harry.

Social and historical contexts are difficult to disentangle, since one influences the other, and drug trends impact people differently. People like Harry, who were incarcerated for a long time, were less influenced by drug trends; others, like Ted, were emotionally alienated from trends in society. Without Teresa, he might have been less influenced by changes in drug preferences. Teresa, however, with her zest for social life and supported by her privileged position as a White woman who began life with a solid middle-class status, was more attuned to changes in social situations and historical drug trends.

Except for a short period of time, when Teresa attempted to live on her own, Ted and Teresa supported each other emotionally, socially, and financially.[49] The social context of their relationship is critical to understanding their drug use. Their marriage survived an intensifying War on Drugs, the unraveling of traditional society, and the systematic destruction of the middle class into which Teresa was born. Ted's drug problems were instigated by his early involvement in juvenile delinquency, which can be attributed in part to a broken family, lack of a father figure, and association with other juveniles who engaged in drugs and criminal activity. His continued drug use is directly linked to his tragic accidental killing of his mother, which left emotional scars that haunted him throughout his adult life. Ted was like a rudderless ship and Teresa was his directional sail. Ted provided Teresa with a focus in life, and they weathered the worst situations together.

As an adolescent, Teresa also was impacted by the social turmoil of the 1960s—the loss of almost sixty thousand Americans in Vietnam, the assassinations of President Kennedy, Senator Kennedy, and Martin Luther King Jr., and bloody civil rights demonstrations. While drug availability and social leniency were certainly important factors in the sudden surge of youthful drug-taking, the social turmoil of this period also influenced the increase in drug use during the early 1970s. Teresa did not identify any historical markers as influential, however, the detailed description of her changing social context and stressful life situations revealed the impact of social forces beyond her control.

Teresa used drugs during times of particular turmoil in her adult life, indicating use as a way to disconnect from volatile emotions. She turned to drugs when she discovered Ted had serious mental health problems she could not help him solve. She entered a difficult drug-using period when her mother died. While these indicators of emotional and relational turmoil are critical to understanding her drug use, the structural barriers to achieving the "American dream" that proliferated during her lifetime cannot be ignored or regarded as not influential. They were humming in the background of her life unnoticed, just as the ubiquitous sound of traffic in modern times goes unnoticed as daily life situations demand our attention.

Despite their drug use, Teresa and Ted maintained a relatively middle-class status until 1990. Due to the restructuring of the labor market, people like Ted and Teresa were left without steady employment, and they joined many other American families who fell below the poverty line.[50] The rapid increase in new labor-saving technology contributed to the loss of manufacturing jobs, but the true culprit was policymaking that increased offshoring of US companies and outsourcing of US jobs.[51] Trade policies led to the loss of thousands of middle-skilled jobs that supported the middle class, which were replaced with low-skilled and low-paying service jobs.[52] Teresa's life was impacted by these policies although she might not have even known they existed—she never mentioned them or blamed any policy for her situation.

A self-described hard-working woman, Teresa was resigned to accepting low-paying and often humbling service positions in retail stores and restaurants. The euphemisms used to make these jobs seem higher status, such as store associate instead of cashier, did not bring better pay or benefits. Teresa realized that her full-time employment paycheck was not enough to afford childcare, and she tried to solve the problem by opening her own home healthcare business. The stress of opening a new business without any business training took its toll. Always anxious and tired, she used crack, which she said "perks me up," and methamphetamine—a drug that provides energy and feelings of well-being.

State policies likely contributed to Teresa's stressful economic situation. During her worst drug-using years, she had been living in states where employees are not protected by unions. These were the first states to enact what are cleverly called "right to work" laws, which really means that employers have a right to fire employees at will, with none of the worker's benefits or protections provided by union membership. These were also states with a paucity of those services that provide a social safety net. Teresa did not acknowledge this political situation. She did, however, note the difference in social services when she briefly moved to the Northeast.

At one point Teresa left Ted in Georgia and took the kids to New York to be near her family. She was surprised to receive some government help.

> They gave me like $600 a month . . . that wasn't even going to be enough. That would be half maybe, if I had found a job. I could have taken the $600 and another $600 if I made it and get an apartment, but it was so expensive, I couldn't afford it. Plus, I missed Ted. He's a pain-in-the-ass, but I did miss him.

At the time of the interview Teresa was unemployed and looking for work. Ted had a blue-collar job that could be terminated at any time. They were living with their adult children in a rented house that was in foreclosure—an impact of the Recession of 2008. Due to the housing market crash, the $175,000 home was on the market for $75,000. They hoped to buy the house with a low-interest mortgage as soon as Teresa found steady employment, although the effects of the recession persisted.[53] I admired her optimism. It was a trait I noticed in others I interviewed, such as Jordan, another baby boomer whose live story illustrates how drug use must be placed in historical and social context

JORDAN

I met Jordan at a homeless shelter where we both were volunteers. She was always neatly dressed, had an easy smile, and talked in a kind manner that indicated friendliness and concern. When she heard about our study she asked if she could do an interview. Jordan is African American and identified as transgender. Her story illustrates the importance of understanding the interplay between agency and structure.

Jordan was born in Maryland and lived with her father, mother, and siblings with no memory of problematic family circumstances. However, her sexual and gender identity were viewed as problematic due to the cultural landscape of her childhood. Although Jordan lived in a northeastern state near New York City, where sexual orientation discrimination was less overt, it was not hidden.

Jordan's sexual orientation and race gave her a double stigmatized status. She was born in 1963, a year before the Civil Rights Acts of 1964 outlawed discrimination based on race, color, religion, sex, or national origin. Legal equal rights for lesbian, gay, bisexual, and transgender (LGBT) persons evolved slowly over her lifetime. Not until 2003 did the Supreme Court determine that sodomy laws were unconstitutional, and sexual relationships between same-sex adults become legal in all states. Jordan was 33 when President Clinton signed the Defense of Marriage Act (DOMA).[54] Georgia, where Jordan lived, passed legislation prohibiting recognition of same-sex relationships in 1996. This was the sociopolitical context of Jordan's life.

Jordan realized she was transgender while in high school and moved away from her parent's home to live with friends when only 14 years old. Although she did not indicate feeling prejudice from her parents, she said she felt more comfortable with friends who were accepting of her transgender status. She finished high school because her parents wanted all their children to have a diploma, and then she moved to New York City. Her drug use followed the trends in large urban areas. She first started to use heroin in the early 1980s and added crack to her drug repertoire in the mid-1980s, right about the time crack was reported as an epidemic. Jordan described crack and heroin as her "rebelliousness of society." She used cocaine in the late 1980s and 1990s, and then switched to heroin exclusively from 2000 to 2007. The year preceding the interview she had stopped all drugs except marijuana, although she acknowledged a brief relapse on crack.

Jordan supplemented her low-income jobs (food service, telemarketing, office work through temporary employment agencies) with sex work and drug dealing. She was engaged as an escort when she met some "high-level mob drug dealers," which ended her time in New York. As she explained:

We were just partying, it was just a party, and what it was, actually, is some-body got a hold of a lump sum of someone else's stuff, not realizing that they were also connected with the mob. Because during my days in New York when I was doing the sex work, I ran into a lot of, I mean some big people. 'Cause I went from sex work to escort, and when you do escort service you have no idea who you're escorting until you get to the event itself. And if you have any brains about yourself, you can realize and, okay, put two and two together and I know what this is. And I ran into some heavy, heavy, heavy dealers. Major dealers, they didn't deal in small quantity. They dealt in money. So one weekend I was in a hotel room and we were just party-ing. I didn't know what happened, I went to the bathroom. I come out the bathroom and lights were out. Gunfire was everywhere, and I just knew to hide. And when I woke up I, I won't say everybody was dead but I would say just about everybody was dead, and there was a couple wounded. But I wasn't interested in staying around to be a witness to nothing 'cause that's all you would need is my face on the news.

Jordan moved to Georgia, where both service work and sex work were much lower-paid occupations. Having few contacts, she was vulnerable to police control on the streets and was arrested a few times for soliciting. She lived with a female sex worker for some time and thought she may have fathered two children with her:

I had custody of them. Their mother was, she was a street worker as well. Back in the day there was this little thing where the lezzies liked the drag queens, and they took better care of us than the men did. So back in the days, that was the thing, so I'm like, let me see what this thing is about. I'm gung ho for anything just about. I'll try just about anything one time.

Although Jordan took responsibility for the children, she was stressed by the insecurity of her status. She said she used drugs to deal with this: "Actually I used a little bit more because I was led on a string, because I didn't know whether or not they were mine or she got pregnant by some trick." Her parental role was cut short when she was incarcerated.

Historical markers in medical discoveries also impacted Jordan's drug trajectory. Jordan was 18 and sexually active when Gay Related Immu-nodeficiency Disorder (GRID) was reported in the news as a disease confined to the gay population. Over time, increased medical understanding of this disease lessened the stigma, but lingering memories of humiliation during the AIDS epidemic influenced Jordan. She was diagnosed with HIV and hepatitis C in 2006, which she said drew her temporarily back to using more drugs, only this time she sniffed instead of injected. "I was never a promiscuous person," she said, explaining that she did not think she got HIV from sexual relations. Jordan's sex work consisted of oral sex, and she claimed to always have used condoms with her sexual partners. She also said she always used her own syringes when injecting drugs and believed she had infected herself by reusing her own syringes.

Jordan was not very knowledgeable of infectious diseases when she first injected drugs, and, despite her claims, she likely shared syringes a few times in the early days of her use before HIV transmission routes were known. At the time of the interview, she was volunteering for a harm reduction program, which exchanged used syringes for new syringes, one of the best evidence-based strategies for preventing the transmission of HIV among injecting drug users. Due to state laws, the harm reduction program was operating illegally.

At age 45, Jordan was one of the youngest baby boomers in this sample. She was hopeful but her situation was not. She still used drugs when faced with a crisis or emotional turmoil, and her life was relatively insecure. In contrast, Moses, among the oldest in the sample, was one of the few Black men in the study whose current life situation was not precarious.

MOSES

Moses was 61 years old at the time of the interview. An African American male with the demeanor of a professor more than a former prisoner, Moses had learned to create a meaningful existence no matter what his circumstances. He was a leader in a well-attended 12-step recovery program, but my impression was that he could have been a leader of any organization he belonged to and performed this role exceptionally well.[55] His life story illustrates not only the impact of historical and social context on drug use, but also the importance of changes in the social and economic situations of individuals over time.

Social context matters because it provides the parameters for access to social networks. As a child and adolescent, *who* you hang out with depends on *where* you live, and this influence carries over in adulthood. Moses spent his childhood in Harlem, New York, a place he described as a ghetto:

At that time, they had projects and in these projects, we weren't, um, rich enough to even live in the projects, which was government housing. We couldn't even get into them because we were so poor. I came from a family where there was no father figure there. In my household there was my grandmother, my mother, and two other aunts. I basically was raised by women, and when I went to school, and I did quite well in school and I was a good student ... I did well in school until I got into high school and started doing other things besides applying myself to the activity that I was supposed to be in school for. I started hanging out with people—they weren't conducive to my education, far as me staying in school. And I wound up, when I got to high school almost completing high school, I think I was maybe two or three months from graduating high school, and I received a felony charge for possession of drugs and distribution of drugs. And I wind up, instead of finishing high school, going to prison instead.

Like Ted and Harry, Moses spent formative adolescent years incarcerated instead of at home and at school. He missed high school graduation and the opportunity to attend college. He did not start working at the same time as his cohort, and he missed other rituals associated with the passage into adulthood.

Moses started using powerful prescription pills illegally at age 17, before their illegal use was widespread. As he explained, "I lived in New York, and there's a hospital two blocks this way and about two blocks that way," gesturing with his hand as if we were there on the location, "and they had all kinds of drugs there. I was a thief, and I went there to get drugs when I couldn't buy 'em on the street—didn't have the money." Living in a big city like New York meant having more access to illegal drugs or, as in the case of Moses, access to obtaining legal drugs illegally. Moses also learned insider criminal skills from an uncle who "was involved in the drug industry" and taught Moses the tricks of the trade, such as "cutting heroin with milk, sugar, magneto, or something" to increase its weight.

The charges that put Moses in prison stemmed mainly from drug possession and distribution, and he often returned to prison due to violating parole. Increased sentencing over the years reflected the popular "get tough" philosophy behind crime and drug laws. As punitive responses to drug crimes increased in intensity, parole violations for behaviors that often were noncriminal in nature continued to expand the number of people incarcerated, which greatly impacted Moses's life.[56]

There was little rehabilitation focus during his first stint in prison as a young adult. "They didn't care whether you changed your life when you got out there," Moses explained. "There was no drug abuse classes, no parenting classes, there was no sex education when I went to prison, none of that." He spent most of his time obtaining and selling drugs in prison, which gave him a trade and meaningful existence until he returned to mainstream society.

> When I'm in prison, I become quite comfortable in prison. 'Cause I get some acceptance about what happened. And every time I went to prison, 'cause I've been to prison many times over my years, it became like something I knew was going to happen in my life . . . so when I went to prison, I got back in the flow. Okay, I'm back in prison. This is what you do in prison, and I went about doing what I do in prison. And that's how I survived in prison.

As one of the oldest baby boomers, Moses experienced therapeutic communities, a popular residential treatment model in the 1970s and '80s.[57] Moses described one therapeutic community where he voluntarily stayed for over a year:

> You heard of that tough love program they do in prisons now? It was something like that where they beat you down by what you were doing with your life. And make you feel ashamed and guilty, and you don't want to do what you did before. You're scared straight, like they say. And that was the treatment they'd use at this therapeutic community I went to. I don't know if you heard of a place like Phoenix House or, what's that other, Synanon? This was something like that. These people that ran this therapeutic community, they were people that graduated from that type of treatment and that's the type of treatment they gave us . . . this was something that was free. All I had to do was walk in there and say, "I'm having a problem with drugs, I need to stop, can you help me?" And they had a bed and a room for me, and they accepted me there, and they started treating me.

> The way they treated me was, say you did something wrong, maybe you were given a pass after a month or something, and you went out and drank a beer or something, and you came back intoxicated. They know that, so they might have you walk around the facility with a beer can hanging around your neck, or they might make you wear a dress for having sex when you aren't supposed to have sex. Like I said, things to shame you or make you start feeling guilty about what you're doing, so you can hopefully change and not do those old behaviors again.

Therapeutic communities were reported to be one of the most successful types of treatment.[58] However, treatment success is often measured by being drug free at the end of the treatment plan; rarely is follow-up conducted to establish if the program was successful a few years after leaving treatment.[59] Moses said the therapeutic community treatment worked for him for about three years, before he returned to using hard drugs.

Drugs trends often depend on what drugs are available, which varies by geographic location. Moses, who was socially linked to drug networks and secure in his knowledge of the New York City drug scene, used a combination of heroin, cocaine, and speed (amphetamine) during the mid-1960s when he was still in his twenties and New York was awash in drugs.[60] "I was what they called at that time a speedball junkie," he explained. "We mixed them together, shot up."

Moses was part of New York City's "heroin cohort," and his drug use practices were like those of young city heroin injectors during the early 1970s.[61] Unlike Ted and Harry, who started with opiates and were lifelong users of heroin or opiates, Moses followed a pattern typical of the young, African American males of his time period, who experimented with heroin when young and moved on to cocaine and crack in later years. He switched to using only cocaine during the mid- to late 1970s, when cocaine was considered a recreational club drug. During the early 1980s Moses had a five-year stretch of using no drugs except marijuana while he was working in a mainstream job that he said made drugs less important. When crack was popular in the mid-1980s, Moses became entrenched in the crack scene in New York, and later in Florida and Georgia, where crack reigned for many years past its waning in other cities. Crack impacted Moses more than other drugs largely due to changes in US policy.

One of the most shameful and racially biased pieces of drug legislation in US history, the Anti-Drug Abuse Act of 1986 instituted mandatory sentencing that increased penalties for possessing or trafficking crack at a ratio of 100:1 compared to powder cocaine.[62] Historical accounts show that this law was imposed more harshly on Black users of crack. For example, while Whites and Hispanics made up two-thirds of crack users, 85 percent of those convicted for crack were Black.[63] Moses was swept up by this historical trend of mass imprisonment of African American crack users and was in and out of prison from age 35 to 50, mostly on crack charges.[64]

Another historical influence on Moses's life was spiritual, which indirectly impacted his drug trajectory. Moses was raised as a Southern Baptist. Although he lived in New York, his mother came from North Carolina, where the majority of African American woman of her time were Southern Baptists. Moses adopted other religions as an adult. He was a Jehovah's Witness for a short period of time. The Jehovah's Witnesses were accused of racist beginnings, but their community-centered approach to religion was embraced by many Black communities, and by the new millennium, African

Americans made up a larger percentage of Jehovah's Witnesses' membership (32 percent) than any other major religion.[65] He became more interested in Islam as the popularity of that religion increased among the African American community, particularly among men who had been in prison.[66] At the time of the interview, Moses said he was more spiritual than religious:

> I became involved in a lot of religions; I believed that there was a God, and that there was a Jesus, and Muhammad and Allah and all these things. But today, because I look at it from a spiritual level, I have a conscious contact, I don't just believe anymore that there is a God; I know there is a God. Therein lies the difference between spirituality and religion. Spirituality is more of a conscious contact that goes past belief.

Moses's interest in spirituality eventually led to his acceptance of the 12-step philosophy and his success as a "sponsor" (mentor) for many new members to this group. Being impacted by spiritual trends did not mean that Moses was easily influenced. The opposite might be said of this thoughtful man who carefully dissected the meaning of life with philosophical precision.

TWO

The Life Course of Baby Boomers

JAN

"I was wild as hell," said Jan, as she summed up her life in five words with a smile. She had something to smile about, having just obtained a coveted bed at the local homeless shelter! I came to know Jan more than most of the people I interviewed since I saw her over the course of three years. When I first met her, she had just found work as a telemarketer, a soul-wrenching job but needed for her survival. The homeless shelter required proof of employment in order to be guaranteed a bed every night and get on a waiting list for transitional housing. Jan knew she was lucky. She told me there are a whole lot of people living in the woods behind the shelter. I saw many of them lining up for the daily meal, which they could get without having a job.

Jan, a White woman on the verge of 50, actually looked pretty good despite having been homeless for months. Her long salt-and-pepper hair had a healthy shine. I observed her hands and nails were clean and manicured—better than my own, I thought, as I commented on her nice fingernails. She beamed at the compliment and said it was because she never did any hard labor. Previously, she worked professionally in an office or clinic. The only visual indicator I saw of drug use or poverty was her lack of teeth. She explained that she lost her teeth over time and recently a free dental clinic in another county pulled the remaining teeth. They promised to get her some dentures. Two years later she was still toothless.

There were a few easily distinguished turning points in Jan's life. Her parents were divorced when she was two years old. During the transition, she stayed with a grandmother. When she returned to live with her mother, she was told she "reverted back to a baby." Some sort of trauma caused a blockage

34

of any memories through the age of four. Her first memories were being ashamed of her mother as a young girl:

My mother was just full-blown alcoholic. Men were in the house all the time. I remember one time, my mother was always drunk, but she got drunk this one particular time. Took off all of her clothes. Like, I don't know what time of night it was. Kinda late—nine or ten o'clock. Put on a short fur coat that just covered herself. Got in her '65 Mustang and drove off naked and drunk. And she would tell me stories even back then that she would sleep with the policemen to get out of tickets and DUIs. Back then they weren't like they are now . . . She, she was just very—I, I really was disgusted with her . . . I had no friends that could come to my house without her making a scene or a spectacle or a drunk—she was a very sloppy drunk. Very embarrassing.

Jan experienced class dichotomy firsthand when every other weekend she left her mother to stay with her father. He came from a "rich" family and remained well off when he remarried. She noted the children with his new family had "different values" and none of them ended up using drugs. Contrast between the family environments was sharpened by the cheerful summers spent in Virginia with her father's parents, after which she would return to her mother's dismal abode. "I had to take care of her feelings, it was draining, and so I would isolate . . . stay as far away from mother as I could. I wasn't a real outgoing personality."

Jan was born in 1960, which means she missed being a teenager during the "peace and love" decade. Like other late baby boomers, she tried to relive it:

I read a lot of books about the sixties' doing drugs and the seventies' doing drugs, and I wanted to do that. I wanted to be a part of that. Kinda like something that I could fit in and be a part of. And alcohol was just the first thing that I could get a hold of. And I didn't really like it. I liked the drugs so much better. And I didn't start drinking heavy—I did drugs, way more drugs than alcohol at first but I—after some years I just enjoyed alcohol. And I hated myself because, not at that time but now, I'm to a point with alcohol that I can't drink the way I want to because I do get like her [my mother]. And I always said I never would do that. And that if I was drinking I would've certainly, of course, never acted like her.

Although she tried to control her drinking, it did not last. When she was in her thirties she started having "blackouts" and could not remember how she wound up in a motel—or an emergency room. She said opiates helped her come down from a blackout.

Jan's drug trajectory followed a pattern more common among White baby boomer drug users; she started with prescription pills, such as Preludin, which she called "very clean pharmaceutical speed." Next came Dilaudid; like many pill users she used both "uppers" (stimulants) and "downers" (depressants). A boyfriend taught her how to inject them. "I fell in love with the rush of the IV use. Actually my boyfriend was already using these drugs when I met him. And he said, "You're not going to do that." And I said, "Yes I am."

She stopped living with her mother at age 15 and moved into her father's house. Although his kids were drug free, dad was not. Jan started using drugs with him:

> It was the late seventies at the time, and he was into the cocaine and the marijuana. But he never let it get out of control. I mean he always had his job, his career, his big house, his cars. He was functional. But it was cool to him that I was kinda doing it too. And it was perfect for me because I was hanging with him and being accepted by him, and it was a very influential time. And I started being a part of the—I mean, I idolized my father because I just thought he was the greatest thing in the world. Because he—I just loved him to death.

At age 17 Jan moved out of her father's house to live with her boyfriend. Bartending facilitated her drinking habit. She was using methadone, Dilaudid, and heroin from age 19 to 20, while also increasing use of cocaine and speed to counteract coming down from heroin. Her boyfriend's mother was "the biggest Dilaudid dealer" in the suburban town and "slept with anybody for drugs." Her boyfriend pressured her to dance in strip bars and turn tricks at the King's Hotel in Atlanta—a place known for its seediness. After her boyfriend left, she continued exotic dancing and tried walking on Ponce de Leon Avenue, the strip in Atlanta where sex workers are in public view after hours. At age 21, an undercover cop busted her for prostitution.

A turning point in Jan's life came at age 24, when she had a long relationship with a "sugar daddy" who was married. He gave her $4,000 for the down payment on a house and a steady income so she could stop other sex work. She attended classes and earned a healthcare technician degree. Once she started professional work, she stopped all drugs for five years.

In the late 1980s, she moved away from the city to a small town along the coast to take a position that would advance her career. Alone in a small town, she met new friends who offered her crack.

He happened to hand me some crack and said, "Try this." I had no idea what it was. And I had no idea what I was doing . . . That rush came back and I was hooked the first hit . . . and it took two years of my life. I stayed on crack for two years.

Still working a professional job, Jan was the affluent one among the interracial drug-using crowd that adopted her. She was "the sexy white girl who had all the money for the dope," and she loved the sense of belonging she felt when was smoking crack with her friends. She used most of her paycheck for drugs, and when that was gone she began "selling everything for crack." Coming to the realization that her life was going downhill, she cut her wrists because she "couldn't resist crack." In the hospital, she found out she had contracted hepatitis C, which she thinks was from sharing needles when she was injecting heroin.

Jan was not a virgin to cutting, and she continued cutting herself throughout her life. She showed me her scars, "That's a cut. That's scars from cutting," she said, pointing to a few pink and purple lines. "From suicide," she said pointing to a deep bone-white scar. "Shooting dope scars are here, here, on my ankles . . . and these are old scars." Some pink lines looked new.

Like most of the baby boomer drug users, Jan was in and out of treatment, and in and out of jail. "I've got a [rap] sheet this long," she said. Ironically she had only one felony charge and that was for marijuana, but since she was 17 at the time, it was not on her record. "That's a good thing because now I have a bunch of misdemeanors but I am not a convicted felon."

Since Jan's drug trajectory depicts a steady use of prescription pills, with intermittent use of different drugs, one might interpret her drug use as less harmful than continual use of heroin. But opioid pills can be just as deadly as heroin, and since Jan crushed and injected the pills, there was little difference in the effect. While injecting prescription pills with one of her boyfriends, he died of an overdose in her house. She did not report his death "correctly" to the police, which landed her in jail again.

After years of opioid addiction, Jan stabilized on methadone for five years, which allowed her to work again. Not able to return to her professional medical career due to her record with drug abuse, she took a job in a retail office. She relapsed after starting a relationship with a woman who was using methamphetamine and had a medicine cabinet full of prescription pills. "She was on pain management, and she had so many pills as far as prescription opiates, which I did like," Jan explained, "but she's a meth addict, so I'm doing both."

Leaving her girlfriend and steady supply of drugs, Jan moved back home to help her ailing mother.

> I was trying to take care of my mother again. Bathing her, feeding her, clothing her, changing her diapers. She's on oxygen twenty-four hours a day. Still smoking with the oxygen on her face. Biting me every bit of the way. And I'm drinking—trying to cope with that. And I can't take care of her. I tried and I would drink, go to the hospital. Starting in October is when I started drinking, going to the hospital, and go to detox. Get out of detox, drink, you know for a couple weeks, go back to the hospital, go back to detox . . . And each time that I went they wanted me to go into the thirty-day program. And I would say no, I have to get back and take care of my mother. Which is the excuse that I gave them, but I also wanted to go back and drink some more.

After another stint in the hospital for detox, Jan went to a halfway house. "I was really serious. I really, really was going to try this time. I had my heart in it. I really thought I was going to make it." After leaving a halfway house, Jan could only find part-time work and was emotionally worn out.

> I'm struggling, you know, really hard with the cravings and was determined that if I ran across somebody that had some pills I was going to take them. I didn't want to drink because I knew I can't control that. I know I'm a blackout drinker, and I don't want to drink. So I did take some prescription pills before I relapsed on the alcohol.

She was asked to leave the halfway house when she was found unconscious after a binge on alcohol.

> I got drunk, slept in the woods for four hours, woke up and was going to commit suicide. Instead of committing suicide, I walked into a hospital and said I was going to commit suicide, and I need to be admitted.

Jan reminisced about the time when she was stable on methadone: "If I could afford to get back on methadone I would. I was very functional on methadone. And I was a pretty good person then." Methadone programs in the area were private and too expensive for someone like Jan. A subsidized program was available in the city, but it had a long waiting list.

I took Jan to eat lunch after the interview and learned a few more details about her early life. Jan said she was depressed since she was a child. She also had a serious weight problem. She was not sure whether she was depressed because of her weight or her mother's alcoholism, or both. Her increasing weight made her feel even more alienated as a teenager. Drug use helped her with both problems. With drugs she maintained a desired weight and kept depression at bay.

Jan called me a month after our first interview. She had been kicked out of the homeless shelter when she failed a Breathalyzer test for alcohol. She still worked at the telemarketing company and was living in a run-down motel. A few weeks later she called to let me know she lost her job and needed to get her last paycheck to pay the hotel or she would be sleeping in the woods.

I met her at a gas station, where she was talking to an elderly man. When she got in the car I learned she was supporting herself by engaging in sex work along the suburban highway. "I am 50 years old, but I look okay to a guy," she explained. Jan had aged years in the last few months and now looked much older than 50. Her hair lacked the luster I had noticed at our first meeting. Her skin was a gray pallor, and her nails were broken and dirty. With no teeth, her cheeks and lips were sunken, making wrinkles more prominent. She said she got $30 for a "blow job." She was propositioning the man at the gas station.

We picked up her last paycheck, and I stopped to get her something to eat while Jan explained her situation. She had befriended Paul, one of the men who lived at the homeless shelter, and he invited her to share a drink from his bottle before going into the homeless shelter for the night. Neither of them passed the Breathalyzer test and they were both banned from the homeless shelter.

Since then she used crack every payday with Paul. When she started missing work, she was fired. When I asked why she took that drink with Paul, she replied: "I wish I knew the answer to that. I wish I knew what would make me not want to take a drink." She sat in silence filled with hurt, and then she provided an answer:

Nobody has the need that I need inside of me. And I am searching for whatever need it is I am searching for. Before Paul I met the guy that I knew in Pittsville; before him, the one that was at the halfway house. So, you know, I am grabbing on to any damn body.

I drove her to the motel where she was staying. It was shabby. The windows outside were covered with dust, and some were cracked. Inside, the curtains were drawn tight, but the sun shone through in torn places, revealing more dirt and drabness than either of us cared to see. I pictured Jan bringing that feeble old man back to this motel and providing him sexual favors behind those closed grungy drapes—the old man sitting bare-ass on the threadbare bedspread, while Jan knelt on the filthy carpet blotched with stains of unknowable origin. Sitting in my car and contemplating Jan's situation, I noticed a patch of dandelions poking through the asphalt of the unkempt parking lot, fighting for survival. I remembered reading that dandelions are the hardiest of flowers. Jan needed to be just as hardy to survive this harsh environment. When I came back a few weeks later to see how she was doing, the hotel was shut down.

LIFE COURSE THEORY

Looking at baby boomer drug user lives through a life course perspective helps to unravel the effect of structural constraints from situational contexts that change over time. A life course analysis focuses on the timing of historical events,[1] with an emphasis on how time and place affect individual actions, called human agency.[2]

What was going on in society and in history at the time when Ted went to the reformatory as a juvenile and to prison as an adult? What did he miss? Why did the timing of a crack epidemic impact Moses more than Harry? How were Teresa's choices in life constrained by her descent into poverty due to economic downturns in society? How was Jan shaped by her situational context growing up with a disturbingly egocentric alcoholic mother and distant father with whom she bonded only through drugs?

A life course perspective reveals how our choices are impacted by the historical and social conditions of the time we live through, but the impact is felt differently depending on when these occur in our life. Jan missed the hippie decade of pot, peace, and love, and she sought the harmony and belonging she attributed to that era. Ted and Harry missed their high school years when friendships are formed and patterns of social interaction are developed. Moses wasted a large portion of his adult life in prison when he could have been building a career. When an individual is out of step with conventional transitions in life, they are at risk of being marginalized and feel alienated from mainstream society.

A life course perspective informs this analysis in three ways: (1) provides a view of baby boomers as a cohort living and growing older during the same historical context; (2) focuses on the variability of trajectories over time and the impact of individual situations; and (3) highlights the importance of transitions and turning points set in social context.

First, a life course perspective focuses on age cohorts as they move through history.[3] Successive generations are constrained by different demographic, social, economic, and psychological parameters as a result of changing social and historical conditions. Macro events, such as the Great Depression and World Wars, impact people differently depending on when these occurred in their life; therefore, children were affected differently than their parents.[4] Cohorts are affected profoundly by historical events occurring in adolescence or young adulthood.[5] The baby boomers studied in this book were born after WWII, living their childhood in the era of American "Happy Days" and a rising middle class.[6] Some were adolescents during the "peace and love" decade, others were teens when the drug scene became a more violent setting. Many boomers entered adulthood during a period of national economic decline. All experienced adulthood during a drug war that led to the highest levels of incarceration ever seen in history.[7] Rarely did anyone in the study blame historical context for their drug problems, but most embraced the American ideal of individualism and blamed themselves for choices they made.

Second, a life course perspective focuses attention on individual situations that buffer or intensify the impact of historical events. For example, Harry missed the height of crack use because he was incarcerated, and by the time he was released, the "crazy crackhead" was a derogatory role even among drug users, a situation that protected Harry from developing a crack habit. In contrast, Moses was free and enjoying a life he called "a bed of roses" while employed by a wealthy family that allowed him to travel from coast to coast. He was introduced to crack when it first appeared on the American scene. With no stigma yet attached to the crack user, he embraced it as a drug he could use on his days off without becoming addicted. Due to the social construction of crack as a drug association with racially prejudicial stereotypes, Moses felt the consequences of the crack era that Harry never experienced.

Age, race, gender, and class interact with situational context in ways that vary over time and place.[8] For example, contemporary norms and formal laws regarding transgender status are very different now than they were when Jordan realized her transgender identity in the mid-1970s while still in high school. The fact that Jordan started to use drugs at the same time as she felt compelled to leave her home and high school is notable as a life course influence. How did gender identity prejudices or racial discrimination constrain employment choices for Jordan in the late 1970s as she entered adulthood? Prejudice and discrimination are difficult to substantiate, and even the subjects of discrimination can be reluctant to accept its influence on their lives.

Jordan, like most people, believed she made her own choices in life and was not constrained by external forces.

Third, a life course perspective focuses attention on transitions and turning points across an individual's life trajectory.[9] A trajectory is a distinguishable pathway across a life span. Turning points are times or events that take a person in a different direction—one of many possible trajectories. These can be positive turning points that turn life in the direction of happiness and fulfillment, or they can be negative turning points that lead to loneliness and despair. Unfortunately, a turning point that looks like it might lead to greater happiness, such as being with a partner, can lead to greater despair when the partner encourages more drug use. Deciphering positive and negative turning points is not always simple. For example, Jan's involvement with Paul, who enticed her to use crack, is easily distinguished as a negative turning point. However, the turning points in Teresa's life are not so easy to distinguish. Was her relationship with Ted a negative turning point even though they helped each other and raised a loving family together? Often, there are many interacting factors that impact a negative or positive turning point, and all factors must be considered when looking for solutions. One-size-fits-all solutions for drug problems do not work.

It is important to point out that correlation does not always mean a cause and effect.[10] For example, negative turning points are often correlated with drug use, but drugs did not necessarily cause the turning point. Instead, drug use might have been a result of another factor that also impacted the turning point. A life course analysis helps to uncover the meaning behind a correlation by disentangling the multitude of factors that interact in a turning point event. One important factor is the timing of role transitions.

Role transitions often mark an age-graded normative passage in life, sometimes called a ritual.[11] When transitions do not occur at age-appropriate times, such as high school graduation at age 17 or 18 marking a transition into adulthood, the societal marker is missed. Sometimes, another transition replaces it, such as obtaining a General Equivalency Diploma (GED) instead of a high school diploma, but these are often laden with socially constructed values that stigmatize the individual instead of providing a comparable replacement. This is important because the synchronization of individual life transitions with societal and generational transitions has an impact on drug trajectories.

Society is composed of many informal social control mechanisms, or norms, which guide individual behavior.[12] Major transitions in life are embedded in normative behaviors linked to roles. Transitions in social roles, such as becoming a parent, influence individual choices based on normative descriptions of these roles. As Teresa illustrated, having a child was a turning point in her life as she embraced the norm that a mother should not use drugs. Even when she started using drugs again, her role as a mother motivated her to regain control. In contrast, Jan, who never had children, had fewer normative guides; therefore, she had less informal social control over her actions.

Individual choices are influenced by the transitional points that occur in one's life, as well as by the social and cultural trends of the period. Jan and other younger baby boomers lamented that they missed the sixties—that short period of time when the first of the baby boomers became adolescents and engaged in risky behaviors. This frightened their parents, who had been through the Great Depression, a World War, and recently achieved conventional well-being (at least for White, middle-class Americans). They reacted swiftly, first with treatment options and then with increasingly punitive criminal justice control. One of the unintended consequences of formal control was disenfranchising a large portion of baby boomers and disrupting the timing of when they would enter normative life course roles. It also presented a barrier to achieving success.

The majority of baby boomers in the study (90 percent) were impacted by incarceration and a criminal record. When Jan and I discussed the continuing educational (CE) credits she would need to reinstate her professional license so she could work in the field she was trained for, she brought up one situation that would forever affect her future: "It's been ten years since I've been in my field, but the CE hours are not the problem," she said. "I mean that's the easy part. I would have to get my criminal history, and all the court documents . . . " She trailed off looking forlorn. I knew what she meant. A criminal record was the "scarlet letter" of her time.

The stories told in this book challenge developmental theories that predict persistent behavior and continuity in drug trajectory patterns.[13] Instead, their lives reveal discontinuous drug-use phases that did not develop or mature over time but changed as they were impacted by social situations and constrained by formal or informal social controls.[14] Some people used drugs in a controlled manner for long periods of time. Others seemed to go in and out of control rapidly. Typically, cessation is the only control over drug use permitted in treatment, which advocates an "addict" or abstinence philosophy. Yet, depending on their situations, many of the baby boomers showed long periods of controlling their drug use by moderating it or substituting one drug with a less harmful drug—a harm reduction approach that will be examined more fully.

SELF-CONTROL OR SOCIAL CONTROL

Drug use behavior is often seen as a loss of self-control.[15] Drug treatment programs almost uniformly depict the active user as an individual who has lost control. A popular theory among criminologists, called *self-control theory,* proposes that self-control is developed in childhood and remains relatively stable throughout the life course.[16] According to the theory, an individual with low self-control will lack self-control throughout life, regardless of the social environment.

The baby boomer lives discussed in this book do not support this theory. All had periods of control over drug use. For example, Ted, a self-identified heroin addict and alcoholic, had 23 consecutive years of not using heroin or misusing opioids before he relapsed, and a four-year stretch in his life abstaining from alcohol as well. Moses's drug use trajectory shows a five-year period and a three-year period of no heroin, cocaine, or crack use. Crack was not the problem for Moses while he had steady employment and used only on days off—it was getting caught with the drug that precipitated incarceration, a negative turning point in his life. Losing the most important social role in his life at the time—his job—he started trafficking drugs between New York and Georgia. Likewise, the social control provided by her parent role helped Jordan to stop heroin and crack use for years. At the time of the interview, Jordan controlled her drug use by using only marijuana, a harm reduction strategy.

The lives discussed in this book provide support for social control theory. In contrast to self-control theory, *social control theory* proposes that delinquency and criminal behavior are a consequence of changes in the quality and strength of social ties. Individuals are more likely to engage in deviant behaviors, such as drug use, when their bonds to society are weak or broken.[17] Informal social control acts through the bonding that comes with attachment to others and ties to mainstream social institutions, such as school, work, and religious affiliation.[18] Situational contexts of jail and treatment break these bonds.

HARRY: SITUATIONAL CONTEXT
OVER THE LIFE COURSE

Official documents, such as school report cards, criminal records, and court transcripts, provide evidence of the impact of social context and how choices are constrained by situations. For example, Harry attended two schools in first grade and three in second grade, moving between three different states. On one report card, the teacher commented: "Harry can do good work, but his attitude toward school is not good." By the next report card, at a new school, the teacher wrote: "Harry has shown improvement, especially in his attitude." These two short handwritten teacher's notes indicate that at the age of eight, Harry made an effort to improve "his attitude" when asked, and he succeeded, showing self-control. However, it also suggests that his new environment might have helped him "control" his behavior.

The differences in his grades from fifth to eighth grade are more revealing of the importance of the social environment. Harry's grades rose from all C's and D's and an F in Arithmetic, in one school, to an A in Arithmetic and all B's and C's in another school during the same year. The teacher wrote: "Harry could be one of the top students of the class but he needs to be encouraged." The good grades were at a time when our family was reunited after the orphanage. Later, we moved to Philadelphia where Harry attended a poor school in a poor neighborhood. His report card shows he was absent for 27 days, and his A in Arithmetic dropped to a D. The evidence indicates that social context was more important than his individual attributes of self-control, although rewards from his teachers also seemed to have an effect.[19]

The situational context of Harry's adolescence included hanging out with an older crowd on the streets of Philadelphia and frequenting the bowling alleys and pool halls in Wildwood and Rio Grande, New Jersey. Additionally, his home life was disruptive, with an alcoholic father and periods of extreme poverty, which are what addiction scholars call "risk factors" for adolescent substance abuse.[20]

Harry received his GED in 1969 when he was in Yardville, the juvenile detention center.[21] In 1970, after release, he attended a community college in Harrisburg for one semester and earned credit for two classes. He adopted a hippie identity, grew long hair, and wore flowery clothing. Another hippie trait—using marijuana—got him in trouble with the law again.

His adult rap sheet started in 1971, in Lancaster, Pennsylvania, with a 1- to 23-month sentence in a county prison for obstructing an officer—a charge that could mean anything from not answering a police officer politely to not showing the officer where you are hiding the weed he suspects you have. The next year Harry got a 2- to 12-month sentence for "violation of a drug act"—vague but indicating that drugs were involved. At the time, he was using only marijuana.

Harry left the East Coast and hitchhiked to California in 1973. He thought he would fit in with the peace-loving state, but the hippie era was over by the time he got there. The police in California had become less tolerant of drug users.[22] In San Diego, he spent 16 days in a county jail for possession of marijuana. Within two months he had another violation in San Diego for controlled substances.

Seeing the writing on the wall, Harry headed back to the East Coast in 1974, but the War on Drugs pushed punitive anti-drug laws nationwide. Harry spent 60 days in jail in Wildwood, New Jersey, for "loitering under the influence of intoxicants" and paid a $250 fine for "unlawful use of marijuana." In 1975 he was sentenced to 23 months in Lancaster County jail for "violations of controlled substances" and in the same year of his release he got 60 days in Cape May, New Jersey, for possession of barbiturates, indicating he had begun expanding his drug repertoire.

In 1976, Harry returned to California, where he was arrested for sales of narcotics and sentenced to 41 days in jail and two years' probation. The relatively little jail time indicated the "sales" referred to an insignificant amount. When he was released he was soon charged for possession of a needle and syringe. The underlying message was to get out of town. Harry headed back to the East Coast again. Landing in New Jersey, Harry received two charges for possession of marijuana with more fines.

By 1977, his growing rap sheet showed mostly drug possession charges. He owed probation fees and court fines on both coasts. His rap sheet also showed he went from being primarily a marijuana user to a heroin addict. With limited opportunity for employment due to his growing criminal (drug) record, Harry starting robbing banks.

In 1978, Harry was charged and tried in the US District Court, Middle District of Pennsylvania, with "armed" bank robbery, although he claimed not to have used a gun. He was sentenced to 12 years in federal penitentiary. He served time in Terre Haute, Indiana; Marion, Illinois; and Leavenworth, Kansas. Counting time served, he was released on March 12, 1986. In 1988, he was given a 10-year sentence, and in 1990, a 20-year sentence to be run consecutively. Both were for bank robberies, and confidential informants were used by prosecutors to win the cases.

I myself left the United States in 1973 and lived in Europe, returning to the states to earn a college degree in 1991.[23] Starting a new life on my own as a single mother, I lived in Georgia because it was where my sister had a house I could rent cheaply. By this time, Harry was only a few years into his 30-year sentence and confined in Huntingdon, Pennsylvania, a maximum-security prison. With children to raise and going to school, I did not see Harry very often. Sometimes when I made the 1,500-mile roundtrip, Harry was in solitary confinement, or what prisoners call the "hole."[24]

Being in the hole usually meant visitor restrictions. Phone calls were not permitted, so Harry could not let me know. Solitary confinement was supposed to be for the most unmanageable, physically aggressive, and violent inmates, although it was being used for the most minor infractions of prison rules.[25] Harry was not a violent prisoner, but he did break rules.

What Harry would not do is snitch. Snitching is against the code of most prisoners, but law enforcement and prison authorities are dependent on snitches or confidential informants. Harry's refusal to snitch, coupled with his loathing of guards encouraging snitching, often landed him in the hole. One of the longest periods in the hole was when he refused to say anything he knew about a successful escape by one of his prison buddies in Huntingdon.

Justin was an infamous member of the "Douglas Gang" led by three brothers who had been convicted of multiple murders among other crimes, many of which they denied doing.[26] After Justin escaped from the correctional facility, the prison officials questioned Harry, who was his closest friend, but he honored the convict's code and feigned ignorance. Since the escape was a huge embarrassment to the warden, in retribution, Harry was put in the hole.

In 2000, Harry was officially eligible to go before the parole board. I started work on a parole plan for him, gathering the necessary mountain of paperwork and signatures needed. Right before his parole hearing, Harry wrote in a letter:

> If I am very fortunate, I should be out of the hole and involved in a drug program in a few weeks, the successful completion of which should warrant my being paroled. There is still to be considered what record there is of my involvement with the escape last year. There were careers ended, political aspirations jeopardized, and millions of dollars spent because of that. And I was commonly known to be his closest friend. How far that knowledge travels and what weight it carries, I don't know.

In my submitted parole plan, Harry would live in my home and was promised full-time employment with a friend in Georgia who ran an organic produce business. Harry had a home, work, and family support, but he was denied parole. He took the news better than I did, writing from the hole:

> Things are pretty much the same for me. I read, exercise, play chess, do crosswords, and daydream. I haven't had any pot in two weeks, and it really sucks. I range from being depressed to being enraged to think that I intend to go several years sober when I get out of the hole so the [parole] board won't have an excuse.

A few months later, Harry was transferred to a special program at another state penitentiary in Camp Hill, a massive institutional solitary confinement program. His letters came more often, indicating his growing despondency.[27] In one he wrote:

> I don't know if I mentioned it, but I am now permitted to come out of my cell without handcuffs for the first time in years. In another month I will no longer be deemed a "threat to the security of the institution" and will be sent to a general population somewhere. It's all such a bunch of bullshit.

I had never known Harry as an adult on the outside. I sometimes worried he would wind up like one of the men I had interviewed who was shooting dope under bridges and in deserted shacks in the "Bluff"—the open drug-dealing market in a desolate community in Atlanta. I discussed my worries with him on my next visit. "Hell, I'm an addict," he told me, "but I ain't no junkie." His answer led me to study drug user types. What I discovered was a wide range of drug use phases. Not all phases were problematic, and problem drug use was often temporary.[28]

PHASES, NOT STAGES, IN DRUG TRAJECTORIES

Drug researchers and addiction specialists tend to model drug trajectories as development stages, suggesting that people progress from one lower stage to a higher one.[29] Others categorize drug users by kinds of drugs used or by drug user types.[30] Classifications, called typologies, are helpful for diagnostic purposes.[31] Yet, they are rarely used for establishing what kind of treatment is needed.[32]

As discussed previously, a life course perspective reveals that drug trajectories do not necessarily develop in stages, and they are not dependent on individual traits. Instead, trajectories are embedded in social and historical context, and often dependent on setting, resources, and drug availability.[33] Most drug use trajectories show a range of using behavior that fluctuates between "controlled" and "uncontrolled" drug use.

Based on drug users' life stories, I developed a "phases of drug use" model to illustrate the movement in and out of controlled or uncontrolled use, which was dependent on the user's social roles.[34] I found the main turning point in the trajectory was when one's identity became linked to being an addict, particularly when others become aware of the "addict" role.[35] A second major turning point was the transition into a "junkie" role, which is when all social roles and control are absent in the user's life.

The nine phases in drug trajectories can be collapsed into three for a succinct and effective analysis: (1) controlled use; (2) dependent use; and (3) uncontrolled use. The controlled phase is when a person can use drugs without it interfering with other areas of life. This is also referred to as functional use. The dependent phase is when drug use is likely to start interfering with conventional life. In this phase, drug use is fluctuating in and out of control but the user can still be functional. If they are caught using drugs or enter treatment, they are often referred to and refer to themselves as addicts. The uncontrolled user is often called a junkie, a derogatory label even among drug users. In this phase, drug use is out of control; however, the important factor in this phase is the social context. If the user is in an unstable social situation or social role (unemployment, homeless, ex-offender), problematic uncontrolled drug use continues. It is difficult to achieve sustained recovery from this phase and instead a recovery and relapse cycle develops, like a revolving door with no exit.

Although each phase should have a different "treatment" response, most drug users receive the same kind of treatment regardless of what phase they are in. The three phases are illustrated in the life of one woman who came from one of the most privileged social situations of all the people interviewed in this study—Ann, a woman with a high social status.

ANN

Ann was 48 when we met. She had recently finished a five-month "professional" treatment program and was attending 12-step meetings daily. A stylishly dressed White woman, her perfect teeth, flawless skin, and silky hair gave little indication of the depths of her drug use. Although both of her parents were alcoholics, she said her father was a functional alcoholic and maintained the family's upper-middle-class status. She recalled seeing her parents drink in the evening until they passed out on the floor. Depressed with her home life, at age 16 she ran away to live on her own.

Ann started using prescription pills she got from a relative illegally at age 12, and by 14 was using cocaine, which was popular in her school. From 14 to 18 years old she used a variety of drugs, adding to her repertoire each year. As I was writing down the list, she smiled and said, "I stopped every single drug on this list when I was eighteen and I was clean until I was forty. Makes it easy."

At age 18 she had a turning point while working and living on her own in Pennsylvania:

> I was completely depressed and I was using speed to kind of counteract the depression to a point and then my supplier dried up and I remember—I was in this little flat. It was like a room in a house, and I remember lying on the bed and going, 'I can't get up, can't go to work, I just can't even do this anymore.' I had no friends anymore, and I just was like 'okay, am I going to die of bed sores lying here in this bed or am I going to live? Okay, I'll live. That means I have to go back to school.' So that's what happened. That's how I got back into school.

> I went back to [parent's home] to start school, but I couldn't 'cause I was so depressed. I was agoraphobic. I couldn't even get out of bed. I couldn't even walk down the driveway. So I actually had to start on antidepressants, and that's when I was able to start school, when I was nineteen.

Ann attended community college in Charlotte to earn a GED, and when the family moved to Oregon the next year, she enrolled in a state university. "School, ambition, and hard work" were her "program" for staying clean. "I needed a project," and because becoming a doctor would be a challenge, she tackled that lofty goal. Using a 12-step analogy, she explained: "my program was school—that was my program, school, ambition and hard work." She earned a master's degree in biochemistry, got a coveted spot in medical school, and earned a Doctor of Medicine (MD) degree before age 30.

Her self-made "program" facilitated almost 20 years of functional life. The year after she got her MD, she went to Atlanta for an internship and residency and then moved to Oregon to start her career as a medical doctor. She married and had two children. Life could not have been more ideal. Although

Ann missed an important ritual in her life, graduating from high school, she made up for it and achieved the American dream of family, work, and wealth.

At age 40, Ann experienced another turning point—this one stemming from her work.

I worked hard, as a clinic doctor and then I'm a hospitalist, which is hospital medicine. That was a new thing when I went into it and then, when I was forty years old, I sent a patient home and I was already kind of following a path towards going into hospice and palliative care so I—at the time that this event happened that I'm going to tell you about I was—I'm really into pain control and easing suffering and all that, right? So I sent this patient home from the hospital and there were a lot of factors, but he went home and overdosed on some morphine I gave him, and I felt like I had put a bullet in his head. That it was all my fault. Again, this is the adult child of alcoholic thing. You're responsible for the entire world. Well, I really felt like that, that I had killed him, and I was distraught. Totally spun out of control, didn't know where to get relief. I tried to get help.

I tried to get help from my med legal department, from the department of psychiatry, from my boss who was a friend, and my bigger boss; another friend. I think it partly—no offense—I think I went to men, and they didn't get it. A lot of them were like, "Mistakes happen, Ann." What? This doesn't happen. So this patient died. He was young, he was a construction worker, and I didn't know he'd had a history of addiction. I mean, I didn't collect and nobody else collected it [drug histories], I mean, when you're doing a quick admission in the ER for something. Anyway, he went home and overdosed—I mean I didn't know a lot of this stuff till afterwards. All I could think of was 'I gave him the drug, and he overdosed and killed himself.' So, I couldn't get any relief from— I was distraught, I couldn't sleep, I couldn't eat. I mean, I was gone.

Ann saw a bottle of pills in the bathroom medicine cabinet at home and took one pill to sleep. "I knew I was jumping down the rabbit hole," she said. "I knew." She started using pills to sleep and pills to stay awake. Soon she relied on the "amped-up feeling" of prescription medication.

I got the Ambien and the Ativan and the Provigil from my doctor—my doctors whatever. So no, I did not self-prescribe. The Vicodin—ten years ago it was easy to get Vicodin over the internet. Get a phone consultation over the internet. You have a couple brain cells in your head you're able to go to multiple sites and get multiple prescriptions, so I had a steady supply of Vicodin or hydrocodone-based products coming in.

As long as she had access to prescription drugs, she used in a controlled manner and fulfilled her roles as a doctor, wife, and mother, without any noticeable effect. Ann was in a functional pill-taking dependent phase for four years.

It was not until age 44 that Ann realized she was "addicted to opioids." She tried to "taper" about "50 times" but would not take time off work to withdraw. At age 47, she said, "I turned myself in, nobody caught me." She told her husband of 10 years that she was addicted to prescription pills.

Her husband staged an intervention, and Ann was sent to a private residential treatment center in Oregon for 28 days. While she was there she met a man who was also in treatment for methamphetamine. "I was just about done and he was already out," she explained. "I ran off with this guy, Donnie, leaving my family . . . and we're just spinning out of control—two addicts." Donnie was abusive and often beat her, once fracturing her skull, but Ann stayed with him. She wrote inappropriate prescriptions for Donnie and lost her MD license and her job.

When she lost custody of her children, Ann checked into a public rehab that she described as a "facility for women who have lost their children because they are prostitutes or street junkies." Without work, she could not afford better treatment.

While in the rehab facility, she had a vision of Donnie dead and stiff lying on the floor of their apartment. The dream bothered her so much she felt compelled to see him.

> So I actually snuck out of rehab—it was lockdown. I snuck out under the umbrella of a doctor's appointment, and I checked on him—he was fine. So as soon as I leave him at the apartment I—again this picture comes into my head—and again I have to tell you I'm off of all drugs. This picture is a very specific picture and it was disturbing me so much that I had seen him, and he was fine. He was drunk but he was fine—this very disturbing picture. So again, a week later I sneak out. Well, you know what the punch line is—I find him dead. Stiff, lying his side, on the floor—on the ground . . . God giving me what they call a warning shot. In medicine when you're gonna give somebody bad news you give them a warning shot. I was horrified because not only did I find him—I found him about six days after he died.

Grieving for Donnie, Ann attempted suicide by taking an overdose of pills. What saved her life was that she passed out facedown on the bed instead of faceup—otherwise she could have choked to death on her vomit.

While Ann was in the emergency room her mother came to visit. When she was released, her parents arranged for her to go to the exclusive long-term treatment center in Georgia, specifically established to treat medical

professionals. After five months of what she described as "intensive, intensive, intensive, intensive therapy," she moved to a halfway house and attended
12-step meetings while working on getting her license reinstated.

TURNING POINTS

Jan and Ann used similar drugs and started in similar situations. Both were
middle class and both had emotionally distant alcoholic parents. Both were
wild teenagers who left home early. Yet, their trajectories of drug use are very
diverse. Jan had multiple turning points into and out of problematic drug
use, whereas Ann had only a few.

Ann was started using hard drugs as a teenager but was drug free for 20
years on her own "self-made" program that involved going to school to earn an
MD. Jan, who engaged in drug use and prostitution, was also drug free while
in school working on a two-year technical degree. Here the similarities stop.

Ann went from being a controlled user to recognizing she was an addict—
a turning point. She continued in her dependent phase for at least three years.
Her turning point into an uncontrolled phase occurred when she asked for
help and was sent to treatment, which proved to be the wrong social situation
for this vulnerable time in her life.

Treatment is the universal response to addiction, and no one can blame her
husband, who was probably advised by the best addiction specialists in Oregon
since Ann worked in the medical field. However, regardless of what phase they
are in or their situational context, people with all different kinds of drug problems are given the same treatment, usually living together in the same residential facility and attending the same group meetings based on 12-step philosophy. Social interaction among vulnerable individuals in such closed social
settings results in reciprocal learning and sharing of skills and knowledge.
Some knowledge is helpful; other knowledge is not. Intimate relationships are
formed. Some might be positive; some, like Ann's, might not.

There are a few exclusive professional treatment "retreats," like the one
Ann went to a few years later, but these are accessible mainly to the wealthy
and not to the vast majority of people who rely on insurance, meager family
finances, or public health programs.[36]

Did Ann need intensive residential treatment the first time she asked for
help? Could she have learned to cope with her guilt by going to a private
counselor for therapy while using a pharmaceutical drug like methadone for

her physical addiction? These are questions that must be asked if we are to address situations like Ann's in the future.

In contrast to Ann, Jan continued problem drug use for most of her life with brief periods of control or abstinence while she was engaged in conventional activities, such as going to school or starting a career. Her positive turning points were facilitated by support from disparate sources, such as a "sugar daddy" who helped her get off the streets and attend college. Her many negative turning points involved drug-using partners or friends, usually short-lived relationships. Always seeking acceptance, she realized she was searching for love she might never find. She also sought to forget the nightmare of her childhood.

The last time I saw them, Ann and Jan were both living in halfway homes for women, attending 12-step meetings and drug free, but their social context and transitional situations were very dissimilar. Ann's highly paid "halfway house" in the suburbs was more like sharing a home with a friend. She had complete freedom, a car, and a credit card. Jan was sharing a room in a city halfway house full of poor women and funded by a small nonprofit. She had rules to follow, no transportation, and no money. However, the critical difference between the two is that Jan, unlike Ann, had a criminal record.

The most common occurrence for people after treatment is relapse.[37] Ann had a good chance of working again as a doctor; Jan will not have the opportunity to work in the profession she went to school to learn. With her criminal record, she can never work in the medical field again. If she fails sobriety, she will most likely go back to sex work, as long as she finds men willing to pay $30 because she still "looks okay."

THREE

Relationships

IAN

I sensed a little anger from this young-looking 56-year-old White man as we engaged in small talk before starting the interview. When he recounted his story, I noticed how he paused, glanced at me, and then quickly looked down at the floor. Ian, I sensed, was lonely, and the pretense of anger was a cover. I learned he had been lonely most of his life. He was sent to an orphanage at age three, the age when we start to remember our bonds to parents.

> I was raised in the Christian Children's Home in the suburbs for about eight years, and from then I went from uncle to aunts, to aunts to uncles, because my mom and dad were separated and remarried again. And both started families with their new marriage so therefore they left me, my brother, and my two sisters [at the orphanage] . . . My two other sisters, they were adopted and I haven't seen them since.

Ian never saw or talked with his mother again after she left him at the orphanage; however, he saw his father. At age 10, a judge ordered his father to take the brothers back. His father's new wife did not want them, so they were bounced from one relative's house to another, and eventually lived with their grandmother in the city. Ian kept in contact with his brother and father over the years, but they were never close. After living with his grandmother, he moved to Alabama, which was where his drug usage picked up.

Ian exhibited one of the most continuous drug trajectories in the sample. Once he started alcohol at age 10, he never stopped. Once he started cocaine, heroin, and methamphetamine at the age of 18, he continued to use them until he entered a methadone program at age 50. He dabbled in crack from the mid-1980s until mid-1990s, the historical period of the "crack epidemic." He usually injected drugs and showed me his arms, which were visibly needle worn. But he was not the proverbial junkie. Ian was a lifelong drug user, but unusually functional.

Ian was a hard worker—mainly blue-collar jobs: "Mostly what I was doing then was hard labor work, construction work, moving and storage . . . I was cleanin' the bathrooms and doing odd jobs and janitorial work." He thinks he contracted hepatitis C from the janitorial work.

He served some time in jail for tax evasion, and when he escaped while on a work crew, he was caught and got more time. During his first jail sentence he was withdrawing from heroin, but he never received any treatment. In his third term in jail, this time on drug charges, he said he was doing heroin or cocaine "basically every week" while in jail.

On one job, his boss was also a drug dealer, and when Ian began to help him with this side-business, his drug use increased. During his dealing days he was involved in a fight and a man stabbed him in the leg with a fish knife, which severed his femoral artery. Ian never fully recovered from this injury, and although he worked occasionally, it was hard to find steady employment with his damaged leg.

Eventually Ian lost his leg and spent years trying to get government disability aid. During this time, he was often homeless. He described some of the problems he encountered living in homeless shelters:

> I was stayin' at the Salvation Army, which was the only place that I could stay at with my addiction and the financial situation I was in at the time. I was stayin' at the Red Shelter or whatever it's called. You had to pay ten dollars a night to stay there.

With one leg missing, no prosthetic, and confined to a wheelchair, one would think Ian was a perfect candidate for government help, but it was not that easy. He had trouble with the onerous paperwork, and the idiosyncrasies of bureaucratic demands did not help. Once Ian started to receive the coveted disability check and was eligible for group housing for the disabled, he discovered that much of his check would be used to pay for public housing.

> They start a program and say it is to benefit the homeless. At the same time, they turn around and tell the homeless individual, if you're on disability, therefore we're going to take a percentage of your check.

While this might appear to be justified in order to keep the disabled from being homeless, Ian had very little left over for living expenses.[1] He said he was having issues with the staff in the group housing program and was looking for alternatives.

Ian began his methadone treatment about seven years ago and remained in the program primarily due to the director, Dave, who also was his counselor and friend. It was only with the director's help that Ian was able to complete the paperwork needed to get his Supplemental Security Income (SSI) for disability. Dave encouraged everyone to attend 12-step meetings, and Ian complied, mainly to please him. He also stopped all other drugs, although he had an occasional beer, something he did not bring up in 12-step meetings. He said he never bought into the alcohol abstinence mandate endorsed by 12-step. Ian appeared to control his drinking. Contrary to popular belief and 12-step teaching, having a few drinks did not make him relapse and start using other drugs.

Since methadone is a pharmaceutical opioid used as treatment for heroin and other opioids, Ian was essentially still using an opioid; however, since methadone is legal, his perspectives and society's view of him had changed. He was no longer considered a "drug user" and did not use methadone to get high. He needed methadone to address his physical pain. His warm relationship with the director helped address his emotional hurt.

As an orphan with no parental bonding, Ian was without a source of emotional support as he grew into adulthood. He had one relationship with a woman for about seven years, and he thinks he might have a daughter from their relationship. However, she left him and married another man, whom she said was the father of the child. He never took a paternity test to find out. Ian said that her new husband "was under the impression the daughter was his, so I let it go at that." He never met his assumed daughter, although from the look on his face, he still seemed to care about her. After this relationship, he had sexual encounters with "occasional partners" only.

Ian was missing the emotional connection provided by a relationship with a partner or children. Until his recent relationship with the methadone program director, he did not mention any friends who provided social or emotional support. His relationship with a former boss influenced him to become a dealer, a dangerous role that eventually caused the loss of his leg with no support from his boss. Even his acquaintances seemed to be transitory. For example, he learned about the methadone program from a man he met briefly at the shelter. "He was a guy that I ran into. He was wasted and he had

AIDS—he died of AIDS," Ian recalled with a hint of melancholy. "His first name was Larry, and I met him when I was stayin' at the Salvation Army."

Following Larry's suggestion, Ian started the methadone program and finally met someone who showed genuine concern for him—Dave, the program director. The respect he had for Dave was evident when he spoke about him. After an addiction lasting over 30 years, his relationship with the director motivated Ian to stop using drugs and find stable housing. He also mentioned that he was looking into an employment-training program for people with disability. A little bit of validation went a long way.

Ian was not the only orphan in our sample. Most lacked family and kinship bonds that act as an emergency safety net both materially and emotionally. They were bereft of a significant relationship during the most difficult times in their lives. Their relationships with friends were fleeting. Ian's turning point came when he began the methadone program, but the impetus for continuing was clearly his relationship with Dave. His life story illustrates the importance of relationships. The social bonds that tie us together are essential for well-being, and without them, drug use is a temporary but effective solution.

SOCIAL BONDS

One of the key principles in life course perspective is that lives are linked through interaction with other people in social networks that change over time.[2] Although this seems like a simple notion, the multiple facets of different interactions throughout the passage of time makes linked lives a very complex matrix of relationships, usually much more multifaceted than seen in Ian's life. Moreover, the strength of relational bonds varies over time. Typically, family is where bonds are first formed and often sets the course of other relationships for many years.[3] Peer networks are very influential during adolescence. While marriages and partnerships are influential relationships in adulthood and provide emotional bonding, the social norms for these relationships are changing rapidly.[4] Ian's one partnership ended before he could verify if he had fathered a child or not, an emotional landmine that obviously affected him even years later. Having been rejected by his own parents, Ian was denied the possibility of having a relationship with a daughter he thought might be his own.

Relationships with friends, co-workers, and colleagues are even more diverse than those with family, and they offer a wide range of social support. Moreover, these relationships are impacted by many factors beyond our control. Ian mentioned few people as friends, and his current relationship with the director of a methadone program was dependent on the program staying open and Ian remaining a client. For Ian, this relationship was enough to stay in the program, stop using drugs, and attend 12-step meetings.

Historical events change the social landscape in which relationships are formed and networks created. They can limit the availability of social networks, force individuals into new networks, and change one's entire life trajectory without much choice on the part of the individual. War is a clear example of how families can be split apart, and young men and women miss important age-appropriate transitions in life. Some come back to their families with experiences that can scar them emotionally or physical injuries that limit plans for family or employment. Likewise, the War on Drugs tore families apart. How one survives after trauma depends a great deal on the social bonds and social support available to them through social networks.[5]

Relationships are essential for emotional, mental, and physical well-being, but they can have positive or negative effects. Strong social bonds to family and friends are critical for people with problem drug use. Unfortunately, too often the bonds are weakened by society's punitive responses to drug users.[6]

FAMILY AND SIGNIFICANT OTHERS

The most significant relationships discussed by respondents were those with family and partners. Lack of strong parental attachment is considered a risk factor for substance abuse.[7] However, an emotional bond with family members can also encourage drug use if the family member was using as well. For example, Jan was proud to be using drugs with her father.

Significant others, whether a long-term partner or a short-term relationship, had both positive or negative influences on drug-using behavior of baby boomers over their lifetime.[8] Typically drug use ruptured a relationship, and non-drug-using partners often instigated the breakup, as was seen in Ann's life. But this was not always the case.[9] Moses had a five-year relationship with a woman who did not use any drugs but was aware that he used.

> She knew about it before and she accepted that part of me for what I was. She knew that, and like I said, she was all right with it. We separated because I got not all right with it. I didn't want to keep stringing her along with that situation. It wasn't a real love thing.

The common pattern found in this study was a male significant other initiating a female into using hard drugs. Ann was introduced to nonprescription hard drugs through a relationship with a man. Jan also started hard drugs initiated by her boyfriend, and she often relapsed when a significant other offered her drugs. However, other patterns of initiation between significant others were found as well.[10]

Relationships involving trauma had the most direct impact on drug use, and trauma occurring during childhood had a lasting effect. The trauma of Ted's accidental shooting of his mother, and his description of trying to put her head back on her body, was a scene he will never get out of his mind. The emotional support of his wife and children helped to keep him alive, but it could not end his emotional and mental suffering. While others told less vivid traumatic events, the tone of their voices, the faraway look in their eyes, or a slight lowering of their heads when recounting childhood trauma gave evidence that they were still impacted.

ELIJAH

Elijah, a 55-year-old African American man, was the son of sharecroppers. When he was 11 years old his father disappeared, and his mother left him with relatives. He did not know why.

That afternoon that my mother left me, she left me without explanation. And the only thing I could think about was standing down there, near the house where she left me at [thinking] it's takin' a long time for her to come back, and I was hoping she'd hurry up and come back. And basically all I was saying 'bout was I [stumbles over words]—all I was thinking 'bout was I was glad that when she was come back—wishing she would return. I never questioned if she would return, I just wanted to know when she would return, and as it got darker, that's when I started to have fear.

He eventually stopped looking for her, but he remembered the specific times he would miss his mother most.

Most specially when I got outta school, 'cuz most of the time she had something prepared for me. And I guess that's when I started missing her, when I started coming home to my aunt's house in the evening. She was saying she hadn't prepared nothing, but I could see her kids was healthy and fed. So that's when I really, really missed my mother in the evening. And quite a few nights as a child I went to bed hungry and that's when I really, really missed her . . . You know, when I was staying with my aunt I never could remember eating breakfast. I never could remember her washing clothes for me. I always been a good child, and in the evening I remember washing my underwear out and socks in a little foot tub that we had and stuff like that. And it felt like at times I'd always been on my own, and, I think I'd shared with you about picking cotton in the evening. That's how I lived. That signified fifty or seventy-five cent every evening. And I did that for a couple of years, and so it felt like I always worked. And I did have some growing up in [those] years.

Elijah's mother came back when he was 16 with money she had saved from working in the city. He lived with her for a year before he joined the military and went to Korea. His drug use started while he was in the military. Elijah's drug trajectory showed continued heroin and cocaine use, only interrupted by five years in prison. He also had a long period of crack use that lasted from the mid-1980s until 2006 when he stopped all drugs. While the lack of parental bonding was not the only influence on his problems with drugs, his childhood trauma had an impact.[11]

Measuring the risk factors related to parental relationships is complex and nuanced. For example, parents can be emotionally absent while physically present. Ann, who was the child of alcoholic parents, and Jan, who was forced to live with her promiscuous mother who drank herself into a stupor, also suffered due to emotionally disturbing parental relationships.

Parents are usually a source of support during times of emotional or economic stress. Even Ann's alcoholic parents came to her rescue in her darkest hour. Some parents, however, practiced what is called "tough love." Tough love refers to an attitude or behavior adopted by family and loved ones toward drug-using family members that can include cutting them off from emotional and economic support. The intention is to force them to "hit rock bottom." While tough love is often encouraged in 12-step programs (Al-Anon) for families of alcoholics and those who are dependent on drugs, others suggest using tough love with caution.[12] Tough love was very popular in the 1980s and 1990s, and adult baby boomers bore the brunt of this historical trend in treatment philosophy.

ALICIA

Alicia, a 48-year-old African American woman, was raised in a violent household. She saw her father beat her mother and heard him ask her mother to prostitute for money. Her mother eventually left him and provided for the family on her own when she acquired steady employment. Alicia did not have a problem with drugs until after she married and was already raising a child. In her early twenties she was given cocaine by a neighbor. Her friend taught her to freebase, a method used to smoke cocaine before crack became popular, and Alicia continued to use cocaine or crack for the next 20 years. Leaving her husband, who did not use drugs, she engaged in sex for drugs and lived from house to house when she moved back in the community where she was raised. She was in prison four times, and eventually all her children were taken from her by government child protection agencies.

During Alicia's problematic drug use period, she had a continuing relationship with her mother. "I kept in touch with her," she explained. "I would call her sometimes when I needed her. If things were going okay for me in the street, when I could come about my drugs pretty frequently, then I didn't call." Her mother's support, however, was inconsistent and conditional.

My mother showed me a lot of tough love. I thought she was the cruelest mother in the world. Okay, now that I am a mother—I thought that was the cruelest thing. So she would say, here take this and just get away from here, out the door. And I would leave and go do what I wanted to do. And then if I ended up in jail, I would contact her and she would send me money. She would come and see me. She would let me talk to my daughter when she was at her house.

Once I was laying on the floor [of her house] during the afternoon. And the police was waking me up. I was asleep. He said, "Hey you got to come with me. Your mom thinks you've done something." She [mother] said, "I know you've got something on you. Y'all can lock her up to save her." And I said, "I haven't did anything. I haven't did anything." And when he ran my name and everything, he didn't get anything. So he brought me back into the house. And he told her, he said, "Mrs. I can't keep her, because there's nothing on her." I said, "Mama, I can't believe you did that! Why you do that?" She said, "You need help. You need help, you know."

Once some detectives locked me up for prostitution. Well, they didn't lock me up; they got me. They took me and they said, "You look like a nice girl. You seem like you come from a nice home." And I said, "I do." He said, "Well, why are you choosing to do this?" And I told him, "I (mumbling), you know." So he said, "If we call your mama, do you think she'll bring you to court tomorrow?" So they took me home. And it was like three o'clock in the morning. They knocked on the door. One stayed in the car with me and one went to the door. One knocked on the door, and she found out who it was and cracked her door. And she said, "Take her to jail." He told her, "I have your daughter and we just want to know if you'll bring her to court tomorrow so we don't have to take her to jail." She said, "No, take her to jail because that's the best place for her." So that's the kind of mama I had.

Alicia stayed in a notably rough neighborhood while she was using crack from house to house, but she had the support of another family member who might have helped to keep her alive. "My baby brother was a cop," she explained. "He sent his partner over to get me because he knew where I hung."

The social setting of Alicia's drug use was an important factor to consider when looking at the impact of her relationships. She "hung" in an area of town that most White people only drove through—the drug market of Atlanta. In some aspects, this community was a protective factor as it provided Alicia relationships with people who protected her. In other aspects, the area was a barrier to forming new relationships with people who were not using drugs.

THE BLUFF

Alicia lived, worked, and used drugs in the neighborhood in Atlanta known as "the Bluff"—a community recognized as one of the most violent open-air drug markets in the country.[13] Once a suburb on the outskirts of Atlanta for the White working class, separating the community from inner-city Black neighborhoods, subsequent White flight to outer suburbs and the development of large housing projects nearby resulted in the area becoming a predominantly African American community. While neighboring communities included the homes of civil rights leaders, such as Martin Luther King, Jr., the community now known as the Bluff was long ignored by city politicians. As crime increased, numerous revitalization projects in the area failed to reverse the downward spiral.

When I was conducting research in the Bluff, the streets were not repaired, the sidewalks were broken or nonexistent, and every other house was boarded up or derelict. Dogs barked incessantly from behind chain-link fences, and I often saw a stray pit bull roaming the streets. There were few grocery stores but plenty of liquor stores and bars. During the day, young males who appeared to be still in their teens stood at corners taking money or handing small packets of drugs to cars that rolled by slowly with their windows open. Streetwalking prostitutes came out in the evening. Gunshots were heard at any time. Once

I heard a round of shots while I was conducting an interview with a dealer in the area. We were in an inner room and safely away from windows. I nervously remarked, "It sounds like target practice." My respondent looked at me with a deadpan face and said, "That ain't no target practice."

Periodically, the police targeted the community with "get tough on crime" programs focused on shutting down the vibrant drug business. The "Red Dog" unit was a drug strike force known for using excessively violent tactics, shady confidential informants, and illegal searches. The name Red Dog is said to stand for "Run Every Drug Dealer Out of Georgia." Instead the Red Dog were disbanded after numerous court cases were brought against it, including the killing of an innocent elderly women in a failed undercover drug bust by Red Dog police who then planted drugs in her house to cover up their mistake.[14] Although the Bluff originally referred to a series of ridges on the edge of the community, the BLUFF is known in the streets to stand for "Better Leave, U Fucking Fool." It appeared to be more aptly named than the Red Dog.

Despite this dismal landscape, some of the best community-led programs for drug users were focused on the area as well. The only syringe exchange program in the state started providing clean syringes to drug users here to address the AIDS epidemic and stayed in the area to provide food, clothing, and showers. A comprehensive treatment program located in the Bluff helped people like Alicia and Elijah find permanent housing and sustainable employment.[15] It also provided Alicia the opportunity to live with her children independently from her mother. However, knowing that her family "had her back" during her most desperate times helped to keep her alive until the point when the community-based program appeared on the scene.[16] Such comprehensive community-based treatment programs were not mentioned by respondents living in suburban middle-class communities, who often paid top price for less support and help.

ABEL

"I have a gift for words," Abel, a 53-year-old White male, told me when we sat down to talk about what the interview would entail. Displaying abundant energy, his zest for life was newly found. Abel was born into a middle-class family in the suburbs of Detroit and lived in an affluent neighborhood growing up. However, his childhood life was nothing like the *Ozzie and Harriet* or *Leave It to Beaver* sitcoms that families viewed on television. In these idealized shows, mother stayed at home cleaning the house and cooking food with an apron on, while father went to work with a kiss from his wife and was welcomed home in the evening to conduct fatherly discussions with his children around the dinner table—a family situation that established the norm at the time. While few families achieved this ideal, most families used it as the model to aspire to and the standard against which to compare themselves to others.

From outside appearances, Abel's family life appeared to achieve the ideal family standard, but behind closed doors life was lonely and frightening for young Abel, who suffered a number of traumatic events early in life. First, his mother was dying slowly of cancer and often in bed or the hospital.

> She had cancer back in the old days when they did really horrible things, and radical surgeries ... and chemotherapy that was poison, and radiation that literally burned her and things of that nature, so it was pretty traumatic. It was one of those, as much as I love my mom, it was a blessing to see her go because she had been tortured for years. Really, really painful! Really just a mess—almost incomprehensible. I kinda zoned out during the whole lot after that, I really wasn't able to feel that much pain at that time.

She passed away when Abel was 15 years old. Although her death was expected, he took the loss of his mother very hard, and his father offered no consolation. "My father didn't believe in therapy," Abel explained. "I cried out on several occasions, and he said only crazy people do stuff like that." His father was also distant emotionally, and he did little to take care of his two sons except to provide a house and food.

Second, Abel endured unremitting abuse from his older brother, who beat him unmercifully. While his mother was sick and his father often absent or emotionally disengaged, Abel had no protection.

> Well my dad was a philanderer, so he was busy doing other things, and my mom was sick. I have the fox guarding the henhouse and [my brother] is a horribly sadistic abusive person. I got beat for nothing 'cause, uh, he had some insane psycho-jealousy that I was going to steal all the affection from the family or something. He's a policeman now. His element, yeah, that was the role he was born to play. He's still a cop. He made sergeant after twenty-seven years in a suburban force then retired. Then re-enlisted in another suburb, because he likes hanging around late at night with a badge and a gun and making people sweat, and being the dominator.

Abel's only stability as a child came from his grandparents, who lived in the same house but in separate quarters. But they both died within a year after his mother died, so he spent his late teen years very much alone and abused. He imagined a better time. Like Jan, Abel regretted that he was born a little too late: "I just missed the sixties and everything—they had everything, you know."

After he graduated from high school, Abel attended college, following the norms of many middle-class boys in his school. However, by this time, his father spent the family inheritance and they had no money to pay for college. Leaving college after his freshman year, Abel married and left his hometown, and never returned. Abel said he did not want to be anywhere near his brother, whom he compared to the "prison guards in Auschwitz in WWII."

Disgusted by his father's behavior, Abel remained monogamous throughout his 25-year marriage. They never had children. Unfortunately, his wife was very sick almost the entire time they were married with a chronic autoimmune disease. Then she had a debilitating stroke. Taking care of his sick wife consumed much of his free time. As a skilled laborer, Abel always had steady blue-collar employment until he started his own business, which took up all of his time when not caring for his wife.

Having lived for so many years with a woman who had a debilitating disease was one reason for his continued drug use. Abel explained: "After she had her stroke and her subsequent brain surgery, she became a permanent acute paranoid psychotic, and that's important because it had a huge bearing on the outcome of everything."

Although Abel used marijuana since he was 18, he never had a problem with it. He said marijuana "causes my mind really to get real clear—it takes the edge off." Abel's drug problems started with a motorcycle accident.

I was in a motorcycle wreck at work, an old lady ran me over when I was test-driving a motorcycle and workman's compensation paid for my injury. I got Demerol shots when I was in the hospital due to the pain. I was instantly addicted. That was a Pandora's box moment right there. I had no clue. After going to la-la-land a couple hundred times on the Demerol express, I um, it, uh, really, really warped my way of thinking, and I'd get a gram of cocaine and sniff a couple lines on the weekend. And it was in the glamour era when people in Hollywood were doing it and stuff—and a line a week, [not a] big deal. And then I started shooting.

I asked Abel to explain how he went from Demerol to cocaine.

Well Demerol, you know, when my knee was busted up, and that's what I took when I got out of the hospital. But that episode came and went. Those were prescription drugs, and they were really hard to get. I didn't have access to them on the black market and, uh, when they just went, I just started doing cocaine and that filled whatever hole it was I was trying to fill at the time for about three years.

Abel, unfamiliar with drug markets, used the most popular drug in his White working-class social environment at the time (cocaine) to ease his emotional hurt and physical pain.

Meanwhile, life at home was progressively more chaotic for Abel when his wife became psychotic after brain surgery. "She started telling every psychiatrist that would listen that I beat her in the head and caused her to have brain damage," Abel said, adding that he still loved her despite the difficult situation it put him in.

It wasn't intentional, and I understand her motivation—when she was psychotic she didn't want to be bothered, and I was a bother. I was trying to drag her back into the real world, 'cause we had a good life when she was okay. And she went to a battered women's shelter, which helped solidify the story about me beating her in the head and stuff, you know. And here I am trying to be the best good guy the world has ever seen, and here she is trashing me at every turn. It's not vanity here, but I should have got a fucking medal for what I did. I just really loved my wife that much, and she didn't have anybody else that was gonna help her pull it back together. Her mom was senile and eccentric on her good days, and off in left field on the others, and her family didn't give a rat's ass. She didn't have anybody but me, and I didn't have anybody but her. And we had everything you could ever dream of as far as middle class goes, except her health.

His wife committed suicide in 2003. As difficult as life had been caring for a sick and psychotic wife, Abel's life went downhill after her death. First he lost his business, and then his home. He became addicted to prescription pills, and when he could not find pills, he used heroin.

After losing his business, Abel worked part-time when he could find work. At the time of the interview, he was without work and living with a roommate. In 2008, he went into a methadone clinic to stop using Oxycontin—the prescription drug highly promoted by pharmaceutical companies as nonaddictive due to its patented time-release mechanism.[17] They were wrong. Oxycontin was one of the causes of the worst opioid epidemic America has ever experienced, and Abel was right there in the midst of it. Without a family or wife, he was alone except for the director of the methadone clinic. Fortunately, he met Dave, whom he now considered a friend. Abel still used marijuana daily to quiet his mind, telling me with a chuckle, "The methadone staff gives me hell for that."

FRIENDS AND ASSOCIATES

Both the positive and negative impacts of a social environment are often conveyed and reinforced through friends.[18] This is particularly true in adolescence, when individuals have very little control over where they live and their range of choices for friends, although baby boomers mentioned friends they met throughout their lives in the context of initiating and using drugs.

Some, however, found it hard to make friends. Jan said she felt like an outsider since she was young, "I'd never really fit in—I wasn't real outgoing as far as my personality." Others distinguished friends from associates. As one said, "I don't have a lot of friends, but I do have some associates. I'm very particular how I say friend, but I have associates, like association with, we were out doing things." Associates could not be counted on for help.

In contrast, Teresa always made friends easily, and it was often through newly found friends that she was introduced to new drugs. Moses, who controlled his drug use, met a new friend in California who turned him on to crack, which led to Moses getting arrested and losing his job. Elijah had a number of friends who helped him find drugs or learn more about administering drugs. Like many, he learned to inject from a friend. "A friend had taught me how to use the needle," he explained. "He told me 'bout where the smaller artery's at and when it come out into the bigger arteries, you get that much more bang."

While friends often introduced drugs and drug use behaviors, they could also be a factor in helping people stop drug use—or give them motivation to stop drug use. Many people mentioned friends who took them into their house when they were down and needed a place to stay. Others mentioned friends who helped them find work. Abel said he had no friends as a child and few while he was married. He mentioned more friends in his story after his wife died. He called his attorney, who helped him avoid jail time when he was caught with marijuana, a friend, and he said friends were part of the reason he entered a methadone program, "I was losing all my credibility and standing with my friends, I just really needed to do something to rehabilitate myself."

For drug users trying to regain a foothold in mainstream society, having friends in the conventional world was critical. The term friend was quickly embraced by those who met a caring person. For example, the methadone director, Dave, was called a friend by several who were his clients. One woman who was in drug court told me the judge was her "best friend in the world." Many of the drug users I met over the years said I was their friend. One man called me months after an interview to let me know he was getting married and wanted me to meet his wife. What they intuitively understood, but might not be able to express, was that beyond comfort and empathy, friends provided access to social capital.

SOCIAL CAPITAL

Social capital is defined by Robert Putnam as the social relations that enhance people's ability to collaborate on common endeavors and to achieve personal goals.[19] Social capital is used as a tool to understand the inequality of status achievement based on social ties and access to resources.[20] The relationship between individuals, their community, and resources available from other social networks is part of what is called social capital. Since social capital exists through relations, its value depends on the social situation where social capital is gained or lost.[21]

Ann was one of the people in the study with the highest social capital. Not only did she have family with resources but she also achieved a high level of education and worked in a professional environment, which gave her access to social networks with high social capital. She was one of the few people in the study who was able to avoid the detrimental consequences of a criminal record. While her drug use was just as problematic as many other women discussed in this book, unlike them, Ann had access to resources that shielded her from law enforcement. When she relapsed after treatment, her mother did not practice tough love, but instead enrolled her in an expensive private treatment program exclusively for people in professional occupations who have problems with drugs.

In contrast, Alicia's mother, who had considerably fewer resources than Ann's parents, called on the police to "help" her daughter. Without the access to resources that were available to more affluent drug users, Alicia and others living in resource-poor communities such as the Bluff used the connections they had available. Social services and nonprofit organizations became vital to help free them of drug dependency and establish a foothold in conventional society.

Although family is a starting point for acquiring social capital, other social networks are arguably the sources of social capital most likely to profit an individual as an adult.[22] As people become imbedded in community they rely on their social relations within the community, and when the community cannot provide the resources, people turn to social networks outside their own community.[23] Alicia was able to survive while she was dependent on crack cocaine because she had connections and resources in the Bluff, where she grew up and knew people in the neighborhood who watched out for her. But even for Alicia, friends and family who lived in the same resource-poor community were not enough for her to stop problematic drug use. Eventually Alicia was linked to a comprehensive community-based program that helped her with the resources needed to live on her own. Without these social services, people like Alicia with little social capital would not have the resources needed to succeed in remaining drug free, such as employment training and reliable housing.[24]

Without conventional social ties and access to resources, disenfranchised people seeking to stop problematic drug use are faced with a nearly impossible feat.[25] Their stories show that as they began using drugs, particularly if they were caught up in the criminal justice system, they lost social roles that provided access to positive social capital. To maintain abstinence or control over drug use, they needed to regain conventional social roles.

SOCIAL ROLES

Roles are used to organize personal activities, guide behavior, and act as a point of reference. Role acquisition, role loss, and role transition help form identity.[26] Both conventional roles, such as being a parent or employee, and unconventional social roles, such as being a sex worker or drug dealer, provide informal social control over behavior.

When people are alienated from mainstream society they are more likely to become involved in unconventional roles that involve illegal behaviors. Losing conventional social roles means losing sources of informal control that help them avoid problem drug use. The informal social control that kept Moses out of trouble was his employment. Even though he limited his drug use to days when he did not work, and it did not interfere with his work role, he lost this attachment to mainstream society when he was caught with crack and incarcerated. This led to years of engaging in the unconventional role of a drug dealer.

The lives of the baby boomers also show that when individuals regain a conventional social role, the informal social control provided by this role helped them maintain or regain control over drug-using behavior. This happened for Moses when he embraced the social role of being a mentor and eventually a leader in the 12-step community, which was a strong social control mechanism to help maintain abstinence.[27] However, as shown in Ann's case, the social context of treatment programs provides more access to other drug users (or recovering users) than access to people in mainstream society. Moreover, for those cut off from society through years in jail or prison, access to mainstream social capital is critical. This is typically facilitated through relationships, particularly relationships that help link them to mainstream social capital.

HARRY: RELATIONSHIPS

Research shows that adolescents who are not incarcerated for crimes fare better than those who are incarcerated for similar crimes.[28] Harry's life supports this finding. Sentenced to a juvenile detention home before he made it to ninth grade, Harry was separated from family members who loved him and thrust into a hostile environment that provided social ties only to other juveniles with problematic behaviors. Scared and alone in the New Jersey correctional facility, he ran away at his first opportunity. He was caught and did not see his family outside of the correctional facility again until he was 18 years old.

By the time Harry came home, our mother and father had separated. Harry lived between father's small apartment and the home mother bought with a HUD loan. Emotionally very close to both of our parents, Harry adored our mother and called her a saint. He also understood our father's alcoholism and never judged him, as I did. Family was extremely important to Harry.

On Harry's first trip to California, he hitchhiked and nearly died of exposure when a driver who picked him up, robbed him, and left him in the middle of the desert. Another driver found him unconscious on the road and took him to the hospital. Harry decided to get a gun after this incident to protect himself. He used the gun the first time to help a friend.

One night Harry got a call from a female friend who was frantic. She was at a bar a few blocks away, where a member of the Pagan motorcycle club had just dragged her sister outside. She was afraid he would rape her. "I'm going out to help her," she cried into the phone. "Can you come help me?" Harry grabbed the gun and ran to the bar where he met the Pagan holding a woman by the arm while pushing his friend away. Then Harry noticed the dog. Harry loved animals, and he was not sure if it was fear or by accident, but when the dog attacked him, the gun went off. The dog was shot, causing the Pagan to immediately let go of the woman to attend to his dog. Harry and the women ran—in different directions. The next day the Pagans ransacked our home looking for Harry, but he had already left the state.

More than 30 of Harry's adult years were spent in prison, so it was hard for him to make friends in the conventional world. Despite the system's focus on moving prisoners often to discourage the formation of friendships, Harry made friends in prison. Justin, a lifer, was one of his closest friends.[29] I eventually corresponded with Justin to learn more about Harry. I asked him to tell me what my brother was like from his perspective. Justin lived with Harry every minute of the day for years, and I spent most of my life separated from Harry as an adult. The following is from one of Justin's letters to me.

> Harry was my handball and running partner for years. He is a good handball player and surprisingly, given the fact that he was a diehard smoker, he maintained a daily running program.
>
> As you know, Harry is highly intelligent. He could fairly easily do the New York Times crossword puzzle, and he is a very good chess player. I would bet a hundred dollars on Harry's chess games, since he usually won.
>
> Harry is a prolific reader of non-fiction and can hold an intelligent conversation on just about any subject. If you emancipate Harry from his addiction, he could have easily achieved any goal.
>
> I've never gotten the impression that Harry rejected society. Harry is a complex person. He absolutely rejects all forms of "authority." Don't misunderstand me. Harry intellectually knows that in a democracy there has to be some form of authority to enforce the treatment of painful consequences to deter one's proclivity for opportunism.
>
> Harry is a student of Karl Marx's "Communist Manifesto." Harry rejects materialism wholeheartedly. But again, Harry intellectually knows Marx's philosophy was never practical, and over time actually proven wrong. But Harry did stay true to Marx's rejection of materialism.

If one didn't know Harry as we do, you can see the dichotomy in Harry's rejection of materialism and him robbing banks. But Harry never robbed a bank for material gain in the sense he was going to buy material things with his loot. Harry's motive for robbing banks was simple. It was a means of feeding his lifetime addiction to drugs, and in robbing banks he understood he didn't need to use a gun or any violence, he simply gave the teller a note and he / she gave him money.

The last bank robbery he had occurred in Lancaster County and he was convicted of armed bank robbery, but nobody said he displayed a gun or weapon of any kind. When he was leaving the bank, a teller incorrectly claimed to see a pistol in Harry's pocket. He didn't have any weapon during that robbery. In fact, Harry never used a weapon to rob a bank.

Harry in his actions is truly a pacifist. Of course, in the prison context, Harry's passivism only goes so far. He will not tolerate disrespect. But all of Harry's friends in prison are convicted murderers and are leaders in the prison hierarchy, so Harry is respected and liked by everyone.

Reading these words confirmed what I believed, but they also revealed insights on friendship behind bars.[30]

In between Harry's two long prison sentences, he lived for a short time in Georgia with my sister, where he established a lasting friendship with Tom, who owned an organic farm. Harry worked on their farm and became close with Tom's family. When Tom signed the parole plan papers saying he would hire Harry, I asked him why he trusted Harry, a convicted bank robber. "I'd trust Harry with my payroll," Tom said. "Harry won't rob his friends."

Throughout his prison terms, Harry kept in communication with his friends and family through copious correspondence. His letters to me were often introspective, revealing how he created meaning in his dismal environment.

I have had several bouts of severe depression in my life. More so on the streets than in jail. In here I am more subjected to extreme anxiety, stress, paranoia, and acute boredom, things that could bring on depression for some persons. The mind controls all of that though, and a firm foundation or belief in destiny, or what some people might call God's Will, does much to combat depression. What a delusion it would be if it were not so. But of course—it is.

The laws of karma, or cause and effect, or divine justice—whatever is the nature of physical and ethereal existence—require things to be as they are, so there really is no need to be depressed. Without this knowledge, or when it is repressed, life can be, of course seem, unbearable, especially to those with severe handicaps or suffering, as opposed to those of us whose suffering comes from thwarted desires, often selfish or destructive in itself.

Harry, like Moses, who also spent a long time in prison, found meaning in his own configuration of God. His letters indicated a more expansive understanding of God than conventional Christianity offers. When I was questioning my faith in God, Harry responded, "God is everything. He is the bad as well as the good. Many have concluded this." Reflecting his knowledge of the Hindu Sanskrit, he added, "The *Gita* teaches that truth is ultimate enlightenment, union with God, and that it takes many lifetimes to achieve this—although of course, this could be that lifetime."

FOUR

The War on Drugs and Mass Incarceration

CHARLIE

Based on his appearance, Charlie, a 53-year-old White man, seemed to be in good shape, although the last few years of homelessness had taken their toll. Our interview got off to a slow start. I reserved a library study room, and while this provided privacy, the bare walls and standard table with straight-back chairs gave the impression of an interrogation room, which I wanted to avoid. Charlie arrived late, so we did not have time for a coffee and a chance to establish more rapport before starting the interview. Yet, he quickly warmed up to the process, candidly sharing intimate details of his life.

Charlie was born into a middle-class family. His parents divorced when he was 10 due to his father's alcoholism, which caused a fair amount of stress in the family. His father died of a heart attack when he was 12 years old. His mother remarried soon after the divorce, but Charlie did not get along with his stepfather. "There was just a lot of verbal abuse that made me not want to be around him," he said. His mother recognized the abuse and got a divorce, but not before Charlie was sent to military school, where he was introduced to drugs. He was arrested for selling marijuana, kicked out of the military school, and lucky to get only probation. He got his GED quickly and attended college but never finished.

Charlie married and stayed with his wife for 13 years, but eventually divorced because of her alcoholism, receiving full custody of their two daughters. He remarried a few years later but soon got divorced because of his own drug problems.

In his early twenties, Charlie had started a photography business with his brother that was very successful for about 20 years, and he lived a fairly affluent life in a wealthy suburb of Atlanta. Charlie began using prescription opioid pills after a serious car accident and became addicted to Oxycontin. He said it did not interfere with his work.

After his juvenile arrest for selling marijuana, Charlie was not arrested again until 10 years later. "They called it aggravated assault on a police officer because I was trying to outrun a police officer or something," he explained. "Because I was speeding. I was driving a Porsche and I was eluding." Within a few years, he accumulated a number of drug-related charges.

> Just a whole mishmash of stuff. It was like ten different charges. I got charged with, what is it called—not kidnapping but—this girl had stolen drugs from a friend of mine and her boyfriend had stolen the truck, and taken the truck with the drugs. And we went to pick it back up. They ended up dismissing all the charges. I paid an attorney down there a lot of money at the time. The girl, I think, kind of disappeared, and she said that she wasn't going to testify. So I think they kind of had to drop the charges or whatever over it.

At one point Charlie started taking methamphetamine to stay awake. "It was keeping me up when I'd take too many (pain) pills," he explained. "I was taking one to relieve the other." He was put on probation for being caught with a small amount of methamphetamine. When Oxycontin was not available he went to the Bluff to get heroin.[1] He was arrested while buying heroin and this time went to jail.

His brother was his business partner for many years. Although they did well initially, their photography business was impacted by changes in technology, and there were fewer customers every year. Charlie blamed himself for the demise of the business. He increased his drug use and was arrested several more times for drug possession and selling. He usually avoided too much time in jail by hiring expensive lawyers. A major arrest in 1996 seems to have been the catalyst for a flood of related problems, including difficult relationship issues with his brother. When the business failed, his brother committed suicide, and Charlie suffered from feelings of guilt.

After his brother's death, Charlie's drug use increased dramatically. He lost his home and squatted in an empty house in the Bluff. He could have not survived in this neighborhood without help from a local resident. "I had met one Black guy down there and he kind of took me under his wing and looked out for me there," he explained. "Trust me, there's not many Whites that live down the Bluff."

Without work Charlie was shoplifting to buy heroin from the "corner boys" in the Bluff.[2] He was arrested for shoplifting. Drug courts had recently started in Atlanta, and based on Charlie's drug record he was offered the alternative two-year drug court program instead of jail.[3] At the time, he was living in a shelter, but drug court required clients to find better housing situations. He looked up an old friend from high school who let him stay in his condo as long as Charlie was in the drug court program..[4] His friend died of cancer during this time, and Charlie remained living in the foreclosed condo, waiting to be evicted. Although he credits the drug court with helping him reduce drugs, he admitted that he did not stop completely. Charlie used heroin just a few weeks prior to the interview.

Charlie knows he will eventually be evicted from the condo and said his mother will let him move in with her. He also has a daughter nearby and grandchildren that he visits, providing him social and emotional support. Finding work is his main problem.

> I have so many felonies on my record that it's very tough for me to get a job, especially the way the job market is now. It gets very discouraging, (long pause) because I think, I figured I have six felonies now on my record.

I knew Charlie was in a difficult situation. In the middle of a recession, men his age were being laid off, not hired. With a criminal record it would be impossible to find employment that would support him even at subsistence standard. I asked why he used heroin a few weeks ago.

> Boredom, probably, boredom. I don't know. It's just something in the back of your mind that triggers, well I'd like to do something. You'd like to forget about some of the problems and stuff. I guess it's more of a thing you like to forget about the problems and get away from the pressures and stuff. (Long pause.)

It was difficult to see a healthy man in the prime of his life so hopeless, and we reflected in silence. Charlie ended the interview on a more optimistic note, "I'm still spiritual. I believe there's a higher power. I believe there's somebody looking out over us."

Charlie started with much more social capital than most of the people I interviewed. Had I not heard many stories like his, I could have easily fallen into the judgmental attitude that some of my colleagues expressed—I might have blamed Charlie for his predicament. But I knew that situations like Charlie's could happen to anyone living under a War on Drugs. Judging Charlie would be like judging a soldier for having PTSD.

Charlie's life shows a number of turning points. One turning point during his vulnerable adolescent years was after his dad died and he suffered abuse under his stepfather. Although Charlie got off to a rocky start with a marijuana arrest, his entrepreneurial spirit allowed him to start a successful business together with his brother. The next major turning point is the accident that led to his addiction to prescription pain pills and eventual drug arrests. While the costs for court fees, fines, and lawyers took a toll on his finances, the punitive response to drug use left him with a felony record.[5] The third turning point was the failure of his business immediately followed by his brother's suicide.

A look at the bigger picture that includes the structural changes over Charlie's lifetime shows how forces beyond his control impacted choices he made. The rise in opioid addiction was due to pharmaceutical companies pushing their drugs with little government or ethical oversight.[6] Charlie was caught buying illegal drugs to address physical dependence when a legal prescription to opioids was no longer available. He was given jail instead of treatment. Changes in technology and the recession caused the failure of his business, but when his brother (business partner) committed suicide, Charlie blamed himself and used drugs to cope. The drug war mandated incarceration for drug users. He was in a drug treatment court after six felony drug convictions—too late for him to avoid a serious criminal record. If Charlie's life seemed bleak, drug users who were not White and middle class faced greater challenges as the War on Drugs ramped up and, ironically, drugs became more accessible over their lifetime.

OMAR

I met Omar as I was hanging out in the Bluff near the Atlanta Harm Reduction Center.[7] Omar is a Black male who came to the center a few times for services. At 50 years old, Omar was tall and thin, with a pleasant smile and deep, penetrating eyes. He always nodded hello when we passed on the street, indicating he remembered me. When he heard about my research, he asked if he could be interviewed. It was early morning when we met, and no one had opened the center yet—relying mainly on volunteers, this was not unusual. It was raining so we started the interview in my car. I offered Omar some coffee and Krispy Kreme donuts I had bought for the center while I explained the interview process and read the consent form. He caught on quickly.

As I expected from our previous interaction, Omar was very amiable, intelligent, and enthusiastic to tell me his life story. He reflected deeply on his life, and I respected his introspection. I vividly remember sitting side by side in the car, the smell of bitter coffee and sweet donuts permeating the enclosed space, the rain pinging off the windshield, thumping on the roof of the car, and splashing in the potholes of the empty streets. The gray light cast a somber stillness over the silences of Omar's frequent pauses. The ambience was infused with his profound sighs—the timeless sound of surrendering to fate. Feeling the depths of his despair, I cherished the honor that he shared this with me.

Omar came from a big northern city. His mother, a nurse, worked hard and was able to take Omar and his siblings "out of the projects" to a house she bought in a middle-class suburb after his father left. Although he said he remembered his father being "crazy," he still missed having a father around. He was just entering adolescence.

> You need a male in your life to tell you, as being a man, to tell you how to be a man. You need a man. Most definitely have to have a man. Because you can't tell me how to be a man, you're a woman . . . What you know and learn about a man? Only a man can make you totally a man. Yeah, that had a big effect on me.

Dropping out of school, Omar married young and got a job at a factory to support his family. The reason for getting fired was beyond his control. "My car broke down and I missed a couple of days of work. And when I came back to work, they terminated me."[8]

Omar started drugs late in life—using marijuana, heroin, and cocaine for the first time on his 25th birthday, all in one setting. He had recently lost his job and was visiting his brother-in-law, who was teasing him for having never used drugs.

> He called me a square, "Square, you ain't gonna do nothing." I told him, "You know what, today I want to see what the hell you're getting out of this." I told him to hook me up like he was doing, 'cause he was shooting dope, and he did.

Sometimes turning points start from small events that cascade, and this is what happened in Omar's life. Having a broken-down car meant he lost his job and ended up with his brother-in-law instead of being at work. Omar, like most people, wanted to feel like he belonged, so he tried drugs for the first time to fit in. Injecting heroin and cocaine is a hell of a way to start, but Omar "fell in love" with a drug that made him forget his troubles. Still unemployed, Omar became involved with "a little ring they had going on" selling drugs to make money. Being new at this, Omar was caught by the police and sent to prison for four years on his first offense. He received a harder sentence because the police said the people he was involved with were a notorious gang.[9] He described what happens when a person is involved in such a group:

I never got rid of them. Even in the prison system we were getting high. Yeah, it crossed my mind, [to get away from them] but it wasn't that easy. You're gang affiliated, and I was, at that point, tied into this gang. And to get out of that is, you gotta get killed, you know, you gotta die. I had to pass through. I retired. Once you turn thirty-five you're allowed to retire.

By the time Omar got out of prison, the gang leader was in prison, and anyone connected to the group was barred from the city. His wife got a separation while Omar was in prison and eventually a divorce. Omar came down to Georgia to start a new life. He worked for five years doing street construction where he started getting drugs just for his co-workers, called "running."

Yeah, basically I was running. You know how you meet people—do a little hustle? I guess I really never had the money, the large amount of money that it takes, you know, it takes a large amount of money to really do big dealing.

The next arrest was for "possession with intent to distribute [and] carrying a firearm by what they call down here a convicted felon, and discharging a firearm in city limits." This landed him back in jail. He was out only seven months before being arrested again:

An attempted robbery, they say, but I really didn't attempt to rob the guy. He owed me some money, and I end up jumping on his ass and taking my money. It [the charges] went from robbery to battery, and I had another possession charge. I had a gun charge, then I had a theft charge—theft by taking. And then when they locked me back up, I end up getting sentenced to fifteen years . . . I made parole in 2006 here, and I stayed out like eleven months, and I made parole . . . I end up, 'cause I had all those multiple charges, and they didn't run them concurrent, they ran one of them consecutive. So after I finished this sentence, I had to start that other sentence, the theft by taking sentence. I end up going to Michigan, with my sister. That's where I end up back in prison.

Omar was speaking fast in unfinished sentences, jumping back and forth over a two-year period as he recalled events that confused him by the injustice of what happened. He went to prison for what appeared to him as a rational act—getting the money owed to him by another drug user. Fifteen years was a lot of time for a fight between two men. And a few months after release, he was put back in prison—he was not sure why.

I took out a timeline and we went over the dates and events again slowly. There were two possible explanations for his reincarceration. One, the prison administration let Omar out early by mistake, not unheard of when sentences are run consecutively. They brought him back from his sister's house in Michigan to finish the second sentence once they realized their mistake. Two, he might have violated parole by visiting his sister in another state without permission—also a common way to be sent back to prison.[10] Omar did not understand why when it happened, and the anguish he felt clouded his memory.

Drug treatment after prison was once again popular in Georgia, and Omar was forced to participate in a program before he was released. He was not impressed.

Omar: I thought it was just a bunch of bullshit to be honest. 'Cause it was too repetitive. You got phase one, two, three, and four. You gotta say this shit called "the philosophy," and then after the philosophy you go into the meetings and you talking about your life. You in prison, and you'll say any damn thing in prison, "I ain't gonna get high no more"—'cause you don't have the access as much as you would out here. Then you had the counselors that was—they were just there, it was just a job to them. They act like they were genuinely concerned but most of them was students, you really could tell they was students. You really teaching them. How the hell you call yourself trying to help me, to help teach me to help myself, and I'm really teaching you?

Miriam: So did you increase your drug use or not when you got out?

Omar: I guess it is increasing. 'Cause I'm out on the streets. Might have me now a couple hundred dollars a day [heroin habit], depends. It depends on how much dope you have and how much money you got during the course of the day.

The rain had stopped. Omar sat quiet and still, reflecting. We took a break and moved to a room in the center, which was now open. I talked to him about my brother, who was still in prison finishing a 20- to 30-year consecutive sentences. I offered Omar a chance to stop the interview, but he had more to say.

You know what, doc, this is like the turning point in my life, you know, right now for me, you know, I'm tired. I'm fixing to be fifty-one. You look at all this, and you, like, like you said, I look over my life now, you know, I got kids, but they grown and married, and grandchild. I'm like, shit, I can't keep doing this same shit over and over. It's getting tiresome. It's getting to the point where I'm getting tired ... I'm a' walking around here saying I need a hundred dollars for some dope, and take the chance of getting burned, get robbed. That's what people come down here every day and do that shit. You don't know if I'm gonna give you some poison. You don't know if I'm a' run off with your money. You don't know what you're fixin' to get. I'm not gonna take that big of a chance, that big of a risk, 'cause I know what the streets are about. I know you can get yourself killed, 'cause I've seen it happen. People get their cars took, get their money took.

Omar paused. We were alone in a small room upstairs in the center. We could hear the noise downstairs, where it was bustling with Bluff residents and passersby coming in for syringes, clean clothes, a sandwich, a shower, or a chance to use a toilet. But Omar was lost in deep contemplation of his life.

This shit right here, I'm getting tired of looking at this, living like this. This is becoming, when you come from one world where you live in this side of life, a decent side of life. You know, my mom was a nurse, so we didn't never really had to live in the hood 'til I was older, you see? I had the opportunity to live in the home in the middle-class neighborhood, go to school. I just chose to go back out in the streets. My brothers and sisters never had to do this. My brothers and sisters don't get high. They never have, so they had the opportunity to go to college with the grants and stuff like that. So they didn't even have to do this. See my mom took us out of the projects after her and my dad broke up. I was like eleven years old and my mother been a RN ever since. So we been living in that neighborhood. But with me, like I grew up in the hood, so I shoot back to the hood I like, when come down here. But then in actuality, you would want to go somewhere you live decent, with some peace ... It's the drugs. It's 'cause, you know, I gotta be here to get the heroin in this area.

Omar revealed a lot in his closing discourse. He knew his mother did not raise him to be a junkie. He had a middle-class upbringing and his brothers and sisters went to college. They smoked a little weed, but they never got into hard drugs. Omar did not start drug use until he lost his job when he was more vulnerable to suggestion and drugs became an opportunity to make money. He was naïve regarding the drug scene and ended up inside the circle of the most infamous drug kingpin operating north of the Mason-Dixon line at the time. And now, after years of incarceration, he was stuck in the Bluff.

Omar realized that something was wrong when he was given too much time for misleading charges, but he did not know he was one of the many victims of "charge stacking"—a consequence of the War on Drugs.[11] He did not realize that the infamous druglord who had ensnared him into the criminal world was also a product of the drug war that enabled the growth of his illegal business, simultaneously with the growth of law enforcement fighting the use and trafficking of illegal drugs. Omar never questioned how and why these both increased together. At the end of the interview, he blamed only himself. "It boils down to it's up to you," he said, repeating what he had been told a thousand times by treatment counselors, drug court judges, and even by the kind director of the harm reduction center.

There are similarities and differences in the life trajectories of Omar and Charlie that point to structural influences. While Omar is Black and Charlie is White, there are a number of parallels in their stories. Both came from relatively stable middle-class families, and both lacked a father figure. Both ended up living in the Bluff, and both spent time incarcerated for charges related to drug use. The clear distinction is that Charlie accumulated much more social capital in mainstream society throughout his life, largely due to his race. Omar accumulated more social capital among unconventional networks, again impacted by race, leaving him with less social capital in mainstream society and much longer prison terms than Charlie.[12]

There were many mutual risk factors found in this sample of drug users, stigmatized and identifying as common addicts and junkies, but their social situations and drug trajectories revealed substantial diversity. Not all had bad childhood experiences, early onset of drug use, psychological or emotional trauma, or lacked social capital. Although these are influential factors, each alone was not common to all respondents. Poverty, addiction, or marginalization impacted many of the people in this study, and race emerged as an important factor. However, Moses, a Black man with little social capital, was in one of the best situations at the time of the interview, while Jan, a White woman with more social capital, was in one of the worst. The thread running through all their stories, even the deviant cases such as Anne, reveals the overarching thesis.[13] One common theme was found in every case in the study and every lived experience recounted in this book—the adverse influence of the drug war.

The War on Drugs negatively affected everyone, prolonging their drug use and increasing the depths of despair. Most were impacted directly through incarceration. But even those who avoided a criminal record were affected by the social stigma of being a drug user—a stigma perpetuated by the War on Drugs. Many lost their jobs, government aid for education, or housing due to a drug arrest or drug testing. Others lost friends and loved ones because drug use was viewed as a moral failing. We might imagine how it could have been otherwise.[14] Imagine if the War on Drugs had never started. Imagine if society provided comprehensive treatment for people with real drug problems and found better strategies to address the social problems that led to drug use. Imagine if the billions of dollars that went to the drug war effort were instead used to fight a war on poverty, heal the sick, and provide better public education. Imagine a world without a War on Drugs.

THE WAR ON DRUGS AND THE MAKING OF MASS INCARCERATION

The War on Drugs was in the making since Harry Anslinger took over the Federal Bureau of Narcotics in 1930, but it was not officially declared until 1971.[15] In 1973, President Nixon established the Drug Enforcement Agency by executive order to fight "an all-out global war on the drug menace."[16] Prevention was based primarily on scare tactics and soon lost its credibility among its target audience—the youth. In response to a high failure rate for treatment programs, policy moved toward control over supply and demand through military-level force and criminal justice solutions, exposing and punishing drug users rather than treating them.[17]

New laws broadened the powers given to the legal system to control drug offenders. The Racketeer-Influenced and Corrupt Organizations (RICO) Act of 1970 allowed judges to give much longer sentences and law enforcers to seize cash and property from anyone involved in "organized crime," including drug-related crime. The Comprehensive Drug Abuse Prevention and Control Act of 1970 incorporated a "civil forfeiture provision" that allowed law enforcement to seize cash or property of suspected individual drug dealers or anyone abetting them, and keep all proceeds from property sales to increase their budgets.[18] Studies show that forfeiture laws increased drug arrests, without decreasing drug use or sales, and provided incentive for abuse by law enforcement.[19] Legislation passed to limit abuses of civil asset forfeiture did not address the profit motive by law enforcement.[20]

Under President Reagan, the bureaucracy of the War on Drugs expanded to include 11 cabinet departments, 32 federal agencies, and 5 independent agencies involved in drug control.[21] Reagan increased use of military equipment, weapons, and personnel used in the drug war effort to stem the supply side.[22] Police departments around the country were encouraged to focus on drug enforcement, at the expense of more violent crimes, motivated by huge cash grants.[23] A zero tolerance policy put many nonviolent drug offenders in jail and prison. Parents and grandparents lost their homes if relatives were providing drugs to others on their property even without their knowledge. Business properties were seized if customers were caught selling drugs on the property.[24]

To coordinate the various agencies and departments, in 1989 President H. W. Bush named William J. Bennett the first "drug czar" as head of the Office of National Drug Control Policy (ONDCP). He also expanded the Drug Enforcement Agency (DEA) and Federal Bureau of Investigations (FBI) drug duties and increased mandatory sentencing for drug-related crime. While President Clinton advocated for treatment instead of jail during his campaign, in 1992 he expanded mandatory sentencing again, and he rejected a US Sentencing Commission recommendation to eliminate the disparity between crack and powder cocaine sentences.[25] The drug czar became a cabinet position under Clinton, and the second Bush president continued the same focus on reducing supply, and paramilitary SWAT raids on Americans increased, eventually raiding medical marijuana clinics in California where cannabis was legal.[26]

Under President Obama, the Fair Sentencing Act was passed, which reduced the sentencing differences between charges for crack and powder cocaine from 100:1 to 18:1.[27] While the drug czar was informed to stop pursuing marijuana dispensaries in states that legalized marijuana, cannabis remained a Schedule 1 drug, which limited its potential for research.[28] The Obama administration also increased funding for the Bryne grant program for drug task forces and local drug enforcement efforts.[29] The ONDCP's budget increased from about $7 billion in 1995 to almost $26 billion in 2015.[30] In 2016 the Federal Drug Control budget was $30.6 billion.[31]

Notwithstanding the immense funding and effort used to stop it, government statistics show that drug use increased since the War on Drugs began. Drugs are as easily available as they ever were, and some drugs are even more accessible.[32]

Instead of decreasing drug use, the drug war resulted in increasing the incarceration of drug users. Since 1980, drug arrests increased by 1,100 percent.[33] In 1980, the year before Reagan expanded the War on Drugs, the total correctional population was less than 2 million people; this rose to 7 million in 2011 and remained around the 7 million mark until 2014.[34] Among the total adult correctional population in 2016, 2.3 million were incarcerated and another 4.2 million were on probation or parole, with one in five charged for a drug offense.[35] Put in perspective of global incarceration rates, the US has the highest number of incarcerated and rate of incarceration among all countries.[36] While prison populations began to decline in 2010, by 2013 incarceration rates started increasing again, maintaining US status as the country with the highest per capita rate of prisoners in the world.

As if incarceration were not enough, the War on Drugs activated harsh changes in sentencing, which included "mandatory minimums" with little flexibility in sentencing for drug charges; "truth in sentencing" that required a minimum time served before parole is possible; and the "three strikes and you're out" provision that mandated extremely long sentences for offenders' third felony conviction.[37] The tactics used to convict and control prisoners included expansion of solitary confinement and the ubiquitous use of confidential informants (CIs) as an easy means of securing a conviction by damaging social ties with family and friends, sometimes with fatal repercussions.[38] Other creative tactics used by law enforcement, such as charge stacking, plea deals, and obtaining coerced testimony from an inmate awaiting trial in exchange for a lighter sentence, made the informant process particularly corrupt.

The War on Drugs has changed the social structure of society and the cultural landscape of communities. The penal system replaced the educational system for many young men, particularly from minority communities.[39] Evidence mounted that showed incarcerating people for using drugs is linked to rising unemployment rates, the severing of families, gang warfare, increased police corruption, decreased educational attainment, urban decay, deteriorating healthcare, and racial inequalities reminiscent of the pre–civil rights amendment era; yet, the War on Drugs continued.[40]

HARRY: THE PRISON DIARIES

Harry's rather pessimistic view of the penal system certainly came from having spent 30 years in prison and seeing the changes over time in both prisoners' and guards' behaviors. According to Harry, the type of prisoners shaped the prison experience. Having been incarcerated before the drug war escalated, he witnessed the increased number of political prisoners entering America's jails and prisons and their influence on the status quo. Over the years, between letters and personal conversations, I gathered additional insight on the changing social context of prison from Harry's insider perspective, recorded in his letters.[41]

Thirty years ago, the typical prisoner was a rebel—a crook by trade or a violent man who had lost his temper. The term "convict" denoted a certain recognition, and most prisoners aspired to such a label. A good convict was a good person who lived by a code. This code involved loyalty to comrades, honesty in dealings with fellow prisoners, unity in opposition against authorities, and above all, no form of collaboration with your captors (i.e., no informing or assistance in any manner).

Such a code is incomprehensible to many of the mental patients, sex offenders, drug addicts, and petty thieves, which filled the prisons during and after the nineties. These prisoners are much more susceptible to behavioral modification techniques and other psychological methods of control. Therefore, they can be packed in and managed easier, as many more of this type of prisoner will collaborate with his captors. Without the code of loyalty, one doesn't know whom to trust.

Standards of living and opportunities vary from prison to prison, but monotony is the overruling circumstance. Not the monotony that exists on the streets, where the option of diversity is always available from moment to moment and its continued state is a conscious choice, but a monotony that is thrust upon you with the knowledge that it was the same a hundred years ago as it is today and the promise that it will be the same tomorrow—unless things get worse. Often a prisoner's boredom alone will be sufficient motive to strike out violently at a fellow prisoner or staff member with the intention of changing his condition, even though a more restrictive situation is certain.

While monotony is the condition in prison, violence is its omnipresent theme. Violence and the threat or fear of violence permeate every aspect of prison life and are used by prisoner and captor alike. The administration will often manipulate or even create violent circumstances or situations between groups or individuals in an attempt to halt any unification process that might be occurring, or for purely personal reasons. This practice of conditioning a prisoner to be a paranoid psychotic leaves a lot to be desired when there comes a time to release him back in free society. Maybe that is why there is a trend toward not releasing prisoners at all anymore. But once on the outside, psychotic or not, "we" are part of the ex-convict population, and the "ex" is always tentative. The only way to survive, inside or outside, as the paranoid psychotic individuals we became, is for everyone to follow the convict code. We have not yet worked out what to do when others don't honor it, except to kill them. As a one-time Buddhist and perpetual pacifist, I could do nothing but hope that those I associate with followed the code as I did.

The "supermax" model is a special housing unit within prisons started at Marion, one of the places Harry stayed during his 12-year sentence in US federal prisons.[42] These are high-security units with intensive management designs. Supermaxes routinely confined inmates to individual cells for up to 23 hours for hundreds or even thousands of days, denying them any opportunity to talk with or touch another human being, and failing to offer any access to programs.[43] The use of solitary confinement was denounced by the United Nations as torture, cruel and inhumane, and should be banned.[44] The place in Camp Hill where Harry was sent during his Pennsylvania sentence was called the Special Management Unit (SMU). Although the name had changed, the SMU was basically another version of solitary confinement (the hole).[45]

Camp Hill was an SMU established to replace or hide controversial tactics identified as violations of human rights, with unintended consequences, according to Harry:

> The cops [prison administrators or guards] came up with a hell of a plan it seems. They throw everyone into a cell and then implement a policy where no one gets around anyone else without being in restraints or behind a locked door. Then when everyone figures out no one can get to them very easily, they start hating and disrespecting each other and it takes a lot of weight off the cops . . . I am sending the SMU Handbook so you have some idea of my situation. Don't show it to Mom if you think that it will upset her.

> I just hope that I can get out of this SMU in time to complete some programs for the parole board. I can't do anything in here and this program doesn't count for anything except to mark you as a problem prisoner.

> I've been eight months without a drag from a cigarette. I still dream about them, sometimes daily. At what point does an addiction to a toxic substance become preferable to the unease of abstinence?

Harry's reflections about prison, from prison, foreshadowed contemporary academic literature. For example, his warnings about mass incarceration and racism were in a letter written in August 1994.

> Once again the issue of "crime and punishment" is being used as a vehicle for political rabble-rousing. It appears that even after we have reached the unenviable distinction of having more of our citizens incarcerated than any other country in the world, we are still not satisfied. Are we really such a criminal nation? I think not.

To begin with, many of those incarcerated have committed no real crime at all. There is a constant flow of probation and parole violators in and out of jails, and prisoners whose misconduct ranges from failure to pay fines to curfew violations. This is hardly criminal behavior.

Then there exist a large number of persons incarcerated for involvement in drugs, which constitutes not a criminal element at all, but a whole bloc of political prisoners. To decriminalize drugs would be to cut the so-called "crime rate" in half overnight. To continue the present course is far worse than whatever might occur should people be left to follow whatever form of self-destructiveness they might choose.

We have in America today a mega-giant prison industry, which must be eliminated. At some point in our not too distant past we changed the function of jails and prisons from institutions of societal betterment to profit-making enterprises. Once jails became a business it was inevitable that so-called "crime" would increase. A natural law of all business is that it (business) must grow if it is to survive. The sequential progression of such a practice would eventually find everyone either a jailer or jailed.

When reason prevails, and a gradual cessation of imprisonment begins, the business of jails will dissipate and incarceration will again become the non-profit government function that it once was. By that time America's policy of mass imprisonment will leave scars that may rival those of its slavery and genocidal past.

Harry's prediction made in 1994 was right on the mark. Eric Schlosser did not publish his famous article on the "prison industrial complex" until 1998.[46] By the new millennium, social science research confirmed Harry's interpretation of mass incarceration.[47] By 2012, after publication of the best-selling academic book *The New Jim Crow,* Harry's description of mass incarceration as "scars that may rival those of slavery" was widely acknowledged among academics.[48] Yet, the drug war remained.

Confidential Informants

People who inform on others (often their friends) to law enforcement are called "cooperating witnesses" if they testify, or "sources of information" if they just pass on information. Confidential informants (CIs) are also involved in trapping a suspect. All are known as "snitches" or "rats" by much of the general population, suggesting a repulsive character. The expanded use of CIs to entrap or otherwise set up a suspected offender is controversial and has been debated for decades. In a 1963 Supreme Court hearing, Chief Justice Warren stated:

This Court has not yet established the limits within which the police may use an informer to appeal to friendship and "camaraderie in crime" to induce admissions from a suspect, but suffice it to say, here, the issue is substantial. We have already struck down the use of psychological pressures and appeals to friendship to induce admissions or confessions under not totally dissimilar circumstances.[49]

People often feel pressured to become informants to save themselves from a criminal charge, or to reduce a threat or actual charge. CIs can be encouraged to commit more crime in order to catch another person committing a crime, or instigate a person to become involved in a crime, a strategy some see as "a retreat from the core purposes of criminal law."[50] Today this remains a common strategy used by law enforcement to catch and convict suspected criminals, including people involved in drugs.[51] The reliability of CIs and veracity of their statements are suspect; yet, it can result in the imprisonment or even death of innocent people.[52] Becoming a CI, or falling under suspicion of being a CI, can have serious personal consequences as well.[53]

Harry was caught and convicted of two 1987 bank robberies committed one month apart because the police used an informant who, under threat of arrest, testified against Harry. Liz was a longtime friend who knew Harry since 1971. In her sworn statement she said, "I met him about the same time I met my ex-husband," indicating she had known him for 16 years. Considering Harry had been in federal prison for 12 consecutive years during the time she knew him, Liz must have been a good friend. She last saw Harry on September 28, 1987. She testified that Harry brought a bag of money to her house, gave her some money for her trouble, and she drove him to another town. He also gave her two envelopes with money: one for his sister in Georgia, which she sent by mail, and one for his mother in Lancaster, which she delivered by hand. Each had $1,000 in it. Her statement shows she was under duress. The transcript of the court case revealed that she testified under fear of incarceration. Her short and mostly noninformative answers to the assistant district attorney indicated she was not doing this cheerfully.[54]

Based on her testimony the police set up surveillance on Harry and caught him in the car with a young man who was driving Harry to Philadelphia. Harry had given him some money for driving, and one bill was marked from one of the banks—called bait money. The young man was turned into a CI, so there is a possibility that the bill was given to him by someone other than Harry. There was no proof that Harry had robbed both banks other than the coerced words of two CIs. The bank tellers gave contradictory testimony on whether or not a gun was involved. Nevertheless, this landed Harry with 10- and 20-year consecutive sentences.

ELIJAH AND ABEL: WAR STORIES

While many baby boomers in the study suffered due to the increased use of CIs and solitary confinement, two incidents were particularly poignant.

Elijah, discussed in chapter 3, said the Georgia Bureau of Investigations (GBI) set up his friend to be an informant, as well as to trick Elijah so that he was caught holding marked bills.

> Yeah, so what it was is my closest friend. I thought I had got smart. I stopped dealing myself. I'd rather take a cut and let somebody else do it. But I didn't understand about informants. I thought friends was friends and to the death. But (laughs) when one of your friends gets busted, he becomes an informant to save his behind. That's never happened to me before and so . . . Yeah, my closest friend, the one that I let him into my home and shared . . . he had got busted.

> And so I was walkin' down the sidewalk and (laughs) it was like OK Corral, 'cuz wasn't nobody else on the sidewalk. So I'm facing this guy and he's comin' with his sports coat on, and I shoulda run then 'cuz everybody walked down the sidewalk, but there wasn't nobody walkin' down this sidewalk if they stopped people. They might have thought they might had to shoot me or I had a gun. It was very peculiar, but I never thought about it. And so he got within arm's length, he opened his sports coat and I saw his gun, and he said, "Elijah Smith, you're under arrest." I didn't say nothin' 'cuz I'm always quiet. 'Cuz I figure, believe it or not, by bein' quiet I cannot belittle you . . . But anyway, he said, "You're under arrest for trafficking cocaine."

> And I'm sure I didn't smile, but it was amusing what he said 'cuz I knew that I hadn't been sellin' nothing. And so what he did—he said "Empty your pockets." So I had about $800 worth of twenties. So I pulls it out and he thumbs through there. And sure as hell there's three twenty-dollar bills with irregular serial number on it.

> "We just give you this money," he says. And sure as hell, my friend had come to me that morning and asks me if I had change for sixty dollars, and he's the one that gave me the twenty-dollar bill. Yeah, I didn't find it amusing. But it was new. No one ever educated me about the drug game. That's what it was.

Learning the hard way that CIs could be close friends, Elijah was incarcerated after he had stopped his criminal activity of drug dealing. While he looked back on this malicious entrapment by law enforcement with a modicum of amusement, others were not so nonchalant regarding their experiences under the criminal justice system. Abel, introduced previously, was put in solitary confinement when arrested for a misdemeanor. He described how he felt being in isolation.

It was a little clique, everybody that was in that jail seemed to know each other and for some reason they were offended by my presence. I don't fit in, in jail, you know. I don't talk like them, I don't act like them, I don't know them, and, uh, they don't want me in their cells. So they conspired and told the guards that I was gonna beat them up. Without any hearing or warning or anything they led me out of the group room and put me in a cement block room with a steel door all by myself twenty-four hours a day, and that's pretty scary.

I can't begin to tell you how horrible it is being in there. They don't let you smoke anything at all and the food, I'd like to see a dog that would eat the slop they were serving humans. And the telephone privileges were restricted, and you can only call people collect, and it was quite the conundrum. I had a real hard time—ten days is an eternity, you know, especially when you're withdrawing from methadone.

They [guards] just don't talk to you, you know, I talk to animals, they don't even talk to the people. I asked why I was in solitary and I was never dignified with any response whatsoever. I'd really like to see an attorney and see if I have any kind of a case against them, because I can't believe in America that you can go from some crap-hole misdemeanor to being put in solitary confinement.

Some people might not be as strong mentally and could suffer significantly from enduring something like that even for four days. I don't understand the mechanism, I refer to it as my sociopathic side that, uh, for some reason . . . you would really think that you would break down and cry or be trembling or scared or something when you're getting arrested and there's so little out there to help, you know. I didn't do any of that, and it's not stoicism. I know what that is, and it just happened that when it happens I picture opening the refrigerator door and just seeing the Antarctic, a couple penguins and a polar bear, that's how cold I can get as far as not feeling any of those kind of emotions. I couldn't squeeze out a tear throughout the duration, and you would really think at some point in time to have gone from where I was to where I am, at some point, you would at least weep. No can do!

By comparing how he talks to animals as he would to a decent fellow human, with the actions of the prison guards, who would not talk to him at all or answer his questions, Abel highlighted the inhumanity of the people who had power over him while he was incarcerated. Abel was more embittered about this experience in jail than other hurtful experiences he had in life, such as his mother's early death, and his wife becoming psychotic and committing suicide. The other incidents were personal tragedies but this, he knew, was a social injustice.

THE SOCIAL CONTEXT OF NO CRIMINAL RECORD

Of the 100 baby boomers in the study, only eight had no criminal justice record. A brief discussion of their lives provides insight into how they avoided arrest despite having used hard drugs for many years. Their stories also show they did not avoid the destructive influence of the War on Drugs. Six were female, three were White, three Black, and two Latino. Socioeconomic status ranged from very poor to very wealthy. The one common factor was that all had access to needed resources (social capital) either through family, friends, or community, although a few said they were "just lucky." Four controlled their dependence on opioid pills or heroin by enrolling in a methadone program, and without these programs they might have been arrested.

Ann, introduced in chapter 2, had an advanced professional degree, more social capital than most of the respondents, and her parents were eventually supportive. Yet she suffered negative outcomes due to the stigma of using drugs during a drug war. When she admitted to being addicted to prescription pills, she was sent to drug treatment, a common response to any drug use. While in treatment, she relapsed with a man she called a "junkie," lost her marriage and children, and eventually lost her license to practice being a doctor.[55]

Joan, a White female, also had a professional degree and strong family support. Her relationships and social capital in mainstream society were protective factors. Even though she was dependent on pills and consistently appeared to have new injuries that required prescription pain pills, she was never reported to any authorities. Joan's interview occurred prior to the establishment of a Prescription Monitoring Program (PMP), an electronic database for controlled substances to help identify high-risk patients.[56] Joan would have trouble with her opioid abuse in our current surveillance landscape. She was still using at the time of the interview, and if she continued her pattern of illegal pill use, it is very likely she has a criminal record today.

Michelle, a Black female, had an extensive network of close family relationships and friends who all lived in the same community with her for a long time. This provided Michelle with social capital among her mostly working-class and poor neighbors, who protected her from risk of arrest. Michelle was never involved in selling drugs and was one of the few drug users in her community who did not have a criminal record. However, her community suffered from the War on Drugs by becoming a street drug market, which increased both violence and police surveillance. Like Joan, in the current landscape, Michelle is likely to obtain a criminal record if she continues drug use.

Sienna, a White female, was raised with an alcoholic father and alcoholic stepfather, which caused considerable turmoil in the family. She married a military man who was abusive, had another marriage with a violent man, and a third marriage with a drug dealer. All ended in divorce. Sienna was involved in running drugs for her dealer husband but was fortunate not to be caught by law enforcement. Her last marriage was with a man she took care of while he was dying of AIDS. She stopped using all drugs while she raised her last husband's child. At the time of the interview, she used occasionally in a controlled manner. She was one of the lucky ones.

Elisa, a Black female, had a difficult childhood after her mother and father divorced. A traumatic accident led to a lifelong addiction to opiates. She was introduced to cocaine and crack by different men in her life, but she said she controlled her use of these drugs and did not put herself at any risks that would get her arrested, since she did not want to lose her children. She was in a methadone program for opiate addiction at the time of the interview, which gave her legal access to an opioid and protection from law enforcement.

Serenity, a Latina, earned a professional medical degree and started using drugs with medical professionals. She said there were few doctors who did not use drugs. She lost her house and all her money in a nasty divorce that started her on sporadic, but more serious, drug use. She ended up in a homeless shelter and was "ticketed" for living in an abandoned house, but since she was not charged, she did not have to make a court appearance and avoided a criminal record. She was not able to avoid abusive boyfriends, a symptom of her hurt.

Chief, a Latino, was a star football player in high school and college, and retired from a 19-year military career in Special Forces. He dabbled in cocaine after his divorce, used methamphetamine to stay awake on military missions, and smoked crack to forget the trauma of war. Although he was arrested once as a civilian for having assault weapons, the charge was dropped when they saw his military record. Chief was unique among this sample by having social capital from being in the military, particularly his status as former Special Forces. Yet, he was never treated for what appeared to be serious PTSD and used illegal drugs to self-medicate.

Arnold, a Black male, was born into a loving family. His father died when he was young, but he said his stepfather was a good role model. Arnold worked for the same company from when he started at age 19 until he retired at age 53. When a company drug test found him positive twice, he was not fired but only denied promotion that year. Arnold married once and stayed married (35 years). During this time, he used drugs in a controlled manner and was mostly a weekend user. He kept heroin use under control by using methadone to decrease tolerance in a controlled process over the years. Although he used crack occasionally with co-workers, he kept his drug use secret from his wife until a year before he stopped. When he lost interest in drugs, he weaned off heroin completely in a methadone program. Arnold maintained positive social capital by having a long-term job and co-workers who protected him (no snitches). He learned controlled use of two drugs (heroin and crack), which are known to be highly addictive. He is an outlier, but his story provides the best example of what the lives of others in this book might have been like without a War on Drugs.[57]

These eight baby boomers avoided arrest because they had positive social capital giving them access to resources (e.g., lawyers, expensive treatment) or protection from police through their connections. The absence of any involvement in the criminal justice system allowed them to lead more fulfilling lives. But the drug war negatively impacted other areas of their lives, extending their drug use as a coping mechanism. Only Arnold seemed able to control drug use for a lifetime. Hiding it from his wife was shameful to him, but if he had he told her, he might have ended up like Ann, who lost her marriage by being honest. In hindsight, this is an outcome of the drug war.

If the War on Drugs had not started when baby boomers were entering adolescence or young adulthood, and if the drug war had not escalated into the most intense and systemic punitive response to nonviolent criminals ever seen in modern history, while fueling racism, gang warfare, and violent criminal activity, the lives of drug-using baby boomers would have played out quite differently. Hurting under the War on Drugs was the common theme in the stories told by drug users.

FIVE

The Racial Landscape of the Drug War

MARSHALL

Marshall, 49 years old, remembered his working-class African American parents with fondness and admiration.[1]

> You know, my mother was, she was real spiritual. She was a Baptist, and she was a Christian. On the other hand, my father, he wasn't a churchgoer, but he believed in doing the right thing for the right reasons. And he kinda felt he didn't have to go to church, to do the right thing, it was just the way he was raised. He was a hard-working guy, you know . . . I grew up in a real nice neighborhood, you know, a lot of elderly people, people that had been there for a long time, and my dad was one of the first homeowners in that area to own his own home.

> Well, I mean it wasn't the ghetto, but I mean it was low-income and my mother exposed us to a lot of things that other kids, they wasn't exposed to, you know what I mean? I mean she, although my mom had a tenth grade education, she knew all the fine etiquettes, and she knew everything from reading. My mom would read a lot, and we knew the proper way, you know. My mother had never been in a fancy restaurant, she had never been to France or anything, but she could tell you the customs. She could tell you things to do, you know, when you go into a restaurant, how you supposed to act, who goes in first, what side dish sits on the left. She knew all those things, and uh, you know, even my, uh, speaking—my mom probably would slap me in the mouth right now, for not pronouncing words right, you know what I mean?

Atlanta was the hub of the civil rights movement at the time Marshall was a child, and his parents embraced Martin Luther King Jr.'s dream to see beyond race, which today is called colorblindness.[2] Marshall explained the culture of the time.

You know Blacks were more inner city. Whites had moved out more to sub-urban areas I guess, and that probably was, you know, I mean that was after the civil rights movement and all that, and, I must say, I'm going to say this, you know—I was raised by my mother. She believed in a lot of values of Dr. Martin Luther King. And I was raised, you know, I mean, Black and White has never been a thing to me. It never was, you know. My mother was a maid. At some times she worked for some Koreans, she worked for a White couple, some doctors once, and it was always, you know, you judge a person by the contents of their character, not by the color of their skin. And she meant that, you know.

Marshall was taught colorblindness, but the failure of the civil rights movement to end racial discrimination was evident in contemporary society. Marshall understood this well.

You know this is America. You can go into some kind of little hick town and you can go into a restaurant or a bar and it's like, you know, like everything stops. You can feel it. And they'll leave you standing there—they won't acknowledge that you're there, you know, hoping that maybe you'll turn around and go away, rather than serve you. When I was coming up as a kid, there was certain water fountains that were Black water fountains and White water fountains, you know, and I was a curious little kid. I used the one that you step on the little thing the water skied up. I didn't want to be trying to turn no little knob, so I was, you know, I would drink anyway. Oh that bothered me, of course it did. It bothered me, and that's still true today.

While Marshall recognized the overt racism of separate water fountains, he did not see a link between racism and mass incarceration.

Miriam: Well I'm trying to see—because we know that, um, there are dispro-portionately more Black males in prisons than Whites, so I'm trying to see if you think that had anything to do with you going to prison at all?

Marshall: No, no. I think it was a direct result of my choices that I was mak-ing. I was making some crazy choices, you know. Um, the things that I was doing it was, you know, a lot of people—this is what I really think about different addicts, and this is just my opinion—but a lotta people just scum from the very beginning.

Miriam: They're what?

Marshall: Scum, I mean they're just trifling, a lot of people just trifling. They grew up trifling. I mean, as little kids they were, they were bad. They stayed in trouble before they even put a drug in 'em. They were stealing, they were, you know, stealing and lying, and cursing, and doing all kinds of stuff. And to me, it's harder for them to bounce back, 'cause they have to learn so much stuff, you know, not only recovery they have to discover, you know, they have to discover a new life. You know, I once had a good life.

Miriam: So you think it was their upbringing that makes a person this way, because you seem to think that you had a good upbringing?

Marshall: I think it does, the environment that you see, you know. I mean I dropped out of college 'cause it wasn't fast enough for me. I mean I wanted money right then and there, you know. And things that I seen in my neighborhood, that people who had things, stuff so to speak, were doing something illegal, you know. And seemed like they were getting away with it, you know. Hey, this is the way to go. They were big-time gamblers, drug sellers who had the big cars, the really nice houses, and popularity, you know, and uh, I gravitated to it.

Although he never married, Marshall helped to raise a son living with his partner and supported them with his steady work. He used cocaine occasionally during this time, but when a friend offered him crack at a football game, he got hooked. "Crack really hit I guess about 1986, and about like '88 it was full blown," he explained. "It was like serious epidemic, you know, in Atlanta, Georgia it was."[3]

Marshall was living during an intense crack-using period in Atlanta, and by 1989 he was in prison for possession of crack—a consequence of a drug law that increased racial disparities in incarceration rates.[4] He described his experience.

Prison is, uh, prison more or less you develop survival instinct and, you know, unless you got like, say if a person got twenty, thirty years you know, you got to serve, then it becomes your life. I mean you try to develop a life inside the walls of prison. But if you got two, three, four, five years, and you know you getting out, you know that. You know it's possible that you will get out in four, five, then it's like just survive until then. All you going to do is just make it through uncut up, beat up, stabbed up—you just want to survive.

Marshall survived, but his father died while he was in prison and he was not allowed to attend the funeral. Abstaining from drugs for nine years after he was released, Marshall relapsed when his dearly loved mother died of cancer. "My mother died in my arms. I flew off the crazy," he said. "It was just so much pain, a lotta regrets the time that I didn't spend with my mom." He ended up homeless in the Bluff. He decided to stop using drugs six months before the interview.

Well . . . if I tell you this, I mean, I know it ain't gonna sound politically correct. But, uh, it's by God's grace that I just had a moment of clarity, just a moment. I was living on the streets. I have lived outside in the cold. I have lived outside just, you know, abandon houses or something, you see, or something like that. Just crawl through the ones, just lay down cold, and just have cried, you know. I have, uh, been to some real dark places, you know. And I had just that little moment of clarity that was just, you know, and something intervened. I had that moment of clarity that I wanted to use, you know. I just can't do this no more, and I just prayed.

Six months was not a long time, and Marshall was still homeless. When I asked if he had a job, he replied, "I'm doing a lot of odd jobs, but I'm outta work," adding with a big grin, "why you got a job for me?" I said I would keep him in mind. He would have to call me since he did not have a phone. When we parted, Marshall shook my hand and looked me in the eye, "This has helped me," he said. "You know, it's always good to make a little bit of money, but this has helped me, you know, therapy with just, you know, uh, sharing. I got a little teary-eyed at one point."

I get a little teary-eyed remembering Marshall. As I read his story I wondered if he would be better off to acknowledge the impact of racism on his life. As a Black man raised in the South, he was shaped by an historical, social, and geographic context that had changed over his lifetime from overt racial segregation to covert racist discrimination under laws that made it legal. Emotionally hurt by racist culture in his childhood, he continued to experience racism when he stepped outside his community as a Black man in a White neighborhood. He suffered under racially discriminatory crack legislation. But like most minority men and women I interviewed, he blamed himself for choices he made in social situations constrained by racial injustices.

THE NEW JIM CROW

Myriad studies have shown that the criminal justice system (from police on the street to prosecutors, judges, juries, prison guards, prison wardens, probation and parole officers) act in discriminatory ways that can legitimately be called racist.[5] The Black Lives Matter (BLM) movement put the racist actions of US law enforcement on an international stage. However, before the BLM movement started, civil rights advocate Michelle Alexander identified the

War on Drugs as a redesign of the old segregationist laws that produced a new caste system, which she called "the undercaste—a lower caste of individuals who are permanently barred by law and custom from mainstream society" due to having a criminal record.[6] She called this the "New Jim Crow." The new undercaste is predominantly Black.

Drug "crimes" usually have no victims.[7] All races participate in the commercial exchange of a product for money, and use the product for pleasure, or to reduce physical, psychological, or emotional pain. While the numbers of drug users change depending on the year of the study and how the data were collected, national surveys show that Black youth in twelfth grade have lower rates of illicit drug use than White youth in twelfth grade,[8] and some studies show that White adults in the United States report more illicit drug use in the past year than Black and Latino adults.[9] Yet, despite that there is little difference in rates of drug using or selling across racial and ethnic lines, Blacks and Latinos are far more likely to be criminalized for drug law violations than are Whites.[10]

The Black population is only 13 percent of the US population, yet they represent 31 percent of all drug arrests, and they are incarcerated at six times the rate for Whites.[11] Among youth this disparity is even greater.[12] Black men with no high school diploma are five times more likely to be imprisoned than White male high school dropouts.[13] Blacks continue to make up the largest percentage of incarcerated population in the United States according to the most recent data.[14]

Learning in a juvenile reformatory or jail is not conducive to gaining positive social capital. The lifelong loss of social capital due to incarceration is difficult to measure, but it certainly is not a setting for acquiring skills and networks needed to become responsible citizens.[15] A former prisoner status carries the shame and stigma attached to being a criminal, which is a double disgrace for people of color who already experience discrimination in everyday life regardless of their legal status.[16] Achieving the so-called "American Dream" is beyond their imagination. The "inalienable rights to freedom, justice, and a fair opportunity" are denied to a person with a felony conviction.[17] And in many states inmates, parolees, probationers, and even former convicted felons who have served their time cannot vote, which disenfranchisement has also been referred to as civil death.[18]

The mass incarceration of large segments of the Black community occurred simultaneously with the deindustrialization of urban areas where they lived, the decreasing power of unions, and the rise of low-paid service jobs without benefits. At the time when employers required greater techno-logical skills, the quality of public education diminished and aid for higher education was cut.[19] As funding for correctional institutions increased, fund-ing for public housing decreased.[20] Contemporary urban conditions, such as absent fathers, unemployment, crime, street violence, guns, gangs, and vio-lent deaths, were instigated by the War on Drugs and directly linked to mass incarceration, but they were blamed on the culture of communities of color.[21]

By the turn of the new millennium, the New Jim Crow was firmly estab-lished.[22] The statistics became too incredibly shocking to blame the racial disparities in mass incarceration on anything but institutional racism in a criminal justice system that functioned to produce and perpetuate a uniquely American caste system.[23] The focus of the drug war was on poor inner-city communities of color, and prisons became their "surrogate ghetto."[24]

Loïc Wacquant argues that the ghetto was built for four purposes: stigma, constraint, territorial confinement, and institutional encasement, and by "locking it in a relationship of structural subordination and dependency . . . [it became] an ethnoracial prison."[25] Today's ghetto and prison are almost indistinguishable in purpose and population, as they are both warehouses of the Black working class. In the new "prisonfare" system, companies can lease prisoners to work for very low wages, a portion of which are siphoned off by the prison administrators.[26]

In Atlanta, Georgia, the proof of the New Jim Crow was most evident in the community called the Bluff.[27] As their stories show, many tried their best with what they had and the opportunities available. But they were sabotaged by a criminal justice system whose strings were manipulated by the War on Drugs. Ex-prisoners returned to drug use when homeless and unemployed, associating with drug-using friends in the only community that accepted them.

JAMMIE

Jammie was one of the few respondents who lived her whole life in the Bluff neighborhood. A Black female, 51 years old, she remembered the neighbor-hood in better times, but she said she still feels like it is a community that looks out for each other.

> We stick together for real. We stick together. We go to jail together, you know what I'm sayin'? We get high together, we go to jail together, we talk about

our problems together. If one of 'em out there that ain't got nowhere to stay—okay, you come stay with me. That's the way it is. We just a community.

Jack from Chicago—he's from Chicago, and see up there and what we do in the South are different. You know what I'm sayin'? Down here we take care of each other. We see 'bout each other. So like if somebody come over here and try to hurt one, you got the whole community to fight. We're not gonna let you hurt nobody. That's the way we are.

Jammie did not start using drugs until age 27, late in life for initiation. Although she started with crack, she added heroin (which people in the Bluff call "heron" with an accent on the second syllable) to her habit; however, in a controlled manner. "I can't be out there sleepin'—sellin' dope." She explained. "I gotta see what's goin' on." Crack (rock) was her drug of choice.

I'm a straight rock. I like it, I ain't gonna tell you no lie, I like it. It's an escape from reality, if you wanna know the truth. Make your problems go away, but they still there when you come back. Now don't get me wrong. You just make 'em disappear for a minute. I wouldn't suggest it to nobody. I wouldn't wish that on my worst enemy.

I just sell heron. Sometimes I sell powder cocaine, to pay my bills and to get my crack. I don't know. I don't know but this 'bout the only place you can get heron at. I don't know why. See, you know what? Seriously, this neighborhood is built on hustle. Everybody over here got some kinda hustle, and if *they* demandin' it, *we* gonna get it. You understand? They gotta new drug out called Lean, yeah, yeah. There's a new one out. It's like a liquid form of heron.

After a series of low-paid service jobs, Jammie learned construction work and found part-time but better paid employment, which she supplemented by running drugs. Jammie was running cocaine for seven years before drawing police attention in 1997, when crack was still the reigning drug in the Bluff and police surveillance was heavy.

Right. I got caught with a sack of cocaine . . . they switch it over to DC6 disorderly conduct . . . they threw it out. That first time they usually throw it out. Then the next time I got caught with some heron, I did six months. This last time, I took drug court like a fool and, uh, when I told them I didn't want that no more, they sent me to prison for a year, so I just got out.

After the crack surge, police crackdown, and resulting overpopulation of city jails, courts began to experiment with alternatives to incarceration. The most notable was drug treatment court, which spread quickly around the country before being tested or evaluated. Some drug courts were better than others, but all were run like a dictatorship by the judge, who had almost complete power over drug court participants.[28] Drug courts became very popular in Atlanta, and although some said they were helped by drug court, Jammie's experience was quite different.

In 2005, I took drug court just to get out 'cause they were offering me a year in the drug court, and I took drug court. Worst mistake I ever made in my life. Because rehab only works if you want it, you understand? Then when I found out what it was, how they was doin' it, I didn't want it because—you don't talk to me like that, you know what I'm sayin?

When I went in there, I was working. I was good worker. You know, I'd get my little part-time jobs and things sometimes. I was biddin' on a house with them, with some people who bid to contract. I was workin' on a house. These people [drug court] called my job and told them. Okay, you don't need to— ya'll need to fire her because she do drugs. Okay, now you handle what—you gonna feel the way I live?

I said, "Well, you want 750 dollars, but you tryin' get me fired off my job." She [the judge] said, "Well, you need to go work at Burger King." So I said, "You want me to leave a nineteen-dollar-an-hour job and go work at Burger King?" I said, "I didn't tell you to leave that bitch and go work at Krystal." You know what I'm sayin? So she said I gotta smart mouth.

"Alright, then you go tell them," I said, "well, so how am I supposed to—you know, my family?"

"Well your family don't need you; you're no good for them."

I said, "I got a husband too, he probably ain't no good either?" I said, "Okay, this is not for me."

This was, a woman judge—they need to do something about her. So got wrote up now, I'm on probation now. She got wrote up to where, like I just left prison right, and that judge—they need to do something about her. She got it wrote up on a paper that I wouldn't report for probation. The man was like, "Well, why haven't you been reporting to probation?" I said. "'Cause I was in prison." He said, "It shows nowhere on this paper that you was in prison." I said, "You ain't got but to call somebody; you better call somebody." You know what I'm sayin'? She's just—she's got it in my papers that even though I can get locked up goin' across the street, she still want me to come to the courtroom. She still would lock me and send me back to prison. The lady is power mad or something, you know what I'm sayin'?

I said I was gonna get, um, try while I'm out—try and get federal marshal or something, 'cause I'm tired of her messin' with me. It's called selective harassment and I'm tired of it. No, she terminated me from her program, but she's such a high judge, that she makes me come to her courtroom no matter what. Like I said, if I get locked up goin' across the street, I still gotta go see this same judge. She will send me back to prison. "Aw, it's all because of drugs you goin' across the street." She thinks everything is because of drugs. They told us that, say if I'm at a Marta [subway] station and I'm being attacked, if I fight back, I get locked up. I said, "So you telling me I can't defend myself?" Not for me.

That big suburban [judge] don't know what's goin' on in the ghetto. Like I told her, "How can you sit up there in suburbia and tell me how to live my life as a Black woman in the ghetto. You can't, you can't. Do you know how hard it was to raise a Black man?"

Come on, baby, I sent my son to college even though I do drugs. My son graduated college. He's in social services. I mean he could do this stuff right here probably. I'm bad, but I got good kids.

I break stereotype, 'cause I love my kids. I love them. There's nothing in the world I wouldn't do for them. My daughter own a little retail business, you know what I'm sayin'? Like, you know, like I told them, "That's a stereotype." They'll get mad at me because I don't do stereotype. Like if I say I don't drink. That's how come I stopped goin' to rehab, "Oh you such a liar. You never tell the truth—you a liar," she said. Huh? She don't believe it, I mean my kids was there. They came to court to see about their mama. She don't care. "Your mother's nothing but a junkie." You know what I'm sayin'? You don't tell my kids nothing like that. You know my son graduated from college and that's not bad for a junkie, baby. Come on, I gave them folks ninety thousand dollars, that was a lotta dope to sell.

Jammie shows that as a Black woman, especially one from a "ghetto," she is immediately stereotyped as a drug user, bad mother, and liar. But she said, "I break the stereotype." Jammie sent her son to a very prestigious college, and coming from a neighborhood in the Bluff, it must have been hard for her son to graduate, but he did. I was impressed that Jammie raised him and sent him to college while she was using and selling drugs, and spent time in jail. Jammie's only arrests were for drug charges—two were for possession only. She was not a "junkie" and did not appear to have much problematic use. She used drugs with her neighbors, but had enough control over her use to raise her four children well. Before she ended the interview Jammie wanted to be sure I got her message.

Let me give you a good insight. You can also let them know that all crack parents aren't bad parents. 'Cuz I got some good kids. I got a son in college now at university, that's my baby. My other son just graduated State University. I got one that just opened a business, and like I said, I gotta son that graduated from [a very prestigious] college. I'm not a bad parent, I just gotta bad habit.

THE IMPACT OF RACISM

Older baby boomers raised in the South remembered segregation, which left an indelible impression on them. Elijah, discussed previously, recounted a poignant memory that illustrated the deep-seated impact of segregation, which he did not understand as a child.

> See, I went to a segregated school . . . And you know, segregated and stuff like that, I never seen a Hispanic until my high school year. And some of the small things that I was afraid to tell anybody—I used drugs to suppress those . . . You know, only today I'm learnin' how to talk about myself. I'm not ashamed to say what I just did, but fifteen to twenty years ago I wouldn't dare tell nobody what I just told you. It doesn't matter anymore. The only thing that matters today is that I've lost the desire to use drugs. It just did a lot to my guilt, shame, and fear issues that I'm just now getting to address. I no longer have to use drugs to suppress those anymore, I have courage enough to face those now. At one time I depended on drugs to help me with my feelings.

Like many southern African American baby boomers who were children during the civil rights movement when colorblindness was the goal, Elijah was hesitant to identify racism as an influential factor in his drug use. The consequences of teaching your children colorblindness in a racist society was personally tragic for some.

Amy was an African American woman who saw a lot of suffering in her 60 years of life. She was raised at a time when African American children were taught to be colorblind. She tried to follow this ideal until she realized it was not reciprocated. Stoically, she recounted how she lost her son in a hate crime.

> It's such a long story. My oldest son got killed and (pause)—Thanksgiving of 1991. And before he got killed, he had just turned nineteen. I said that I was the only child for seven years and I didn't want my child to be here in the world by himself. So that's the only reason why I had my second son. You see how things happen? He ended up getting killed. Now my baby boy is here by himself.
>
> Racially motivated. They (pause), they robbed him, put him in a van and took him to an abandoned house, stuck him in the chimney and set the house on fire. The only reason why we know what happened—it happened

Thanksgiving and it was a five-alarm fire. And the very next day the only thing standing was a wall and the chimney. And when the steam shovel hit the chimney, his body slid out. And do you know, he was not burnt, nowhere on his body. Nowhere on his body was he burnt. Now, what is that?

He was last seen with two Caucasian individuals, 'cause we didn't teach that in our household. He had all types of friends, all colors, races, and whatnot. And he was a very friendly person anyway. And he was last seen with these two Caucasian guys, (pause), right before the fire started. Nobody was arrested, 'cause nobody could identify them. Nobody knew 'em in the neighborhood.

We sat in silence, sharing a pause in our worldly thoughts as we contemplated the terrible impact of racism on the life of this hurting mother.

CHIEF

There is a "class advantage" that offers some protection from the worse effects of racism and the criminal justice system.[29] The stories discussed in this book show that not all Black baby boomers came from a ghetto or returned to a ghetto. Discussed in chapter 4 were eight baby boomer drug users who avoided incarceration. Three were White, three Black, and two Latino. Two of them, both White women, had considerably more economic resources and mainstream social capital than others. One of the Black / Latino men had a different kind of social capital that protected him from incarceration.

Chief was 49 years old at the time of the interview and an active drug user. He identified as half Black and half Hispanic / Latino.[30] Born in Virginia, he spent his childhood in military bases across the states and in Europe. Both of his parents had military careers.

A star athlete in high school, he was recruited to college sports but had to stop due to injuries. He joined the Army and eventually trained as a Special Forces sniper. He was sent to Iraq and Afghanistan more than 50 times. Up until his first sniper mission, he had never used any substances, not even tobacco or alcohol. But immediately after his "first kill" in 1985 he began smoking marijuana and drinking beer and liquor.

Chief married only once when he was 22, and divorced when he was 26. It became harder to relate to his wife and kids every time he came home. He also worried his children's hyperactivity would set him off. After the divorce he became a regular user of cocaine for a motivational "pump" and to keep awake through long periods of waiting while on a mission.

Chief was reticent to talk about his real job in the military and where he had been, but he was forthcoming about the drugs he used while in the military traveling from country to country. Once he was sent to a South American country to "burn crops"; he said they kept some to bring home.

> Burn so much and you take so much. We took what we wanted, and when the camera crews came to film, yeah, we showed 'em burning a little bit of stuff. But other than that we were putting shit in airplanes, helicopters, in your duffle bags, if you wanted ten or twenty keys. We were taking so much shit. That crap—the War on Drugs? There's no damn thing, War on Drugs. You bring that shit over here.

Sustaining injuries and multiple surgeries, Chief now lived on a pension and Supplemental Security Income (SSI) for disability. He was plagued by flashback episodes ("reliving all of this stuff"), sometimes lasting for hours. He said his life was "boring now." Resigned to his condition, he continued to medicate with methamphetamine, crack, weed, and liquor. He goes to the Veterans Administration (VA) for detoxification and treatment when his drug use becomes a problem.

> Yeah. You just go in there for thirty days but you can leave if after a week you get that itch. I mean, you can go and nobody holding you. You just go in there. I usually go, spend thirty days in there, come out and I'm alright for a little bit, until the dreams and all that stuff starts happening again . . . When people talk too damn much. I'm not joking. It's just like, you get high or whatever and then you always have one or two people that just won't shut up. And I just—I tell them a couple times, "You're talkin' too much." And they look at me, and they don't think too much of anything, and when I get up . . . it's over 'cause I'm gonna shut ya up. That's why I don't hang around a lot of people.

Despite his race, Chief's military ID offered a protective factor:

> Yeah. I got charged three times with assault and . . . spent a couple hours in there and all that's said is like, "You can go." The last time I got arrested was about three months ago. [Suburb] County. 'Cause when I broke this guy's arm—he just would not shut up. [Suburb] County came and they were telling me I was going to be in jail for up to eighteen months for criminal assault. And I was like, "Yeah, yeah, just do what you gotta do." They put me in the car, took me down, and they never asked me for my ID the whole time. We got down there, took out my—showed 'em my driver's license, my military ID and stuff. Guy said, "How long were you in the service?" And I said, "Longer than you've been a cop." He's like, "You're a smart ass." I said, "Man, just put

me in the holding cell 'cause I don't have time for this." Forty-five minutes later the guy slipped me my wallet and he said, "You can get the hell up outta here." He didn't even ask any questions.

Chief was not the only respondent who had been in the military, but he was the only one who made a career of it. His story about drugs in the military is unique in this study sample but characteristic of stories that others on our research team heard from people they know personally who were in military.[31] His story serves as an illustration of the impact of the War on Drugs on military personnel.

ANTHONY

A charming man who was 51 years old at the time of the interview, Anthony was sharp and conscientious, often asking us to go back in the interview timeline to check on a date. Born and raised in Atlanta, his parents separated when he was 13, and he lived with his mother. Although he also kept in touch with his father over the years, he said it was hard not having a father at home when he was a kid. He left college to work full-time when his wife was expecting a baby. Although he did not climb the ladder in the southern company he worked for, he stayed with the company until it downsized. He never blamed his situation on racism, but the fact that he was Black in a company run by White men may have been a factor.

> So they had this thing called Bumping and Rolled. So I got bumped from one position then I'd go to another position. And I'd be the lowest man on the totem pole in that department. And I'd get bumped out of that department. And I got bumped out the door and didn't know where to go.

With a family to support, Anthony was determined to find work and soon landed a job with an airline company based in Atlanta.

Anthony used cocaine and heroin for 15 years while he worked steadily. He indicated no social or work problems arising from his drug use, even though he was probably addicted to heroin at the time. His wife knew he was using, but she did not complain as long as he was working and supported his family. His drug use was not a problem until the company he worked for shut down, a result of the government deregulation of the airline business. Without a job, and still addicted, he engaged in illegal activities to support his habit.

Anthony's first arrest was for injecting drugs in a car. After that, he was in and out of jail every year until he received a four-year sentence for buying crack in the Bluff for a friend.

> He liked the crack rock. I don't like crack. (laughs) So he said, "Man, stop and let me get a rock." And then I said, "Man, I don't feel like going over there. Let me go get my stuff first and then I shoot over through there." So I went and got straight and then took him over there. Okay, so we was over getting his thing, getting the crack. Red Dogs [police] pulled up . . . I can get charged with all this dope. You see what I'm saying?

By this time Anthony was only "dipping and dabbing" (occasional drug use) with his friends; he did not have a problem and was careful not to use before a parole office visit when he might be drug tested. Like Omar, Anthony was sent back to prison because he had more time on the books to serve. When he got out, his drug use increased

> Well, something happened and then I started doing it every day. What happened? Oh, 'cause when I first got out, [Suburban] County came back and told me that my time weren't ranked—all my time was supposed to be ranked concurrent. And, so they was telling me to come out there and report, because I was going to have to come back and do that time. And they were talking about three months. I was going to have to go back and do three months. That really messed me up for a minute, because I had got stuff started. So I said, shit, that's what up, you know. I went and did the time and when I got out it was kind of like . . . I was so pissed off. I tried not to do it, but I got pulled into the drug scene, going over there [the Bluff] every day.

His wife divorced him while he was in prison, so Anthony was alone after his release. He was hurting emotionally, but his main focus was finding work.

> It was kind of hard because I had, you know, been a convicted felon. It was hard to get the type of work that I was used to getting. So what I did was go back to school. I went to a tech school, took up heating and air, and started work. I'm still doing that.

Once he had steady employment, Anthony stopped his problematic drug use by going to a methadone program. With daily doses of methadone, Anthony felt his life was now on track. Even though the mandatory drug tests showed he was occasionally using cocaine, he was not kicked out of the program. He remarried and stayed in touch with his two children from a previous marriage, both college graduates.

Other Black men in the study recounted similar stories, which show that despite occasional or even daily use of hard drugs, it was possible to control drug use so it did not interfere with other parts of their lives. Anthony always worked and supported his family while using drugs. Although we have not heard his wife's perspective, the fact that she did not divorce him until he was sent to prison for four years provides some indication that she accepted his drug use, as he said, and he did not deplete the family's income for drugs. It is also noteworthy that Anthony knew when his heroin use became unmanageable and voluntarily enrolled in a methadone program. Controlled use of potentially harmful substances is not an ideal solution, but it is certainly a better solution than incarceration.

HARRY: ON PAROLE

In 2004, Harry was released on parole to Wernersville halfway house near Reading, Pennsylvania. Due to his record of using drugs in prison, he had to go through another drug treatment program to show he was "treated" for his addiction before he could be released into society. The halfway house was run by the criminal justice system and only for prisoners on their way out. At the end of the program he received a "certificate of completion" and he was free to go. This time our home plan was for Harry to live with our mother and a sister in Daytona, Florida.

I drove from Georgia all night so I could be at the halfway house early in the morning when Harry was released. The thought of seeing my brother on the outside, knowing he was now relatively free to take a walk whenever he wanted, choose where and what to eat, and listen to music he liked, kept me awake with anticipation as I drove through the night. The feeling was temporary. As he threw his one black garbage bag full of all his worldly possessions in the trunk of the car, he asked me to drive him to a friend to pick up something.

"I am not picking up drugs for you," I said cautiously. "No, it's a bottle of whiskey, really," Harry insisted. "A good bottle a guy was holding for me for when I got out."

I wasn't against Harry drinking—it was a long ride to Florida and I would not mind—but I was not going to drive him to a "friend." What kind of friend would he have in this town, I wondered?[32] What I saw of Wernersville looked like a ghetto. I told him I would buy him a bottle somewhere in a liquor store on the way. Unfortunately, it was Sunday, and Pennsylvania was a dry state on Sunday. We had to go to Maryland, where I pulled off the highway and parked with other desperados sitting in their cars on Sunday morning waiting for the liquor store to open.

With a fifth of whisky reassuringly in his possession, Harry took a few swigs and we were off for a long ride. A few hours later, I saw Harry eyeing a police car driving past us, and I thought to ask him the question I ask all my study participants when I drive them anywhere.

"You don't have any drugs on you, do you?" I asked. He shook his head no. "Marijuana is a drug," I reminded him. "Well, okay then," he said, "I might have a little joint here somewhere."

He checked his pants pockets as if looking for small change and he found one. I pulled into the next gas station and told him he had to throw it away or smoke it in the back. I wasn't getting in trouble for having drugs in my car. He chose to smoke it. The rest of the trip was tranquil.

Our sister Rose lived on 10 acres with her husband and our mother, near a large state reserve between Orlando and Daytona. We went down a dirt road about five miles before arriving at her property. They had parked an Airstream behind the house for Harry. Rose set Harry up with a job as a busboy in a nice restaurant where businessmen and lawyers brought their clients for lunch or a drink. Rose knew the owner and cashed in on her social capital to help Harry.

The Airstream was a temporary solution. Our mother used the money she had left from selling her house up North to buy a one-room efficiency apartment in a converted old hotel in Daytona—a sort of working-class vacation timeshare that had seen better days. Because of the deteriorating neighborhood, it was unbelievably cheap. Harry only had to pay the utilities and maintenance fees, and he could afford that on his busboy pay, leaving the tips to buy food, phone, and transportation.

Harry had some difficulties adjusting to living on his own. He was always lonely and called everyone he knew at night until he fell asleep. He never liked television and preferred listening to a jazz station on the radio. When I talked with him on the phone, I often heard Billie Holiday, one of his favorites. At the time, phone plans did not come with unlimited minutes, and after a few months of nearly not being able to pay outrageous phone bills, Harry learned to watch his minutes. Unfortunately, this meant less time talking with someone to ease his loneliness.

On my first visit to Florida I helped Harry fill out the paperwork for a Pell grant and we submitted an application to Daytona Community College.[33] After a few months he was in college. He got a driver's license and with our mother's help bought an old used car so he could drive to college from work and not be late waiting on Daytona's unreliable public transportation. The first months seemed too good to be true, but only because criminal justice processes move slowly.

Everything changed when Harry's parole officer turned up at the restaurant to check out his place of employment. Harry had already been working there for months. His boss was happy with Harry and gave him extra hours, filling in when they needed a dishwasher. But the parole officer said he could not work there because it had a bar and sold alcohol. Part of his parole conditions stipulated that he could not be physically present in a bar or anywhere that sold alcoholic beverages. The parole officer said that included working at a bar, and he had to look for other employment.

Harry found a job at the 24-hour Denny's downstairs in the building where his efficiency apartment was located. He worked the graveyard shift as a dishwasher. Since there were few dishes to do from midnight until 8 a.m., he usually helped out in the front dining room. Daytona was the crack capital of Florida, and Denny's seemed to be the crack haven in Daytona after hours. Within a few weeks after starting work at Denny's, he made a lot of new friends—all people using crack who had nowhere to go at night but Denny's. Harry did not like crack, but he used it occasionally when offered to show camaraderie. Harry became their designated driver to pick up crack, since he was the only one with a car.

His involvement with Daytona's crack-using community started when Harry befriended a young couple, Jim and Cindy, who were parents of a four-year-old daughter, Lucy. They had recently been kicked out of Cindy's parents' house for stealing from them and were living on the beach during the day. They came into Denny's at night to put their little girl to sleep on the cushions of a booth. When they got to know Harry, they asked him to watch her while they went on some "errands." Sometimes they were gone for hours. He assumed they were smoking crack. Harry felt sorry for the little girl, and since he was working all night, he offered the parents his key to the efficiency apartment so they could have a place to stay and be with their daughter at night. The little efficiency soon became grand central station for crackheads.

Harry and I kept in touch almost daily, so I knew what was going on, but I could not ask him to put the young couple and their daughter out on the street. I warned him about taking people to buy drugs in an area where the police are looking for easy targets, although I knew he would risk it for friends. He was still going to school and still working, but all he needed was an unlucky day.

I also noticed, that at least in Daytona where Harry was staying, crack users were a racially desegregated population. White, Black, and Latino / all used crack together. Jim and Cindy were White; most of their friends were Black. All of them became Harry's friends, and he enjoyed their attention. I sometimes called Harry when he was taking his friends to the crack houses and we talked while he waited in his car. I could understand the sense of belonging he felt with this group of people who respected him because he was the only one stable enough to have money in his pocket and sober enough to drive them around. Former felons cannot pick their friends. However, Harry got more than friendship out of this exchange, since at least one of his new friends paid for the car rides with prescription drugs.

Once Harry called me from a crack house. He was calm and there was no indication that he was using crack, no stress or excitement in his voice despite the situation he described.

> I just wanted to call and let you know that I might be back in jail tomorrow. I'm sorry. You did so much for me. And mom—please tell her I am sorry. I drove some friends here to get some crack and now there's some cops banging on the door. If anyone opens it, I'm in trouble. I shouldn't be here. I know you told me. I am sorry, I let you down.

I could hear a cacophony of yelling in the background. I heard pounding at the door and a man screamed, "Don't let them in—they ain't got no warrant, and they ain't coming in." No one opened the door. The police eventually left. Harry got away before the police could come back with a warrant, and he avoided the cop car he saw waiting at the end of the street. He called me the next day to say he was safe and was heading downstairs to work.

I could tell Harry was not using crack, or if he was, it was not interfering with his work. However, he was using prescription pills illegally, and this is what got him the parole violation that sent him back to Camp Hill Penitentiary in Pennsylvania.

SIX

Women Doing Drugs

INGRID

I first ran into Ingrid when I was working as a research assistant on a heroin study and recruiting at night on Ponce de Leon Avenue. At the time, the street had a reputation for being one of the seamy streets to hit after dark. After the sun was well below the horizon, a section of the Ponce became heavily decorated with pretty women in short skirts or hot pants. I met Ingrid before she started work and took her to the Phoenix Cocktail Lounge, once known as Atlanta's seediest dive bar. Frequented by older gay men and young male drug users who made extra cash as sex workers, the Phoenix was an undignified cement block and later was shut down during gentrification of the neighborhood. Dark inside, even for a bar, two women in this establishment were easily ignored. It was early and the patio in the back of the Phoenix was empty. We began our interview as the sun set, casting an eerie glow on the dreary parking lot. After the interview, I drove her over to the Krispie Kreme donut shop on Ponce. She worked a corner in the area.

Ingrid had a heroin chic look—rail thin with dark circles under her bright blue eyes. She was in her mid-forties at the time. She covered her track marks and bruises with strategically placed clothing but showed them to me during the interview. There were many scars of various colors and shades; the more recent ones were livid. Once we got to Krispie Kreme under bright fluorescent lights, I could see that years of drug use and streetwalking had taken their toll on her face.

Ingrid had just learned that she was HIV positive, and she was not feeling good about her prospects. She had no intention of telling her tricks—men who often belittled her and beat her when they noticed her track marks. She already was paid very little, telling me the "crack whores" had lowered the rates, and as a heroin addict she needed a certain amount every day. I saw her a few times on the Ponce strip—each time she looked more and more like she was wasting away slowly. I stopped hanging out on the Ponce when the heroin study was over, and although I looked for her when I drove by, I did not see her again for years.

Recruiting in the Bluff for the older drug user study, I was surprised when I saw someone who looked like Ingrid walking down an empty street early one morning. It was rare to see a White woman alone on these streets during the day, so I drove closer and pulled up next to her. She turned around and beamed a toothless smile, her eyes lighting up. I thought she did not recognize me but was happy for the opportunity to ask for a few dollars from someone who was not from the neighborhood. We chatted and I reminded her that I had interviewed her about ten years ago. She said she remembered. Still a heroin user, she was living in the Bluff. She told me she needed money for her AIDS medication and went into a long story about how she lost her Medicaid. I gave her some money and we made an appointment to meet at the Atlanta Harm Reduction Center (AHRC) to do an interview later that week. Her story was much the same as she told it before, but with more years of drug use, prostitution, and in and out of jails and emergency departments.

Ingrid was born an orphan and ran away from foster parents at age 10. She said she never went to school after that, although she could read and write— skills she was quite proud to demonstrate. She also demonstrated a remarkable memory, perhaps a survival skill needed for people with no phone, no computer, and no stable home where physical memories are stored.

Ingrid was in the worst social situation of anyone in the study, and she might be considered an outlier, but as discussed previously, outliers can point to important truths about humanity that are missed when we dismiss them.[1] Although I have heard about life events similar to hers over the 20 years I have been listening to drug users' stories, no one I knew was as old as Ingrid— now 56 years old—and a continuous daily drug user.[2] For over 40 years as a heroin user and sex worker, she had not died of an overdose or at the hand of a trick. She had lived with AIDS longer than expected, but the years of living on the street with no stable residence and no steady relationship with someone to support her emotionally was beginning to be more than even Ingrid could bear. My research assistant helping to conduct the interview had never seen someone in such dreadful physical condition. Her body was covered with open sores that she made little attempt to hide. She covered a few on her face with Band-Aids that were now peeling off, some hanging by one flap and exposing oozing deep red marks. She was nodding off during the interview and kept shaking her leg to stay alert. Nevertheless, her story matched what she had told me years previously. The AHRC staff were familiar with Ingrid since she had been using their services since they started syringe exchange. Ingrid was a legend simply by staying alive in the worst environmental and social circumstances imaginable—in the richest country in the world.

Ingrid was told her mother was only 12 years old and her father only 15 when she was born. They immediately gave her to an orphanage. By age 9, she was living with a foster family.

> And they had other foster kids and other kids, and it's just a lot of trouble. I didn't feel like they cared for me or loved me. I guess I didn't get the attention that I wanted. And then my foster father—I had a brother that was slow and he'd get in fights and stuff and I'd get my ass beat. He used to hit you in the ears or in the face you know, where it hurt the worst, if I didn't take up for him or if I did so—either way it was a losing battle. And I didn't feel like I was loved, so I ran away.

> And when I ran away, they caught me and one time I brought a kitten back. They already had cats and they made me put the kitten in the shed when we went to church—come back and the kitten was dead. To me that kitten gave me the love and attention that I wasn't getting there. So I ran away again and the first people that I ran into that gave me attention, I jumped on it. And they were shootin' dope so I wanted to fit in, so "hey, do me." I continued to do that for two weeks and I thought they were my friends, and little did I know they were just using me basically to go into people's houses and stores to steal for them, to keep their habit up. But that's how I started with that. I didn't actually start prostituting till later, probably about fifteen, no about sixteen.

Her first sexual experience was when she was raped by a police officer at age 15. Ever since then she has had sex exclusively in her role as a prostitute, usually working on the street. She never had an intimate relationship with a long-term partner. Other than being a sex worker her entire life, she held a few short-term jobs and engaged in buying drugs for others to get free drugs. Her whole life appears to have been one never-ending trauma. She said she used heroin to ease the hurt.

Ingrid stayed in Philadelphia until a man from Florida offered her work in his landscaping business.

> I got paid under the table. But basically I met him as a trick, 'cause, you know, I did more sucking his dick than I did workin' the job itself, actually out

there in the yard. I mean, I actually did the work, but I did more spending time with him.

Ingrid left Florida and came to Atlanta, where her criminal record grew as the War on Drugs expanded. She recalled precisely, "I've got like 401 arrests, 81 alias names, 56 felony convictions. I've been in jail more than I can count . . . I've been to prison four different times but the most I've ever done is 17 months."[3] Ingrid recounted the story of her first arrest for extortion.

Ingrid: The guy, basically his wife found out about me 'cause I was still young and he worked at Sarah Lee, and I had nowhere to stay so he'd let me sleep in the car, but he told me to be quiet in the back. Well, they had a dog and the dog heard me, or whatever. Anyways his wife found out about me. So to keep his ass out of trouble, he told them that I had pictures, and if he didn't give me any money that I was gonna tell his wife about me. That's what was said in court.

Miriam: What were the felony charges?

Ingrid: Drug related. I'm on five different probations now—all for drugs. Possession of heroin intent to distribute; possession of heroin; possession of cocaine; possession of cocaine; possession of cocaine. I've got a few theft by receiving because sometimes I'd pay somebody to use the car even though I don't have a license, come to find out it was stolen. I have arrests for being in drug-related areas, disorderly conduct, and jaywalking. But my whole history is based on drugs.

Miriam: All the felonies have been drug related?

Ingrid: Right. The only reason I really never got—the last time they tried to get me for habitual—the only reason they didn't 'cause they didn't catch up with all the names then.

Miriam: Did you ever use any violence in any of your crimes, like have a gun?

Ingrid: No, well, I've been locked up for armed robbery and possession of a firearm, but they dismissed it because first of all I didn't have a firearm, and second I didn't rob nobody. See what it was is I gave a guy head [oral sex] and I didn't get him off. And he wanted his money back, and I didn't give it back. So he caused me to stay in Fulton County [jail] for a year. That was back in 1998.

Miriam: How many times do you think you've been in treatment?

Ingrid: I've been in three. All three times I didn't stay in but a day, two days.

Ingrid was incarcerated at least 50 times for drugs and prostitution and offered treatment only three times because she lived during the War on Drugs. As jails filled with drug users, Atlanta was ordered by the federal government to reduce their jail population, and treatment alternatives became popular. By the time she was offered treatment, it was too late. She had adapted to a life of drugs and prostitution. The chaos of street life came with an acquired taste for freedom that was difficult to contain in the constricting environment of treatment rules and regulations.[4]

Ingrid discovered she had HIV when she was in jail in 1998. In 2008, she learned she had AIDS.

> Miriam: How did you find out you had AIDS?
>
> Ingrid: Just recently, well the doctor, when I was in jail, I got locked up for a piece of peppermint about a month and a half ago and they charged me with possession of cocaine.[5] But my T cell was so low that he said you're right on the borderline of being AIDS and HIV. See that's why I'm saying—that's why I was desperate for this, 'cause see I have to pay for my own medicines because I'm not on Medicaid yet. I'm waiting for them to find out what's going on or whatever . . . But see my main concern today is getting my medication. Somebody's already gave me fifty dollars. My medicine cost a lot of money, it costs a hundred and three dollars.
>
> Miriam: But can't you go to Grady [hospital] and get that?
>
> Ingrid: No, I don't even have a Grady card. I had one. I was in the hospital back in April. Either way, I don't have Medicaid. I have to pay the price of the medications. Mine's like a hundred and three dollars. But you know, like I said, I ran out yesterday, but I was blessed. Somebody else helped me with fifty. So now like, fifty-three dollars lacking, so that's why I'm desperate, you know.
>
> Miriam: Why don't you have Medicaid?
>
> Ingrid: They haven't approved me for anything. I already put all my paperwork in.

Ingrid said the AHRC staff, experienced in Medicaid paperwork processes, was helping her obtain her Medicaid status, something the jail and hospital failed to do. I later called the AIDS nonprofit organizations in Atlanta and found out Ingrid would not qualify for any of their services.[6]

Ingrid talked about her current situation candidly. She was staying in the Bluff "to cop" drugs for other people, thereby getting a little cut for herself. I had mistakenly interpreted her nodding as being high on heroin.

> I hardly get high anymore. I basically just do enough to get well. When I nod off it's because I've been up for too many days. Just been up too many days. Sleeping here and there in abandoned houses and stuff.

I asked what she did about withdrawals from heroin. "I come up on something," she explained. "Somebody I cop crack for, I take their crack and try to trade it off [for heroin]."

When I asked Ingrid why she did not stay in treatment when she was offered a free program instead of jail, she responded with what I heard from many people who left treatment or relapsed: "I wasn't ready. I wasn't really ready. I wasn't tired." This is the treatment "script" that encourages self-blame for any failure in life—particularly relapse.[7]

After I paid Ingrid the $40 for the interview, she flashed a Starbucks gift card and asked me to buy it.

> I'm still needing thirteen dollars. It's got sixty-three dollars on it. The guy [a trick] that gave it to me, he bought it. It was on his receipt. He didn't have any money, so he gave me that. I don't drink coffee, but I was gonna keep it, but because I'm going to be short thirteen dollars. I've got fifty and your forty's going to be ninety.

I gave her $20, for which she thanked me profusely as she rushed out the door.

> I gotta hurry . . . I'm on schedule, you have to stay on point with your medication. And I usually take my medicines at 9:30 to 10 o'clock. I take Combivir and Viramune. It costs an arm and a leg and that doesn't include the Bactrian, the antibiotics I'm supposed to take.

I was encouraged to hear that Ingrid was trying to take control of her health, but even if she ran out to get heroin, I could not blame her. The medical doctors who diagnosed her should have made sure she had coverage for needed AIDS medication, like they do in almost every developed country and many developing countries—but not in the United States.

The Starbucks card actually had 68 cents, which was a surprise since I thought it would have nothing. I saw Ingrid a few more times in the Bluff and always gave her a twenty or offered her a ride somewhere. But then she disappeared. The AHRC staff said she stopped coming around and suspected she was in the hospital or jail. No one had heard of an overdose victim with her description, and almost everyone in the Bluff knew Ingrid.

VICTORIA

Victoria, a 45-year-old Black woman, was born and raised in the Atlanta area. She never knew her father and lived with her mother, whom she saw injecting drugs when she was young. After her mother remarried she also lived with a stepfather who sexually abused her.

> I think I was about ten—ten or eleven. My mama never knew. I never told my mom. She never knew. I still haven't told . . . I was in the bed one night and he came to the room. And he said if I didn't let him do me, he was gonna do my sister. (pause) It was rape.

> He was living there. He had just got out of prison, and my mom let him move in with us, and I think he did it when my mom was either asleep or gone. Well, he did me like, probably like—I don't know. I don't know if it was every day or it was like—I know he did it quite often . . . I guess, because he said that he was going to hurt my mom (long pause). And I know he used to beat my mom, so I felt like, I guess, that I felt like that he would hurt her if I say something. She was scared of him. She was very much scared of him.

She told her story with many sighs and pauses. Her sentences were short and hesitant, as if she were filling in the missing parts in her head visually. She both blamed and excused her mother, yet she understood her mother's position as a poor Black female.

Victoria had her first child before she graduated from high school, but she finished high school and then attended a year of college before she had another baby. The father of her children moved in with her and her mother. She thought he was a good provider. "He bought everything I needed for high school prom, junior, senior fees," she explained. "He pretty much took care of me. He fed me. We stayed with my mom, but he did everything that my mom was supposed to been doing."

They were officially married after their second child was born and still married at the time of the interview. He stood by her during her worst years of drug use, and even bought her drugs when "he didn't want me to walk the streets."

Victoria started using crack late in life, at 26 years old. It was the late 1980s when crack was called an epidemic in the community.

> My family was doing it. My cousins, my uncles—I was working everyday. My cousins, my uncles—and when I go to bed at night, it's there like when I wake up, people sitting at the kitchen table . . . Well, actually it was my apartment. Me and my husband and my kids. And actually they were his kin people that usually come to the house. And they always come when I sleep. And I was wondering why every time I wake up there is all these peoples in the house walking around, everybody quiet. And then one day I got out of work early and my brother was smoking [crack]. And for years I just blamed my

brother. And I asked him let me try it. I just wanted to see how, why—I was just curious.

Her life quickly became a "big blur." She was using, copping, and in and out of jail or treatment for many years. "Darn. I can't get them dates down," she said in frustration and consulted the timetable. Eventually she organized her life around her children's birthdates. "That's when I start my addiction," she said, pointing to 1990 on the timeline. "I'm positive because [my baby] was born positive for drugs in his system. And he was the one who was born addicted." Her mother took her children while Victoria was living out of her "addiction" for 15 years.

As long as Victoria had a house, she seemed to control her use to some degree.

> When I first started, I was working. I was trying to work. It was just like any jobs, like working at all. Like working at different barber shops, like sweeping hair up. Or working, like, any little grocery stores, cleaning their windows or emptying trash . . . I pretty much just stayed at home then because family was letting me use—they were using my house to smoke. When I lost my apartment, that's when I had to start hustling . . . I was just hustling. I was buying me a nice piece [of crack] and selling some of it and smoking some of it, and whatever money I made off that person, I would buy me some more.

Eventually she used sex to get money for more crack, but her process for finding clients (tricks) was much more systematic than streetwalking.[8]

> Because, I just, I guess I just didn't care no more, to be honest with you. Crack was in control of me. I really wasn't thinking. I really didn't care. I just wanted to get more drugs . . . They [tricks] was the one that I know they'd get a regular check every month. And I knowed they were one to trick off. You know what I'm saying? Them is the ones that I pretty much messed with. I had a book. A little black book. I had a little black book with the phone numbers. I promise, I had a little black book. 'Cause sometimes I just had the numbers in the book. I didn't have no name by it. But I'd put a star by it, 'cause I know he gonna pay. And I put a lot of smiley face that he gonna be alright. So I just call them like on Fridays, I just went through the book. I will have a cell phone, but I will use pay phones, or whatever or whoever phone I could use. And I would get in touch with them. They would have me meet them that night or whatever.
>
> The dealers, I mostly tricked off with the dealers. I didn't trick off too many with the people in the streets. I mostly tricked off with the dealers because I know after I got through tricking off with them I would get money. I would

get beer. I would get whatever I need when I got through with the dealer. There were even outfits. They would even buy me something clean to put on and I would be able to sit at their house and chill out for a couple of days. 'Cause they would trust me. They usually asked to come and clean up their house for them ... It was just like, I would sit at their house and then they would be like—you know, 'cause I had all of their numbers. And they'd be like, my boy here, you know, he got some money. He want to spend money. Or they would call me and tell me that they got somebody at their house spending money. One of their customers, they were spending money. And they would call me because they know I didn't steal nothing from my customers. They know that if I felt like one of my customers was in danger, I made sure that my customer would leave the environment where we at.

So the dope boys would mostly like tell me to come deal with their customer 'cause they know that I'm going to make sure their customer didn't get hurt or nothing. Because you know in the neighborhood, in a trap [crack house], when people find out that you tricking off with somebody who got some money, they're going to try to rob that person. And so the dealers just ask me to take care of them and make sure that nobody try to rob them. And people knew that you couldn't do that with my customer because I'm with a dealer's client. So they pretty much knew not to try it.

Like many women in the drug-dealing scene, Victoria's privileged status was dependent on the "dope boys," and when she was less attractive to them, she was forced to change strategies.

I guess because I really stopped taking care of myself as much as I was doing. Because when I was taking care of myself real good, dope boys were like, they wanted to be around me. I was taking care of myself better and they didn't have a problem with taking me out with them.

After a few years, this crack-using lifestyle affected her looks. Instead of asking Victoria to hang out with them in their house, the dealers gave her crack to sell to her own customers.

And the dope boys would give me the dope—you know, if I go to the dope boy and be like this guy has a lot of money. And if I go to the dope boy and be, like, can you just break me off something and I'll bring your money back? They would give me so much dope that I could sell it to my client. And I made my own money.

Victoria's husband, Antoine, was an exceptional father. When he discovered the extent of her drug use, he tried to help her at first. Only after he saw that he was not able to stop her from using, he separated and took custody of all five children from her mother, even the two he knew were not his own. He still allowed her to see the children. Victoria's mother also kept in touch and was there when she needed her.

> As a matter of fact, while I was out there, my mom, when I get tired or need some rest, I would go and knock on my mom's door. And my mom would open the door and let me in. And I would go in there and go to sleep in my room. I still had my own bedroom.

Her first arrest was for something she did not do, but since she did not want to snitch, she was charged with the crime.

> I was with some peoples that was driving out of town. I guess they call them pill pull. They would go in the store and pill pull—Tylenol, steal a whole bunch. And I woke up and the police was standing up over me like this and I was looking at him. And he was looking at a whole bunch of pill bottles in the car, like Tylenol bottles and Motrin. And I didn't know that he had stole all this, because I woke up out of a sleep. And when I woke up they told me I was being arrested for theft by receiving. And I didn't even know. And they put a charge on me because I couldn't tell them—I mean the boy would not confess that he did it. So he made everybody get a rap. [The police] told us, "I'll let you go if he say he did it." But the boy never did say he did it. So they gave me a charge.

She was in and out of jail for the next five years. After another baby was born, Victoria followed the advice of her family and enrolled in a private treatment program.

> They discharged me because they said I didn't meet the requirements. You had to make a certain amount of money and give them your check . . . I asked them not to do that, because I know I'm going to use. And they discharged me and I used. I got back high again.

I discussed what "choice" meant with Victoria. Did she "choose" to leave treatment if she did not have the money to pay for it? Should treatment be free? Her response indicated that she took full responsibility.

> I think it was okay to pay, because I caused that on myself. They would take your whole check and that's what I didn't like. I was working two jobs and they would take your whole check. I caused it on myself.

Victoria did not try to hide the fact that she was using while pregnant. Even though she knew the stigma attached to pregnant mothers using crack, she filled in the details of her last pregnancy.

But what happened was, all the while I was pregnant with him, I used. And right before I got ready to go into labor with him, about a month before I went into labor with him, I call the treatment center then. Because I found out that you get locked up, you get locked up for using and for having a positive child on drugs. So I made an appointment for me to go to treatment. And that's when, after I made the appointment, they never did have no room for me.

Other than her drug-related activities, Victoria embraced conventional values. For example, Victoria and Antoine did not divorce, although they never lived together again. "I'm still married twenty-three years," she said proudly. "I told him to death do us part. We're best friends. Actually all my kids call him Uncle. The ones that aren't his, they call him Uncle."

By 2004, treatment alternatives to incarceration proliferated, and much of the treatment expense was paid for by the city or nonprofit organizations. Victoria was offered free treatment in order to regain custody of her newborn child. She insisted it was her choice to go to treatment.

When I got to [the hospital], they didn't lock me up because—they had it on record that I tried to get some help. So what they did, they gave me a choice to call somebody in the family to come and get my baby and I'd go to treatment. So what happened was my sister got custody of him, and a DFCS [child services] worker told me to get clean for thirty days and then my baby could come to treatment with me. And that's what happened—it were me. I wanted to get clean. Because like I said, I were the one that called the treatment center and rat on myself. Didn't no DFCS worker made me call. Didn't nobody make me go. The only reason DFCS became any part of it was because my sister was going to get custody of him from me. So DFCS had to come and do the paperwork at the hospital. The DFCS worker told me to just go for six months. I stayed fourteen months.

When it was time for her to leave the treatment program, Victoria requested another program, where she was eventually offered a job as a peer counselor.

When I left [the treatment program], I asked to go to another treatment center while I was in treatment. I went to the director and I asked her if I could get some more treatment while I was there; which was really strange that somebody asked for extra help. So that's when they sent me to drug court at Fulton County ... Once I graduated ... I had just finished drug court when I came here [the housing program]. So I asked the director where I was working, I told him that I wanted to go and volunteer at juvenile court every week, so that's what I was doing. So Judge Jones, the judge that died in the plane crash, me and him, he was like my best, best friend in the world. He really helped me get the job. And I'm the peer counselor over that program. So I went down there every Wednesday to talk to the ladies and work down there every Wednesday. And Judge Jones asked me would I speak for a Humana grant. So I went and spoke for a Humana grant, letting them know the importance of an aftercare program. And they gave a $100,000 grant. And I'm the peer counselor over that program.

It's like aftercare—it's not a transition. It's a place where the ladies will come. I'm the receptionist and the peer counselor there. And it's where the ladies will come and they'll do their drug screen. We will feed them and at two o'clock they go to court. This happen every Wednesday. At two o'clock they go to court. I go to court with them in front of the judge. The judge may ask me how is they progressing, do they see their kids, do they go to their classes? And I would tell her. So I pretty much help advocate for them to get their kids.

Victoria had six years of comprehensive treatment, including her time as a peer counselor. By 2008, a number of transitional programs for women and children were opened in the Atlanta area, and Victoria's situation dramatically improved when she was helped through a program using a Housing First model.[9]

Independent living, transitional housing. It's where the women come when they get out of treatment. They pretty much live on their own. We have our own apartment here. We don't pay no light and no gas bill. Our rent is subsidized. I don't know who—I think Families First pays some, HUD pays some of the people's apartment rent. I don't know but I pay real rent now 'cause my job I got. I pay what everybody else pays. It's pretty much a safe place. You have to go to [12-step] meetings. You have to have kids to stay here. You can't have a man staying with you. No. A man can't be there.

Victoria continued working with women recovering from problematic drug use. I asked if her own experiences helped her better understand the needs of her clients.

I think, so, because a lot of my clients now—a lot of my clients at my job, they, they've been molested. So I found out a lot about a lot of them now. Since I been working, because I work with recovering addicts. And a lot of ladies in their interviews, a lot of 'em talk about how they was molested, how they were raped. And a lot of my client's kids is getting raped to right this day. Well, not raped, but molested. And we have to talk them into going to the law.

Although she recognized the trauma of rape, Victoria never blamed her drug use on her own rape experience as a child. She thinks women make their own choices to use drugs. "It depends on the individual if she's willing to listen to what they've got to say," she said. "It don't work for a lot of the women. A lot of the women don't want to listen. They want to relapse."

The social context of Ingrid's and Victoria's lives were about as different as their race: Ingrid had no family, no steady relationship, and no structure in her life while Victoria had all of this, which ultimately helped her regain a life she desired. Yet they experienced similar situations as women. Both were molested as children, both used their bodies to make money for drugs, and both worked hard to have some semblance of control over their lives. They shared these traits with many of the women in this study who came from different social situations and held different roles as they fluctuated in and out of control over drug use.

THE GENDERED CULTURE OF DRUG USE: MULTIPLE ROLES, MULTIPLE RISKS

Gender plays a major role in the lives of people who use drugs, but the influence of other demographics cannot be easily disentangled from gender. Race, class, and age intersect with any discussion of gender and shape how women are viewed from birth to old age.[10] They also shape how the women view themselves. Yet, there are more similarities than differences when focusing on the demographic status called gender.[11] First, most were abused before they started using drugs, and they were more likely than men to be subject to violence in drug-using environments.[12] Their lives were also constrained by gender roles. When women cannot perform their roles to society's standards, or when they cannot cope with multiple roles, they face social stigma and loss of self-esteem.

One of the most critical roles to the women in this study was that of being a mother. Although mothers are not the only parent who provides for children, mothers remain the primary caregivers for young children and often are expected to provide more continuous emotional support than fathers.[13] Partially due to their role as the primary caregiver for children, mothers are also stigmatized as "bad women" when they violate gender role expectations.[14] Women who use drugs while pregnant are identified as having "moral failings" and ascribed a "spoiled identity."[15]

Even though research shows that poverty, low education, poor mental health, physical health problems, and social environment are direct or indirect causes of child neglect and abuse by parents, drug use is the easily identified culprit.[16] When mothers are caught using drugs, child protection services become involved, and instead of helping the mothers, children are forcibly removed and mothers have to prove themselves to get them back.[17] Fear of losing their children presents barriers to mothers seeking needed healthcare and treatment.[18]

The increased punitive responses and harsh legislation brought about by the expanding War on Drugs led to a greater focus on women who used drugs. This often resulted in more intrusion in their personal lives, loss of social services, loss of welfare benefits, and incarceration. Their multiple roles as mothers, partners, and friends were often in conflict. Women lost their homes or were evicted from public housing if their children or partners were caught using drugs on the property.[19] Women were encouraged to inform on their own children or significant others who were suspected of dealing drugs or other criminal activities.[20] As shown in Victoria's story, some women chose jail over becoming an informant.

Although women can become empowered in the drug-using world by being "cooks," runners, and dealers, these roles also come with more risks.[21] Younger female drug users may find empowerment through their involvement in the underground economy, since their youth supplies bargaining power, but older women generally face a reduction in resources in the drug-using world.[22] Jan and Ingrid were forced to take greater risks to survive as they aged in sex work. Victoria, who had more control over relationships with clients, was nevertheless influenced by the "dope boys" to sell crack to her customers, which put her at greater risk for incarceration and violence.

Because of their multiple roles and multiple risks, women need more resources. The turning point for Victoria was when she was provided sufficient resources. Without the resources she received from alternative treatment programs, she would not have found steady and fulfilling employment, a home, and a drug-free life with her children. She benefited from programs implemented after the new millennium to address the rising crisis of addicted mothers separated from their children through incarceration or treatment. Within a few years, Victoria was self-sufficient and contributing to society, saving taxpayers tens of thousands of dollars in jail costs, hospital visits, and child protection services. Victoria was in the right place at the right time to be offered the right amount of resources needed to turn her life around. She was one of the lucky ones.

Alicia, discussed in chapter 3, did not have the family support that benefited Victoria, and she also spent more time in jail. She explained that the Bluff was the only place she could go when she was released from jail.

> Now this old man adopted me through the years. He was old, no sexual nothing. He treated me like, "there's my niece." He was like on disability and stuff. And that man opened his house up to me. "You can stay here." That was my living area. I had somewhere to live. Somewhere to stay—that man got his check. He got two checks a month. Every check he got, he'd give me some money. He would let me bring my dates there, everything. But he treated me... "That's my niece and you don't mess with my niece." He would drink. He drank alcohol. That was my home. I lived there.

Alicia also exchanged sex for money or drugs, but unlike Victoria, she did not want to work with a "dope man." Empowerment for a woman in the drug culture came with risks; Alicia understood the risks and did not like it.

> 'Cause during that time, I'm still pretty fresh to people. I just came back from Alabama after three and a half years. I'm getting in the mix and I'm new. See, mostly I would get with the guys that were getting high. They're spending money. Over there you got guys that do crack. They get money because they get high. I'm saying they go get some money. Those are the kind of people, guys, that took to me.

> You can get high—not too much with a dealer. I've always been pretty strongheaded when it come to you trying to tell me what to do. I ain't fixing to hear that. 'Cause if you're giving me, if you're a dope man, you're trying to make your money. I would get killed. I ain't getting involved in nothing like that.

Having used drugs during her pregnancy, Alicia was offered treatment when she birthed a baby with drugs in her system.

> They didn't take her from me, but they sent me to Recovery House for a ninety-day program. I went there. I stayed clean them ninety days. I worked at a vegetable packing company. I worked there. I did what I was supposed to do. I graduated out. I got out. I came back... what, a month's time I'm back getting high again. But I'm with her daddy. I'm just, like, I'm with him, before I went. He helped me raise her. She looked at him like, she know her daddy. We're staying with his daddy. We're staying with his daddy and we leave. And that's when we go back to the Bluff. He's getting high now, her daddy. We go back to the Bluff. He'd get his income tax and we'd go to the Bluff. We're

staying with the man, who I told you adopted me; like an uncle to me. We're staying with him.

Treatment for 90 days was not enough. Without sufficient aftercare resources as a single parent, and trying to keep her family together, she lived with her child's father. She relapsed with him, and they returned to the Bluff.

MARTHA

Many of the women who recounted stories of rape and sexual abuse said they never reported it. Martha, a 53-year-old White woman, was one of them. She told me this story when I asked what was the worst thing that happened to her.

I guess this is the worst thing that ever happened. At seventeen me and my girlfriends used to hitchhike down to another town. I couldn't find my friends that day so I decided I'll hitchhike by myself, and this truck pulled over and I got in the truck. And he drove me the nine miles and everything was fine, and I'm like, "Oh here's my stop, I'm ready to get out." And I'm trying to get the door open and I couldn't get it open. I'm like, "I can't get the door open." So he comes over, you know, trying to kiss me, and I started fighting, and he put a knife to my throat. No, that's right, at first he started choking me, and I would fight. And then he would choke me and each time I would fight—it was on pretty much the interstate, but you could pull off sort of where trucks could pull. So he wouldn't let me go, and he just put a knife to my throat, and I kept fighting and fighting, and I don't know why I just didn't give in but I didn't. I fought and fought and fought before finally he pulled me by my long hair into the back of the truck and proceeded to rape me.

And then he wouldn't let me go 'cause I gave him such a hard time. So we stayed there for a while . . . He finally said, "Okay, I'm gonna let you go, bye baby," and I just took off running . . . I ran all the way to my girlfriend's store, she owned a store down there, and as soon as I walked in she goes, "Jesus, you look like you just got raped." I had marks all over my neck. But that was the worst thing that probably ever happened to me, and that, that's traumatic.

Martha wanted me to know why she never reported the rape to the police, recalling each detail vividly, filling in how she felt at the time, and what she was thinking.

When you think he's gonna kill you, you don't even think about turning him in. I just wanted outta there. I was petrified. And you know, his truck was rigged, I should have turned him in because he probably did this all the time. But see, I just wanted outta there. You couldn't get the door open, I mean he, I could not get the door, that's how he—I couldn't get out, I was trapped, so that's why I was so scared, there was no escape. A big, big—with the cab—and he pulled my long hair, I had long hair and he just pulled it, into the back I was fighting trying to kick the window out. And he just, it was scary. I pushed the knife away, and each time he choked me, he choked me longer. You see, the last time he choked me I was on the verge of passing out. So I knew then, if I didn't give in, I would be dead, 'cause each time it was longer. He meant business.

He just said after he was done—you know, it didn't take that long. He wanted me to have oral sex, and it was all over like and then he just says, "Since you gave me such a hard time, you're gonna stay here a while." I stayed there a while. I just laid there. I think he was like rubbing my arm and stuff, and then he finally said, "You can go." And then he said, "Bye baby." I remember that.

After this horrific experience, Martha began a conventional life. She was happily married with two children, when a snitch reported that she and her husband were selling marijuana. Martha's father was a police officer, and she lived in a prison community, where almost everyone worked in the local prison and where drug use was severely punished. Martha was let off with probation because of her father's connections, but her husband went to jail and was on parole after his release. The surveillance of her probation officers was overbearing.

My probation officers were a pain, and when he [husband] lost his job, they turned our heat off in the house. My probation officer alerted children services, "There's no heat in their house." So now I've got a probation officer on my back, and I got children … Once they got on me, it was, they wanted me to have an abortion for our third daughter. They said, "You already got two kids." I said, "No, I'm not." They said, "Then you need to give her up." I said, "No, I'm not giving her up," So it was just, well then, "If you don't leave your husband"—they didn't like him or something—"then, we're taking your kids." So, we weren't getting along all that well. So, I chose my children, left my husband, and moved into an apartment. My dad loaned me the money to get my first month's rent and then I went on welfare. So now I'm on welfare— I'm a welfare mom. I was welfare mom for quite a few years.

Martha's husband had never been abusive, and his only crime was selling marijuana. But threatened by social services, and stressed by constant surveillance, she got a divorce and began a life as a single mother.

Martha became so lonely she began to pick up men at bars. One was a federal probation officer who proposed marriage. She was ready to accept when she learned he was touching her daughters inappropriately. She moved to Georgia to escape him, but since he was a federal agent, she was in constant fear he would follow them. Like many women who were raped, she was very sensitive to abuse issues, and the fact that her own daughters were molested under her care hurt more than she could endure. Martha started a downward spiral into alcoholism and drug use.

Ironically, even though she had divorced her first husband so she would not lose her children, and moved to Georgia to protect her daughters from a child molester, the Department of Family and Child Services in Georgia took her children away because of her alcoholism. After her children were gone, Martha started using crack, methamphetamine, and morphine tablets. She was living with different men who abused her until she eventually was homeless.

> Yeah, I end up living under bridges, sleeping in abandoned buildings, just— I'm dying. It's raining out, I have no clothes, I mean, the clothes on my back. To change clothes, I'd go to these food, these clothes dropboxes, I'd rummage through and that's how I'd change my clothes. I was resourceful. I'd take showers in the creek. I used to bath in the, in the river.

> I had been out on the streets all winter alone, all winter for about three months, just surviving. I'd go to grocery stores and eat samples you know, a little, they got some good samples and when you're hungry. So then the last night I spent [outside] that Express Holiday Inn curled up in a ball, throwing up, cold. The wind picked up, it's raining, I'm getting so sick. I'm just so sick and the next day I went to the homeless shelter up there on Highway 41. They give me a bed, food, a structured environment, AA meetings, a little counseling. I cleaned up, got a clear head for the first time in years, didn't drink. Now I'm on unemployment, looking for work. I'm going to a training session this Thursday to do roadwork. Women are gonna do, like hold the signs or whatever. They're gonna train me for free, so I'm hoping that may be my ticket.

At the time of the interview, Martha seemed hopeful she would get a job through this training program, but she was still in a vulnerable situation. She never mentioned that her drug abuse problems might have stemmed from her own sexual abuse. She never talked with anyone about the "worst thing that ever happened." Although she appeared strong at the time, she was still suffering the loss of her children.

Harry was the oldest of six children and the only boy. He was a protective older brother when he was around, and always had a soft spot for women when he was not in jail. As discussed previously, when a woman called Harry to say her friend was in danger of being raped by a motorcycle gang, he rushed to defend her, not considering his own safety.

It was another female friend, Liz, who bandaged his arm after a bank robbery. He gave a fistful of cash to Liz herself, and envelopes with cash to deliver to his mother and sister. Liz became a reluctant informant who testified only because she feared she would have been charged as an accomplice if she didn't. Although Harry detested snitches, he was not angry with Liz since he realized she was threatened by the police. He seemed to understand women's vulnerable roles in society, having seen how hard it was for our mother.

Harry came to the rescue of another woman who cost him his freedom. As recounted in the last chapter, while on parole in Florida, Harry allowed a homeless couple, Jim and Cindy, to move into his efficiency apartment when he realized their child was sleeping in Denny's all-night restaurant. They stayed at Harry's place until Cindy's mother let her back into the house, contingent that she come only with the child and obey a curfew.

One night Harry had just finished work and had taken a pill and a few shots of whiskey to go to sleep when he got a call from Cindy. She was at a crack house and needed a ride back to her mother's house.

"My mom's gonna kick me out of the house if I don't come home by her stupid curfew," Cindy cried in desperation. "And she's threatening to get custody of Lucy (the child)." Harry felt sorry for her, so he went out to pick her up against his better judgment. The pill and whiskey kicked in on the way, he nodded off and hit a tree. When he woke up, the cops were already there. He had not hit anyone but he had a deep gash in his forehead. When the police booked Harry, they found out he was on parole from Pennsylvania. His urine turned up dirty and he had a pill in his car that was not prescribed to him. He was sent back up to the Pennsylvania state penitentiary.

Harry, like many people who are hurting, helped those in worse situations, and he was especially concerned for women and children. He could not bear to see them sleeping outside while he had a bed inside. In some countries, women with children are provided a home and a guaranteed income, and in most developed countries they are provided free childcare.[23] Many advanced governments allow children to attend afterschool programs of their choice at no costs and provide tuition-free higher education. How different the lives of mothers and children discussed in this book would have been had the United States embraced the cultural understanding that all children should have a healthy, loving, and intellectually stimulating environment so they can be better citizens contributing to the well-being of society.[24] The best way to do this is provide the same for their mothers.[25]

SEVEN

Aging in Drug Use

FRED

Although he was 60 years old, Fred's drug trajectory is very relevant for contemporary society and reflects many of the same issues that men and women of all ages have experienced since pharmaceutical companies began marketing pain pills. Raised in a middle-class family, Fred was given Dilaudid for a sports injury at the age of 15. After his first encounter with this strong opioid pain pill he told the doctor, "You should six-pack this and sell it." Using a beer marketing analogy, he aptly described his initial reaction to this wonder pill. Although Fred eventually used heroin, crack, cocaine, and methamphetamine sporadically over the years, he used pain pills continuously throughout his life from this point.

Fred was an orphan; however, he was lucky to have landed with great parents who adopted him and raised him as their son. He was nine months old when he was adopted, and his sister was adopted five years later, when she was six months old. He remains in contact with her today. Fred is White and was middle class for most of his life. Raised in a small southern town, he became a sports star in high school until he injured his knee, and he was given the fateful pain pill that changed the course of his life. It was the first substance he ever used, even before alcohol and cigarettes. Fred was prescribed pills legally throughout his adolescence due to multiple surgeries between back and knee injuries. He seemed to react differently to opiates than most people, explaining, "Pain pills gets me up, not down." Eventually, the prescriptions stopped. "When I was in my late twenties, I started forging prescriptions," he explained. The forgeries continued for most of his adult life.

At the time of the interview, Fred was living in an assisted living facility housing people older than Fred. But due to his health condition, he was on a Supplemental Security Income (SSI) disability program and received government aid. He walked with a cane but he hoped to become more mobile and leave his assisted living situation.

Fred's life story seemed like that of the typical man next door, except he had been using opioids for 45 years. He went to college and joined a fraternity, where he engaged in popular drinking habits. He was introduced to a number of drugs that were popular over the years—heroin and cocaine in the early 1970s, methamphetamine in the late 1990s—but he used mainly opiate pills illegally after he discovered he could forge prescriptions. Married four times, Fred's last wife was a nurse. He taught her how to get prescriptions pills for him using her insider status.

Despite his constant use of pain pills, and occasional use of heroin when he could not get pills, Fred maintained a functional life. Fred always worked and had a succession of successful careers. He used responsibly, explaining he never had a car accident or any accident due to drug use. Yet Fred had a lot of accidents, for which he was always supplied more prescription pain pills. Fred insisted they were not on purpose.

> Every wreck I've ever had, somebody has hit me. That, and I was helping a friend move, and we were throwing boxes down to each other from my truck. And I caught one and I had to go down with it. I don't even remember how.

Fred did not avoid the criminal justice system, but for most of his life he could afford to stay out of jail long term. He was charged for prescription pill forgery in his late twenties, mid-thirties, and early forties. Each time he bonded out after an overnight stay in jail. On his own volition, he attended 12-step meetings for about a year and stopped using, but he said he got tired of attending group programs. He always went back to pills.

His mounting criminal record impacted his work opportunities, but due to his substantial social capital, Fred always found blue-collar work. Typically controlling his use, Fred said it became difficult after a divorce. "I was just out of control," he explained. "Just feeling bad. Emotionally. Just thinking back about things was making me feel a lot worse. All the stuff I had done was starting to feel worse."

Fred always supported his family while married, and he took care of his son after the divorce. However, he eventually served two years in prison, losing all contact with his son during this time. Being in prison was very hard on him physically and psychologically. Although he said it was a turning point in his life, he continued forging prescriptions and using opiate pills illegally after he was released.

Recently, he suffered what appeared to be a stroke.

> I woke up one morning. My sister called me and she said that I was talking to her and not making any sense. She came down to Atlanta and took me to the hospital. They kept me in there for two weeks. Then I had to go down to physical therapy for thirty days to learn to walk again and everything else. Now I'm here, I've been doing good.

At 60 years old and with a number of other health issues, Fred was not sure how much drug use impacted his memory or if this recent health crisis was the result of sports-related concussions. He was still hurting from physical injuries acquired over a lifetime. Fred stopped using pain pills and started a methadone program since he left the hospital. He expected to stay on methadone for a long time.

AGING DRUG USERS

Baby boomers appeared more accepting of illicit drugs as they aged than were previous older cohorts.[1] The first of the baby boomers reached age 35 in 1981; the youngest baby boomers reached age 35 in 1999. Instead of maturing out, they continued to use past age 35, making them the fastest-growing age group of drug users. Data collected annually over this time reveal that drug use for all age groups declined steadily except for the age group 35 and older.[2] The impact of this phenomenon is already overwhelming substance abuse treatment, health care, and social services.[3]

All people need more health care as they age and their bodies wear out, and people who use drugs tend to have more health needs. A closer examination of older drug users shows that poor health often is not due to their drug use but instead to their social situations. Being homeless, engaging in sex work, and living in unsanitary conditions and close quarters with others, such as in jail, prison, and homeless shelters, result in poor health.[4] Sharing syringes was common among baby boomers when they were young and unaware of infectious disease transmission. The delayed implementation of harm reduction programs, such as needle exchange, increased the transmission of HIV and hepatitis C among this age group.[5]

HIV / AIDS is increasing among the older drug-using population, a phenomenon contributing to what some call the "Graying of the AIDS Epidemic."[6] Older drug users with AIDS are significantly less likely than younger users to have social support through friends, which is critical to coping with this disease. Few social services are prepared for an influx of older drug users with HIV / AIDS.[7] Prisons are even less prepared.

THE AGING OF THE PRISON POPULATION

A 2013 study of state prisons made a startling discovery: in the past 20 years the number of state prisoners age 55 or older increased 400 percent.[8] The researchers of the study attributed this to the longer sentences and increases in older adults entering prison. Even while the growth of state prison population slowed, those sentenced to more than one year increased. Prisoners age 55 and older more than doubled every 10 years and accounted for almost 10 percent of the state prison population in 2013, making them the fastest-growing age group incarcerated.

Loïc Wacquant predicted an explosion of elderly prisoners, warning that the aging of the inmate population would present the greatest financial challenge to the prison industry.[9] Due to increased health needs, the average cost to incarcerate a prisoner over age 50 is $70,000 a year.[10] The prison industry does not want to absorb the exorbitant costs of required healthcare, and "geriatric release" or parole is becoming more popular.[11]

How will older ex-prisoners survive outside prison? Many have had few years of work and might receive a meager Social Security check when they reach retirement age, but most will have no other retirement benefits. Some might qualify for Supplemental Security Insurance (SSI), or Social Security Disability Insurance (SSDI), but the monthly payments are not enough to live on. Many people do not give much thought to older adults, especially older adults who were in prison. But they might start paying attention when they realize how much incarcerated older adults will cost taxpayers, and how much older adults subjected to poor living conditions in prison will cost Medicaid and Medicare after they are released.

Ian, discussed in chapter 2, was in very bad physical health at only 56 years of age. After years of homelessness, Ian was not able to obtain SSI benefits to be stably housed. He was in a methadone program, but his living conditions were temporary. He pieced together any kind of help he could find.

> Ian: And got a lot of medical issues that need to be addressed, which can't be addressed in this situation that I'm in right now. I just recently underwent a cervical spine surgery out of [the local hospital]. My neurosurgeon, she had to go into my cervical spine because one of the discs was pressing against a nerve and it was paralyzing my whole right side. So she had to go in, you probably can still see the scarring where she went in, and she had to go in and remove that disc so it wouldn't press against the nerve.
>
> Miriam: Why is it that you're still on methadone?
>
> Ian: It's something that keeps me from going out and buying something off the street or going to a doctor to get something to control the pain—the pain I get from my neck.
>
> Miriam: So it's not so much the addiction to heroin but you have physical pain so you need some painkillers?
>
> Ian: Yes, ma'am. Chronic pain.

Jan, discussed in previous chapters, found it easy to support herself as an addicted drug user through escort services when she was younger, despite her "junkie" appearance:

> At that time, I was probably looking more like a junkie . . . I was twenty-one and my sugar daddy, he was like a twice a week thing. But he didn't want to keep renting motels so he set me up in a little apartment by the airport. And I got sick and had to go to the hospital with the hepatitis. Still dancing. But, yeah, didn't have to really walk the streets much because I had this older man—married man that took care of me. I mean for four years he was really good to me. Yes, but I was still very much a junkie, and I messed up that apartment and ended up going with another drug dealer who mostly dealt marijuana. But I met him in a club and he's like "well, come live with me" and I did. But I was still seeing my, this man—I mean he, it was a combined thing. I mean he took—we went on trips. He was a friend. I mean he was a big part of my life.

Jan's description of being a "junkie" at age 21 might be glamorized, as it is in movies. But they do not grow old in movies. By the time I met Jan at age 50, she could not work as an exotic dancer, and she could no longer attract a sugar daddy or a drug dealer to support her. Instead, as an older drug user, she was walking the highway asking men if they would give her $30 for a "blow job" in a dirty motel.

While aging as a drug user is harder for women in many ways, it also takes its toll on men. Omar, discussed in chapter 4, was nearly in tears when he said he could not take it anymore. Stuck in the Bluff, he was hustling every day to get his heroin hit and keep his withdrawal symptoms at bay. When I suggested he try to get into a methadone program, he explained why this would be difficult in his current situation.

> When you know yourself at this age, you have to be honest with yourself, I can have the methadone, and I could have the methadone pills, and I'm cool, drunk the liquid meth, I'm not gonna be sick. And out here . . . I see you and, "Oh man, we got this, let's go get high," and sit in your house. Now I'm sitting up here, I really don't need the dope, but since it's around I want it. But if I'm away from these people, then you got a little time to get a little stronger, so I ain't gotta walk into you.

Omar was referring to his current living conditions in the Bluff, and how hard it would be to avoid a friend or associate who would entice him to use drugs. He also lamented how hard it was to find work, and he was only 50 years old.

Charlie descended into a "junkie" phase after the failure of his business followed by his brother's suicide, as discussed in chapter 4. Participating in a drug court program, Charlie was able to control his drug use, but at his age, his situation was still precarious.

> Right now, I'm just coming up to that point where I know I'm going to be getting into a situation where I'm going to be losing the place where I'm staying again. I'm going to get back in the job market and be able to hopefully be able to find something. I'll just have to take what I can get at this point, but I think that's the most discouraging thing about it is that I'm going to have to take a mediocre job, if I can find one at all that one will hire me.

> Unfortunately, nobody will give you an opportunity, even though I had many years in sales experience, unless you go into a commission basis or something, and even then a lot of people won't give you the opportunity. It's tough.

> Actually I'm coming into the age where it makes it tough for anyone to think of you relative for a job. They think well he's already fifty-five, or he's coming on fifty-five, you know, what do we want. He's not going to be—his longevity

is not going to be that long. He's not the kind of person we're looking for. We're looking for somebody energetic, you know, younger, energetic. That part of it, it's discouraging.

HARRY: AGING OUT OF WORK

By the time Harry was up for parole again, our mother's health was failing. She could no longer make decisions about her life and my sister made them for her. Regarding Harry's situation, Rose thought it was time for "tough love." According to the tough love philosophy and practice, a family member should love the user but not enable him or her to use drugs.

I was never a fan of tough love. Having read former Senator George McGovern's sad memoir of using tough love with his daughter, who died alone in a snowbank, I was skeptical. However, some of the former self-identified "addicts" I interviewed insisted that tough love worked for them. I was still looking for better solutions, but I thought we might try a modified version. If Harry wanted to use drugs—he knew where to get them no matter where he was living. If he wanted to socialize with drug-using networks—he knew where to find them. I would not refuse to help him if he was drinking or using drugs. But I would try to give him incentives to *not* use.

Harry submitted a home plan to live with Justin's family in Pennsylvania. They had a big home and Harry was welcomed. The plan was denied. Instead, the board paroled him to live with a former prisoner Harry knew in South Philadelphia. Bill had served his full sentence, so he was out free with no parole obligations. He managed his own contracting business for home improvement services. He offered Harry a room and a job. The parole board in Philadelphia approved the plan.

At the time, I thought it sounded like a good option. At least Harry would have work, I thought, and work was hard enough to find at the beginning of a recession even for men his age without a criminal record. Being paroled to Philadelphia offered another benefit. Mayor Nutter of Philadelphia was focused on helping former prisoners reentering in his city. On his hundredth day in office, he announced a program that would give $10,000 a year in municipal tax credits to companies that hired former prisoners and provide them tuition support or vocational training. It was an encouraging initiative that we did not have in Atlanta.

Again, I drove to Pennsylvania from Georgia to pick up Harry at the same halfway house in Wernersville, this time driving him to Philadelphia. Seeing him for the first time, I immediately noticed that he had aged more than I expected in the two years since he lived in Florida. In Daytona he had a nice tan, and he ate healthy food that he cooked for himself. But it was more than the loss of a tan and a few pounds. He seemed less confident, and there was no spring in his step. I offered to get him a beer but he said he was not allowed to drink—an odd thing to hear my brother say.

We stopped to buy some warm clothes for the coming winter weather and a cell phone—this time with unlimited minutes. When I stopped for gas, he got out to smoke a cigarette. I looked at him as he stood on the curb of the convenient store—tall, very thin, sunken cheeks, and wincing as he pulled a drag from the tiny cigarette he had just rolled, holding it in cupped hands against the wind. With his oversized jacket draped on his shoulders, he looked like a character out of a 1950s Chicago gangster movie.

Night was approaching when we pulled up to his new residence. As soon as I stepped inside, I knew the situation was not good. The house was in disarray, since it was being repaired and remodeled. But there were other troublesome indicators. The kitchen walls were only built to the studs, and the stove was not functional. Harry could not cook in this place—a huge disadvantage for a vegetarian.

Bill was a short, wiry, White guy with a ready smile, but unable to hold a gaze. He looked away quickly when we met, and he began to twitch like a person using crack. He spent most of the time going up and down the stairs with men who came to the door. There appeared to be some drug activity going on upstairs. I asked Harry about it when we were alone, after Bill went upstairs again with a stranger who barely acknowledged our existence. He shrugged and indicated that it was Bill's affair, not his. I left Harry with a sick feeling of despair, realizing what the "tough" in tough love really meant.

The situation got worse. As I suspected, Bill was addicted to crack. He spent most of the money he made from contract work to buy large amounts of crack, which he sold and smoked. Harry was not fond of crack—not even when he lived with crack users. If Harry had any money left after rent, food, and parole fees, he bought marijuana and alcohol, maybe a pill. Harry told me that when Bill ran out of money he borrowed it from Harry and never paid it back. Since Bill was his boss and landlord, he could not refuse him. They had a few contract jobs, but Bill wasn't really working anymore, and Harry had few remodeling skills (he was the clean-up guy), so the income would not last long. Harry needed to get a different job and another place to live, but that meant seeing the parole officer, and maybe Bill getting a visit from the parole officer. Harry did not want to put Bill in any jeopardy, even if he was treating him badly.

One of the ex-offender programs established by Mayor Nutter's new initiative was an employment program. Harry enrolled in it, following my advice. I first called the director of the program to make sure Harry was eligible and to find out what time and days he needed to attend. It was a jobs program called the "Reentry Services Program" (RESP) sponsored by the Pennsylvania Prison Society and managed by the Impact Services Corporation. The program required Harry to attend one full morning of intake classes and weekly half-day classes for the next two weeks. I sent him some money to help until the program was completed. Many of the classes covered areas Harry knew already, such as how to dress, how to write a resume—all things he was taught in prison in a pre-release program. Other classes were on cleanliness, how to interview, and other skills that Harry had learned many times in many different programs. Interestingly Harry also had a class on "minority rights" since almost all the people in the program were Black. Although I knew it was repetitive and must be boring, I encouraged Harry to continue attending the classes so he could get the job list and the mayor's personal recommendation, promised to those who completed the program.

Everyone who graduated from the reentry work-training program received a letter of introduction to prospective employees on the letterhead of Mayor Nutter's Office for the "Reentry of Ex-Offenders." Harry graduated and took the letter to all the places on the job list they gave him. He called each job on the list and went in person to those who requested a face-to-face application as well. After a few weeks of daylong employment seeking, he checked off the entire list and was not hired anywhere. I called the director of the program to ask for advice on what to do next. His answer was not encouraging.

I am sorry, but your brother is unemployable. He's been in prison too long, and he's also older than our usual clients. I will ask the staff to give Harry another list for day labor sites—that's what people like Harry usually end up doing.

Harry was given a list of places to go for day labor—basically street corners where men stood around to be picked up for a day job in construction. Harry went every day for almost three weeks and stood all day in the cold. He was never selected. He said he saw an interesting pattern.

First they pick up anyone that looks Hispanic, no matter what age. Then anyone Black or White, but young. The older Black men get picked up if anyone comes around who knows them. By this time, all the old White men have left. I'm usually the only old White man left, and always the last man left standing in line.

Harry understood that if a White man is standing on the corner looking for a job, many people know there is something wrong with him. Why? Because people understand what research shows, that even with a criminal justice record, it is easier for a White man to be employed than for a Black man without a criminal record.[12] So, they wonder, why is this White guy doing day labor? Something must be wrong with him. He must be a criminal. But Harry's problem was not only his criminal record—he got a job in Florida with a criminal record. Harry's problem was that he was aging with little record of employment or work experience. He was too young for Social Security checks and his health was too good for SSDI.

SOCIAL SECURITY WOES

In 1935, after the Great Depression, the Social Security program was enacted at the federal level. Primarily an old-age insurance, the program was the foundation for unemployment insurance, aid to families and children (welfare), and disability insurance. Social Security is a payroll tax on wages that funds pension checks for the retired. Workers can receive full benefits at age 65 if they were employed for at least 10 years. The age for when people can retire and receive full benefits has been creeping upward toward age 67 since 2000. People may retire at 62 but receive only 75 percent of the full benefits. Medicare, also funded through taxes on employment wages, was started in 1972 to provide basic healthcare for the elderly.[13]

Baby boomers, as the name implies, comprised a much larger number of people than the generations before them and the generation after them, which was great for the Social Security of their parents. Since working baby boomers paying into the Social Security program exceeded the number of retirees receiving benefits, there was a surplus in the Social Security program every year. The benefits to retirees are paid out of the annual tax income received, and, by law, the surplus had to be loaned to the US Treasury every year, called the "Social Security Trust Fund," which should be paid back to the Social Security program with interest.[14]

As baby boomers retire and stop paying into the system, there will no longer be a surplus, and, since there are so many more baby boomers retiring each year, eventually there will be a deficit. This occurred in 2010, when expenses exceeded dedicated taxes received by the Social Security Administration. Since then, expenses have exceeded income every year, drawing from the Social Security Trust Fund. Although this fund had a balance of $2.8 trillion in 2013, this money is considered national debt, and it is predicted to be exhausted in 2033.[15]

Supplemental Security Income (SSI) is another kind of government aid for people 65 and older or disabled people, but this also comes with restrictive criteria. As a means-tested program, it has very strict financial guidelines (only for the very poor). Social Security Disability Insurance (SSDI) is an entitlement program, which like Social Security benefits is based on how many years a person has paid into the program. Medicaid is a joint federal and state health insurance program for very low-income people, who are generally eligible to receive other federal aid.

Just because these programs exist does not mean all older people in need will be automatically enrolled in them. In fact, due to the restrictions, many people who apply for SSI or SSDI are denied. Long-term prisoners have an even harder time. People who were not employed for enough years to receive Social Security benefits, at least 10 years of their lives, and who worked illegally (under the table) and did not pay into the system, receive only a minimum SSI.

A pamphlet called "What Prisoners Need to Know" distributed by the Social Security Administration warns:

> Social Security pays retirement benefits to people who are age 62 or older. Generally, you must have worked and paid Social Security taxes for 10 years to be eligible. We pay disability benefits to insured individuals who are unable to work because of a serious medical condition that is expected to last at least a year or result in death. A person who is a recent parolee, or who is unemployed, doesn't qualify for disability payments.[16]

As revealed in the interviews, older adults who were injured or acquired chronic illnesses that restricted their employment applied for SSI or SSDI. Not many were granted these benefits. Only two men in the sample were old enough to qualify for Social Security benefits. Since they were the earliest baby boomers, they lived some of their adult lives before the start of the War on Drugs, and most of their adult lives before the dramatic increase in sentencing for drug offenses under the Reagan administration. These two men were less impacted by mass incarceration compared to younger baby boomers, so they had at least 10 years of employment and were eligible for Social Security. They both had stopped use of hard drugs by the time of the interview, but they took different routes.

JAMES

Sporting a ponytail, James, a 65-year-old Black man, hobbled quite well with a cane due to what he jokingly called "Arthur Itis." He was conceived during World War II, born in Georgia, and raised by his single mother, who he said was a "singer." Living in the countryside as a kid, he smoked "rabbit tobacco," which "looks like cotton stalks" and "made you high."

James graduated from high school and moved to New York City for six months. He explained in his folksy way, "I didn't like it, so I moseyed on back to the South and from there I was always here."

A functional alcoholic, he supported his family and his habit with his own repair shop. When his drinking became out of control, he started other drugs.

> I looked at that damn fifth of Cutty Sark Scotch that I used to keep in my office and said, "What are you doing in here? I don't need you no more." (laughs). So I grabbed hold of myself and was able to come out of it, but then I turned around and grabbed his cousin: weed and cocaine. (laughs)

After his first divorce and the death of his mother, James began to snort cocaine. He lost his own business, but stayed employed in the same line of work. His second marriage lasted two years. By his mid-thirties, he was using heroin.

A debonair ladies' man, James married a third time, saying, "I made changes in my life." He was a steady worker and "enjoyed my kids," so when his wife asked him to leave, he was surprised. This separation occurred immediately after he spent three months in jail.

James was a romantic and wistfully longed to be in a marriage—a social institution he respected.

> Marriage is very beautiful. It is beautiful. It's a bond between two individuals, that if you bonded right it's the most beautiful thing I've ever seen. I experienced some of it. When it started getting to the point to where . . . it eventu-

ally helped me in my life as to make me the man that I am now. That's what the third marriage did for me. It made a change in my life. It took—although we weren't married that long—but the flow plan that I had discovered that was happening to me, I [would have] chosen to continue it.

Without a stable relationship, James was sucked deeper into what was already a 15-year career of heroin and crack / cocaine use. For the next four years he was increasingly in and out of control. He went to methadone programs to help control his tolerance when he could not afford the costs of heroin bought on the street. "I started methadone back in the eighties because I was trying to cut out addiction, and taking methadone was a help to me because I didn't have to have a large sum of money."

At age 42, while in methadone treatment, he started another repair business on the side, along with his steady work in a government job. At the same time, James was "dippin' and dabbin'" heroin and cocaine, a term meaning occasional use.

Employed all his life, when James's health deteriorated to the point that he could no longer work, he applied for disability income (SSI) at age 55. While waiting for approval, he supported himself through illegal activities. "I hustled, stole, and I'll just put it point blank to you, I was a naughty fellow," he said with a chuckle, "all of the illegal things I did to survive."

For the past 10 years, James has been in the same methadone program, although he still used heroin occasionally. He described his controlled use of heroin.

> Heroin is a drug that (pause) relaxes you and (pause) sometimes I can get real tensed. And sometimes I can use a toot or two and calm myself down and I'm okay. You know? Before, when I was on it religiously, it was like a medication that I had to have. Now I don't have to have it, okay? And I'm going to keep it that way. I don't have to have it.

During a time when law enforcement focused on the open-air drug market, the narcotics squad caught James for "being in the wrong place, in the wrong area." He explained, "You know we've got a law here called DC6, and that's being in a drug area for no reason." He was in and out of jail until age 56 when he called the director at the methadone clinic where he was on a waiting list. The director, Dave, brokered his return to the clinic.

> Moving up on the methadone, so the heroin kept right there dropping off. I was using less and less of heroin. I was using a lot more methadone. You see

what I'm saying? So when I got up to about fifty, okay, fifty milligrams, the heroin wouldn't do me no good. It [methadone] was blocking the heroin slap out. So then that's when I realized who and what I was supposed to do. So I stayed here with the clinic.

James seemed very sure of his stability at the time of the interview. He had last used heroin two months ago, but he was trying to stay on methadone without using. When asked if he would ever use heroin again, he replied honestly:

I'll put it this way. A druggie is going to be a druggie. And I can't never say that I'm never going to use drugs again. I can't say that I'm going to get clean again completely, but my goal is to do that . . . My goal is to do that, but as being a twenty-five, thirty-year junkie—the urge hits you every once in a while. It's like smoking. I just don't know at that time, how can I handle it. It might be to a point where I can say no and go about my business. It might be important to say the urge is just too dadgum great; I got to try it. Then you get disappointed when you done tried it and it ain't no good . . . Methadone puts you in your game, but heroin takes you out of your game.

Although James always thought of the 12-step program as a gimmick, he had come to appreciate the meetings. Attending them was required to stay in the methadone program. He was finally approved for SSI and no longer needed to hustle.

JOHN

John was the only other person in the sample who was eligible for Social Security because of his age. A 65-year-old Black male, he spent years incarcerated, but he had more time working and building relationships in mainstream society than in jail. He also had a college degree.

As an early baby boomer, John experienced a different drug environment in his youth. Displaying entrepreneurship since a child, he said he had a "strong work ethic" and held many jobs. He also embraced various religious faiths. His father was a Spiritual Israelite minister who converted to Nation of Islam and then to Christianity. John considered himself a member of the Nation of Islam when he was young, but left to join the Jehovah's Witnesses. Like his father, he later converted to Christianity.

John's juvenile life was rough. Coming into adolescence when the Black Power movement was strong, he rationalized his criminal behavior as political action "for the Movement." Soon after his first release, he robbed a bank, a skill he learned in jail.

> Revolutionary spirit (laughs). But I was telling my son about an hour ago, I said back then we'd robbed a bank, you'd rob a bank, you was, you had all this notoriety and what not. You had your clenched fist and all that kind of stuff, and it was all in the name of the Movement. It was big deal to me. Now it's so commonplace, every day. There was a lady talking on the telephone today robbing a bank. It was on the news earlier. I said, boy, this is amazing.

Rehabilitation through educational programs was still popular when John was in prison, and he finished a college degree while in "the joint." Interested in continuing his education, he enrolled in a university when he got out of prison, where he met his first wife. He moved to Georgia and was a teacher for many years.

At age 40, he was back in jail for a robbery that he said he did not do. He stayed for three years, describing himself as a "senior citizen" in jail.

> It was unbelievable. I was like in my forties . . . behind me having a track record. I was highly notable and respectable . . . The old kids, the young kids, they want to hear your stories, and then it's a means of survival also. You get their respect. He's an old-timer. He know the ropes, he's been here. You get an awful lot of respect, an unbelievable amount.

John was also introduced to experimental forms of behavioral change while he was in prison.

> I was in a group, but it wasn't for drugs. We were studying behavioral sciences and this young brilliant doctor was in the Fed joint. He started this program, and we was studying. We was learning how to psychoanalyze, and we was learning how to psychoanalyze ourselves. When I was in the Federal joint back in '67 to '71, it was outstanding. This guy didn't believe that guys would go off in the joint. He didn't believe in medicating them. He put them in padded cells. He didn't believe in medicating them or anything. You might have heard of Dr. Eric Berne, *Games People Play*. Well, that was our focal point. I believe it saved me—it helped save me. Transactional analysis. First, second, third order analysis and all that good stuff. Makes it real plain. It helped me so much.[17]

Despite the experimental program, John started using heroin after his release from prison when he began dealing to make some extra money. Even though he had other work, he continued his drug dealing operation, using his exceptional acumen in the business.

It wasn't my drug of choice. I considered it a business decision. I was always turned off with drugs 'cause I had an older brother that was strung out and I was, it displeased me. However, when I got in the business to earn money, I would have guys test the drugs, and they would lie to me, and so I ended up testing them myself.

His drug use increased in quantity and variety, but through the years he learned to control his use. When asked how he was able to do this, he explained:

Well, mostly my spiritual, my spirituality primarily. Then it's a real moral issue with me, and now in addition to those—is age. Age has become really the primary factor. I ain't just trying to leave here, and I know that's suicide on the installment plan.

Throughout this time John raised a family with his second wife. He still has a good relationship with all his children, and he shares the wisdom he gained from life experiences with them. Regarding his drug dealing days, he has no regrets.

I'm glad I had the kinda relationship with my family, I took care of them when I made money, all of them, "Here's a grand, here's a grand, what do you need, this, that, and the other." But I'm glad I had the kind of relationship, I always had defined a difference between a drug addict and a junkie, and I've never allowed myself to cultivate a junkie mentality, 'cause a junkie'll do anything. They'll steal from they mama, they'll kill they daddy, they'll do anything . . . Makes a big difference, and that's what saved me. And also the guys that introduced me to this lifestyle coming along, they were good decent people. And although they was introducing something to me that was destructive, they were instructive on how not to just mess myself up.

John stopped using heroin on his own. He was adamant that he stopped without treatment.

You got to be in control, or you're going to lose it. It became problematic. That's why I eliminated the problem. I don't subscribe to AA [12-step]. It's not that I don't think it works, but I think people get hooked on AA as opposed to the drug. I have different views about a lot. I don't believe there is such a thing as drug abuse. I think it's self-abuse. Drugs don't do anything. They just lay there. They don't cry for you. They don't talk to you. They don't do anything. You put that life into them and the action, and that's why I don't buy a lot of these concepts and theories that people are into.

I used to shoot several grams of heroin every day. I kicked through prayer. I'm not saying that that's for everybody. People deal with what they need. But I don't buy all them stories about, "Well, if it wasn't for my wife, I wouldn't." I tell them guys all the time, "You do it because you like it." That's the bottom line.

I don't think it has a whole lot to do with addiction and nothing else. I think it's simply a matter of choice. I want to get high today. You got people who are chippers [occasional users]. I know guys that own homes, got nice cars and this, that, and the other and every ninety days or so, they might want them a weekend of dealing with what they call recreational drugs. Buy a couple grams of cocaine, sit around with the ole lady and sniff it and freak off, and do this, and do that, or whatever. But they ain't fixing to lose their home, and they're not fixing to lose their car, and they're not going to not be able to buy their kids what they need or whatever. They're just grown to where they can exercise that kind of discipline. And then I know guys that are sixty-five that's out here on the street that's just completely burned out. Women sixty, sixty-five years old selling their body and all that, but I think those are excuses.

John certainly had a wealth of experienced-based wisdom, but not everyone had the same opportunities that John had in life. Even though he was in prison, he was there at the right time, and he had the opportunity to take college courses. He left prison with a college degree. When younger baby boomers went to prison, educational programs were no longer provided. While in prison, John also had the opportunity to participate in some very experimental programs that gave him greater insight into his own life and thoughts. Few of the baby boomers in this study were exposed to this kind of therapy. However, his concept of addiction was avant-garde, and he did not embrace any of the models used in addiction treatment programs.

THE ENDURING QUESTION: WHAT IS ADDICTION?

Addiction has been called a troublesome concept that can indicate a range of drug use behaviors.[18] The classical definition of addiction was based on opiate use and distinguished opiates provided under a medical doctor's supervision (e.g., prescription pills, morphine) from heroin obtained through illegal markets.[19] The main characteristic of most addiction models is a compulsive loss of control.[20] Yet, most drug users in this study were able to control their drug use for long periods of time, indicating that addiction comes in phases. Many stopped all drug use without treatment or medical attention—even those who were forced to withdraw from heroin in jail. However, they almost always relapsed, sometimes many years after stopping. Most defined their desire to use drugs as an addiction, although this meant different things to different people.

Diagnosing addiction is less problematic than defining it, since most treatment professionals use the *Diagnostic and Statistical Manual* (*DSM*) developed by the American Psychiatric Association, which is in its fifth edition.[21] The word addiction is not used in the *DSM*; instead the patient is diagnosed with a "substance abuse disorder" or "substance dependence." The physical aspects that are often associated with addiction are not as important in the *DSM* diagnostic formula as the psychological aspects. In the *DSM-5*, tolerance and withdrawal are neither necessary nor sufficient for a diagnosis of drug dependence; opioid use disorder, which always includes physical dependence, has a separate list of criteria.[22]

In chapter 1, I discussed the concept of social construction. By now it should be clear that the definition of addiction and the *DSM* criteria for dependence are socially constructed to explain something that cannot be tested empirically. Although attempts are being made to achieve empirical evidence of addiction under the brain disease model,[23] addiction as a brain disease has its own set of problems and academic debates.[24] Most addiction scholars agree that addiction is multifaceted, has many causes, and is influenced by physical, social, and cultural factors.

Carl Hart, a neuroscientist who spent 20 years conducting research to understand "the addict brain," contends that "neuropsychopharmacology does not have the answers but instead leads to the wrong conclusions about drugs and the causes of social problems."[25] He eventually came to the conclusion that social factors are more important than the "dopamine hypothesis" of brain disease or any other biological explanation of addiction.

> The vast majority of drug users never become addicted. And in fact, social support itself is actually protective against many health problems and multiple types of risky behavior, including addiction. Indeed, a great deal of pathological drug use is driven by unmet social needs, by being alienated and having difficulty connecting with others. The majority of people who avoid drug problems, in contrast, tend to have strong social networks.[26]

I might add that having strong social networks in mainstream society is also important for people who are struggling with drug use, poverty, and unemployment. Despite the multitude of research showing the importance of the social environment, most people in society—whether doctors, politicians, treatment specialists, friends, or family—either punish or treat the addicted user, and only superficially attempt to address the social context of a problematic use. Rarely are the social issues that might be the underlying cause of problematic drug use acknowledged by treatment specialists or policymakers. Almost always, the "addict" must first stop using drugs (through treatment or jail), and only then the "recovering addict" might be given some of the social services needed. Even in the most expensive treatment programs, primary attention is on changing the individual and minimal attention is given to social context.

Some baby boomers stopped using or learned to control their use on their own without treatment. Their lives and experiences show that what we know about addiction—what most people think addiction is—might not be true.

As I worked over the years to help Harry get over his dependence on heroin, he never provided a definition of addiction. When I suggested to him that he was just in a phase of uncontrolled drug use at times, and that when he had more social roles, more opportunities, and more control over what he wanted to do in his life, he would have more control over his drug use, he smiled at me and said, "I'm very disappointed to hear you talk like that. You still don't know what makes me tick." Having been in prison for so long, Harry had less time in social settings where he could learn to tick differently.

Some of the older baby boomers in this book matured out of drug use given the chance to learn how to do this. Perhaps Charles Winick was right—that addicts eventually mature out of drug use by engaging in social situations that require their time and attention, or learning to cope with the issues that instigated drug use.[27] The life stories of baby boomer drug users suggest, however, that the War on Drugs extended the age of maturing out.

Those who spent most of their adult years incarcerated, or were in and out of jail and treatment programs without success, had little time to become engaged in social roles that replaced their drug user role. They had little time to engage in new social activities. They had little time to learn to handle the hurt that caused continued drug use. Since differences within age groups increase with age, we have yet to discover the age of maturing out for the drug war generation.[28]

EIGHT

The Culture of Control Expands

JOE

The pleasant and physically fit White man sitting in front of me looked younger than 53 years old. He had been raised in a solidly middle-class family. He was married until recently and kept in touch with his children after the divorce. Joe said his whole family was "a hundred percent behind me all the way." Joe had the critical social and economic support needed when he was arrested on drug charges. Without the lawyers his father had provided, his life would have been very different after the tragedy.

In high school, Joe experimented with the typical substances used by kids his age at the time—alcohol, tobacco, marijuana, LSD—but the horrific accident had nothing to do with drugs.

I accidentally shot and killed my best friend . . . I wasn't using [drugs] at that time. I was hanging out with some friends and a buddy of mine came and borrowed his dad's car, and picked me up and my brother. And we went and picked up Sam, and we were gonna go out that night and party. It was like five o'clock. We had just all got picked up from my house. I was in the front seat; my brother and Sam were in the back seat. I had never been around guns my whole life. I reached under the seat and his dad had a little 22. I thought it was a fake gun, so I picked it up and—pointing it around, and pointing it at the back seat, and pointed it at my brother and Sam, and I pulled the trigger. It hit Sam right in the chest. We rushed to the hospital, and he was dead on arrival.

Nobody got in any trouble. The mother, the lady, the mother of the son, the kid that died, wrote a long letter to the judge when I went to court. He threw it all out, you know. She knew that it was an accident. There was no charges filed, everything, it—it wouldn't be like that today, but back then, nothing happened to anybody.

Joe never had any counseling for the traumatizing accident. Although he said it left emotional scars, he did not link the accident to his increased use of a variety of drugs, especially cocaine. He was the only one in his family of six children who got in trouble with drugs and the law. His first arrest was for marijuana, and with a lawyer to defend his case he received a year on probation.

His heroin use started when he was 20. Joe had no doubt what caused his addiction to heroin. "It was my motorcycle accident," he explained. "I was fed so many pills for two years straight that, you know, I liked them and I always wanted to get that feeling again." He continued to use prescription opioids or heroin all of his life, with short intervals of less than a year. He learned to control his dosage and never overdosed. "I'll just start out real small with heroin. You don't play. I respect it. I start out with just a little bit. I know it'll kill ya."

Although Joe went to college, he dropped out and took a blue-collar job. A reliable worker, he was promoted to an office job, bought a house in the suburbs, and achieved the middle-class dream—all while using drugs. He was functional as a father and provider until his arrest for possession of Oxycontin and methamphetamine, when he received five years' probation. Another methamphetamine possession charge six months later landed him in court again. "I had a good attorney," he explained, "and he [the judge] ended up saying as long as I did six months in-patient rehab he gave me eight years' probation."

This started a long string of treatment rehabilitation programs—all paid for by his parents. One of the treatment facilities was a popular program mentioned by others in the study—Narconon, a therapeutic community reputedly developed by Scientology.[1] "My dad paid like thirty thousand dollars for that," Joe said. "It was like going to a country club out there."

Within a few months he relapsed and was caught with methamphetamine again. Called an "epidemic" at the time, the state received federal funding from the High Intensity Drug Trafficking Areas (HIDTA) program to address the methamphetamine problem with more police control. This meant that methamphetamine users were under heightened surveillance, so more were caught. Joe was arrested five more times—always on drug charges.

> My father's just always been very supportive of me. He's always hired lawyers to get me out of my trouble. I had charges in different counties, and my attorney got all these charges wrapped together . . . The judge in the county that wanted to give me the full eight years in prison agreed to get all the counties

to work together. As long as I successfully completed the drug court program, then I wouldn't have to do any prison time.

Joe was in a methadone program and living at his parent's house at the time of his interview. While in drug court, he used heroin on purpose so he could get into a methadone program, which drug court allowed only for those addicted to heroin.[2]

WHAT HAVE WE LEARNED IN 45 YEARS OF WAR?

In recent years, as the news of mass incarceration of drug users is beginning to reach the public mind, the disease model is again replacing the moral model to explain addiction, and the criminal justice system is bracing for an erosion of power and funding. As a country, we face a potential turning point in policy. Will taxpayer monies stop going to law enforcement programs and instead fund the best treatment programs? What have we learned from the War on Drugs that can help lead us into a better future?

After a 45-year expansion of the prison industrial complex, the emergence of alternatives to incarceration, such as drug treatment courts, are part of a new culture of control.[3] The primary agents of social control as the War on Drugs escalated were police, courts, jails, prisons, and drug treatment programs. As discussed previously, addiction is a debated concept that many believe is constructed to serve the interests of those who benefit from addiction being a problem.[4] The vested interests of the drug war have grown beyond the criminal justice system and infiltrated medical and social services.[5] Mimicking the scare tactics of Harry Anslinger, but with more advanced technology, science, and propaganda techniques, the masters of the War on Drugs became adept at the game of manipulation and understood the importance of influencing public opinion. Historically, the pendulum swung from an emphasis on a punitive response to an emphasis on medical treatment for drug users. But in contemporary society, these two are merging.

THE PRISON INDUSTRIAL COMPLEX

The term "prison industrial complex" is attributed to Angela Davis, whose 1997 speech, "Masked Racism: Reflections on the Prison Industrial Complex," argued that imprisoning people for alleged crimes takes care of social problems like homelessness, drug addiction, and unemployment by hiding them from public view.[6] In the same year, investigative journalist Eric Schlosser explained the idea of an industrial complex to aptly illustrate the profitable relationship between government and corporations in which "the raw material of the prison-industrial complex is its inmates: the poor, the homeless, and the mentally ill; drug dealers, drug addicts, alcoholics, and a wide assortment of violent sociopaths."[7] However, the raw material was not free.

The total cost of the entire prison industrial complex is difficult to establish and varies over time due to changes in federal and state laws and budget decisions. According to the US Department of Justice, the 2015 budget for federal prison alone was $6.9 billion. To put this in perspective, the average costs of incarceration for one prisoner in federal prisons was $30,619.85 annually or $83.89 per day. In California, one state prisoner costs three times the maximum welfare benefits paid to a family of four.[8] The *combined* state and federal prison budget in 2010 was $80 billion, a per capita expense that had tripled over thirty years.[9] However, prison costs estimated only by government agency budgets can be misleading.[10] What we know is that the total budget of the federal and state criminal justice system is larger than the share of the public funding for the poor.[11]

With money at this level comes corruption, particularly through government contracts with private industry. A plethora of private services (transportation, food, healthcare, repairs) and materials (beds, bedding, clothes, kitchen equipment, cleaning materials, locks, arms) are provided by small private companies and large industries—all relying on taxpayer money. Public funding for incarceration includes facilities such as detention centers, processing centers, halfway houses, and immigration detention centers. The profit incentive for the special interests of the prison industrial complex is far-reaching.[12]

Private prison corporations were proposed as a solution to reduce waste in federal spending, which allowed for-profit prisons to increase shareholder dividends while minimizing their costs of incarceration. This was a recipe for greed on the backs of prisoners who had no rights. Private prisons "saved" money by overcrowding prisons, decreasing services, or providing poor-quality supplies for prisoners, with little oversight.[13] From 1999 to 2009 the private prison industry grew by 1,600 percent.[14] Lobbyists paid for by prison industry organizations influenced legislatures, and campaign contributions were made to legislators overseeing prison government contracts. High-level federal bureaucrats became well-paid board members of for-profit prison organizations after leaving office.[15]

One need only to look at the increase in super-maximum security facilities, or "supermax" prisons, and Special Housing Units (SHUs) to understand what government and industry collaboration can lead to when lobbyists, legal bribes, and promises of lucrative industry board positions are allowed to persist unhampered. Fueled by media-led panics of drugs epidemics, crack babies, and drug-related violence,[16] the public allowed corruption to continue despite increasing reports of human rights violations and injustices.[17]

This brief historical look at the rise of the prison industrial complex through public funding provokes a number of questions. Should people be incarcerated for drug problems? Did the billions of taxpayer funding spent to incarcerate them make a difference in their drug-using behavior? How did time in jail impact their lives? How does locking up nonviolent offenders help society? The baby boomers' stories in this book provided insights into how incarceration influenced their drug use, impacted their lives, and affected their communities. A few selected excerpts from the lives of those already introduced further illustrate the pattern of corruption and injustices perpetuated by a prison industrial complex fueled by the War on Drugs.

ABEL: SOLITARY CONFINEMENT

The 53-year-old man introduced in chapter 3 whose bullying brother became a police officer, avoided the police at all cost. He succeeded until his wife committed suicide, his business failed, and he suffered from "the kind of depression where you can't get out of bed in the morning." He was in a methadone program when his house was foreclosed and the police evicted him from his home. They also took him to jail.

> I left to pay a phone bill for fifteen minutes, and I'm gone and I come back and the sheriff's there toting a shotgun away, and there's six thugs [police officers] in my house throwing my stuff over the railing into my front yard. And my four cats are inside there, and they weren't gonna let me back inside to get my cats. They weren't gonna let me back in for anything . . . The couch where I had my things stashed was out in the front yard. I reached down and found a couple Xanax, and I like to do Xanax and just off and on for the last ten years. I liked doing them 'cause they really, really take the edge off anxiety. Here I find these two Xanax and a minute later one of the thugs found, it's called "dirt weed" [marijuana], 'cause it looks like dirt. It's just crap, you know, and

I've had it for probably nine or ten years. I completely forgot about it, and I stashed it in a piece of cat furniture—a nine-foot tall scratchy post for the kittens. So when they tipped it over this dirt weed came tumbling out and they just threw me up against the car and put me in the car while my possessions are being put out in my yard.

This little Johnny law knew exactly what it was and stuff. He reminded me of my brother so very much. Oh, here's a funny one: they were hauling me in, the last thing I see is my stuff being put outside, and I says to the cops, "Why don't you just pull me over and shoot me now?" And he didn't say anything. He took me to the suicide department when they took me to jail because that constituted a suicidal threat. So for seventy-two hours those rights were abrogated while I sat around in a chilly room in a ninja turtle outfit and these assholes are coming around asking, "How do you feel today, Mr. Jones?" I say to myself how do I answer this question you know, I'm feeling pretty crappy, and I'm starting to have withdrawal from having no methadone. And the last thing I saw was my shit being put out on the lawn, and don't know what happened to my cats. I haven't been able to contact anybody.

The next year, Abel was arrested for a misdemeanor drug offense and spent time in solitary confinement.[18] His early experiences with his brother and subsequent encounters with police left Abel with an abhorrence of law enforcement. "Actually I took a vow to break the law every day that my brother was a policeman," he explained, "'cause someone had to be there to keep the scales of justice even." I asked him what scales he was referring to. "In the world! With his [brother's] thug ass out there hassling the crap out of otherwise law-abiding citizens, somebody had to do something." Abel relished breaking the law every day by smoking marijuana.

Even up to this day, I don't drink a drop, so, you know, I get together with my friends and we'll burn one [marijuana], and sit around and shoot the breeze, and it's just not that big a deal. Apparently it is to the police.

Abel was not a violent criminal and going to jail did not influence him to stop using drugs, but it did make him even more mistrustful of public servants paid to protect us. And for a man who suffered a lot of pain, the harsh actions by the criminal justice system made it hurt even more.

JORDAN: GUARD-ORGANIZED SEXUAL ASSAULT

The transgender baby boomer introduced in chapter 1 was in jail when a group of guards attempted to rape her.

I was supposed to be there for seven years, but something happened where they tried to molest me, and they made a deal. Either I sue or they cut my time short, and so I took the time, of course . . . I'd say the second week I was in jail there the guards sent about six guys in my cell. The guards did (pause). Yeah, and the camera turned every five minutes and when it turned which direction my cell was, it got stuck and it stayed there for about fifteen to twenty minutes, and caught everything on film. Yeah it was just a freak accident. Actually we had no idea it got stuck until I told them [lawyers], I says, "Well, look at the camera." My lawyer went to look at the cameras and it showed about fifteen to twenty min of what was going on—the fighting actually. Well, I grew up with some brothers that taught me how to fight. And I fought my way. Well, they got my clothes off, I will say that. They got my clothes off. That's as far as they got. My cell was kind of tore up and my TV, everything in there was kind of messed up. I wore a couple of bruises, and there was some stitches here and some stitches there, but they never really got a chance to do anything sexually to me. But they knew what the intentions were. You know, you got six guys and this trans-sexual—what's going on here? It's like the second week I was there.[19]

Jordan experienced humiliating stigma and pain due to her transgender status, but as she told her story, she told it with pride, not withholding the brutal details of sexual abuse while under the control of her jailers.

IAN: CIVIL FORFEITURE SEIZURE

Ian, introduced in chapter 3, was in Florida when he was involved with a small-time drug supply operation and realized that the police were negotiating with drug dealers.

I was meeting people, I was in demand for that certain product, like marijuana or heroin, or Dilaudids or whatever they wanted and Mr. Friend [his boss] could supply. So I would sell it to them and turn and hand the money over to him, and he would give me my percentage . . . It was basically people on the street and people who held jobs also. And there were a few people that were homebound that were livin' off of the government and getting disability and stuff like that.

A Florida highway patrolman area at the time started the drug interdiction team and later on became sheriff of the county because he stepped on some toes of politicians that were involved with drug trafficking. So they wanted him off the streets, so they put him off the streets and made him a sheriff of the county. Now, they [the highway patrol] are not after the drugs, they're after the money. Back then, they were just strictly after the drugs. Now they're after the money that's going down to Florida, South Florida to buy the drugs.

What Ian observed and described supports the argument that the Comprehensive Crime Control Act of 1984 motivated police to focus more on confiscating property and money, such as the money the drug dealers were transporting, since they are allowed to keep it.[20]

MOSES: DRUGS IN PRISON

Several baby boomers in this study confirmed the availability of drugs in prison. Some said they preferred to withdraw—cold turkey—than to have to keep up a habit in prison. Moses, introduced in chapter 1, adapted to the prison culture by becoming a middleman for drug dealing:

> I remember the first time I went to prison, there were guards there, staff people there that brought in the drugs. And sometimes the visitors of other inmates, they was able to slip the drugs into the other inmates. I was used as someone to sell these drugs, because I had access to large areas of this prison. Because, like I said, I did very well on a test, that GED test and I became a teacher's aide. And that gave me access to a lot of other areas of prison that normal inmates wasn't able to go to. So because I was able to get around so much, I was asked to, "eh, help me do this, with this." People used to tell me, "eh, I got this, could you help me sell this." I was a middleman for a lot of deals that was going on. We used to have a number system, and I was a bookie like. There was all kinds of activities that happens in prison. And I became involved in all of these criminal activities.

> It's something I willingly participated in. When I'm in prison I become quite comfortable in prison. And every time I went to prison, 'cause I've been to prison many times over my years, it became like something I knew was going to happen in my life. Right, so when I went to prison, I got back in the flow, "Okay, I'm back in prison, this is what you do in prison." And that's how I survived in prison, 'cause I've been in a lot of situations in prison where I know it's only God's grace that I'm still alive today. People getting killed, me getting caught up in someone else's stuff between gang rivalries, between race riots and stuff like that, all kinds of different things that would happen in prison . . . 'Cause when I go to prison I get access to things 'cause I know how to operate in prison. I learned how to be at peace in prison so I can go there and survive. I'm a survivalist when I go to prison.

The question that this story raises is why—under a 45-year-long War on Drugs and billions being poured into stopping drug use—are drugs still being sold in the one place where law enforcement has the most absolute control? If drug use cannot be stopped in prison, how can law enforcement stop it in society?

The lives discussed in this book show that the drug war's mass incarceration plan has failed to stop drug use and instead increased violence on the streets and corruption in the criminal justice system. But public support for this might be changing due to a real epidemic of opioids started by pharmaceutical companies.[21] As more young people die from opioid overdoses, distraught parents are joining human rights advocates to help keep their loved ones out of the criminal justice system and alive.

Incarcerating drug users is beginning to be viewed as an unsustainable cost in both financial and social terms, and societal response to drug users is moving away from punitive toward treatment solutions. Instead of a pendulum swing, however, treatment is being incorporated under the criminal justice system to maintain more control over drug users and receive drug war funding. Drug treatment courts are managed by court systems.[22] Prisons operate in-house and halfway house treatment for prisoners. Parole and probation officers mandate ex-offenders to treatment programs under the threat of jail. The line between punishment and treatment has become blurred.

TREATMENT INDUSTRIAL COMPLEX

The American Friends Service Committee is a Quaker organization that has been working to promote peace and justice for over 100 years. One of the forerunners focusing on the injustices and corruption inherent in the prison industrial system, they also are one of the first to identify a disturbing collaboration between prisons and treatment.

> While the prison industrial complex was dependent on incarceration or detention in prisons, jails, and other correctional institutions, this emerging "treatment industrial complex" allows the same corporations (and many new ones) to profit from providing treatment-oriented programs and services. As a result, this emerging Treatment Industrial Complex has the potential to ensnare more individuals, under increased levels of supervision and surveillance, for increasing lengths of time—in some cases, for the rest of a person's life.[23]

Collaboration with the treatment industrial complex lent law enforcement not only a stamp of legitimacy to control drug users but also ensured the flow of money from public and private entities. In response to the community's cry to stem the rising tide of opioid addiction, law enforcement embraced the "prevention sector," aware that doing so diverted more funding into its own coffers.[24] In addition, instead of being the "bad guys" who were arresting and sending their citizens' sons and daughters to jail, they now were offering them an opportunity for treatment.[25] It was a win-win situation for law enforcement and treatment industries, and policymakers praised the new collaborations.[26]

Alone, the prison industrial complex and treatment industrial complex were in competition—together they were a gargantuan Trojan horse that could stop the tiny force of intellectuals and activists who were demanding an end to the War on Drugs. But how did treatment gain so much legitimacy in the public mind? Perhaps because the construction of addiction as a disease was legitimized by biomedical science.[27]

The preceding chapter discussed how addiction was socially constructed. Suggesting addiction is a socially constructed phenomenon does not mean the phenomenon is not real. Whatever addiction means to different people, it is objectively *felt* by many of those who have problems due to using drugs and cannot stop using them. Their loved ones see them change into uncontrollable individuals they do not recognize. The biological reasons for this are still being studied, debated, and disputed.[28] But even supporters of the leading scientific model (brain disease) call addiction a complex phenomenon with more than one causal factor, and many scientists agree the social environment is the most important factor.[29]

Yet problematic drug use continues to be viewed as an individual character flaw, or a personal disease. All the baby boomer drug users in this study mentioned one of these as the reason for their drug problem. Many said they were bad *and* sick. Few blamed the social environment. Even those like Omar, who acknowledged that it was difficult to stop using while living in the Bluff, blamed themselves for being there.

In contemporary society, both incarceration and treatment are solutions that are widely accepted. Treatment is better than jail if one is sick. But if part of the problem is the social environment, then treatment programs must include this as part of the solution. Merging treatment with law enforcement will not allow a focus on ameliorating the social problems, it will only create a bigger and more powerful industrial complex diverting public funding away from addressing the root of problematic drug use. The lives of baby boomers introduced in this book, and description of their lived experiences with past and current treatment models, provide insights on why we should be wary of an emerging treatment industrial complex.

The 12-step program (AA, NA) was used in every treatment program mentioned by people in this study, whether private, public, or court-mandated. Group meetings based on 12-step were the only treatment option for people who could not afford private treatment or get a bed in a public program. Everyone had an opinion of 12-step—mostly negative. Criticism was centered on too much talking, too spiritual, or too much access to drugs through the people attending the meetings. Those who liked 12-step enjoyed the talking and were comfortable with having a belief in a higher power. The one aspect of 12-step that appealed to everyone, however, was the social support and networking it provided.

According to Thomas McLellan, founder of the Treatment Research Institute, good treatment is rarely available to those who need it.[30] McLellan, who lost his son to a drug overdose, believes 12-step is based on an outdated model of addiction, which he calls "the washing machine model . . . dirty old addicts go in, clean new citizens come out"[31] Conducting an intensive treatment evaluation, he found the majority of the treatment offered is "dismal," and "it's a dirty little secret, but none of these [treatment] places want to be evaluated."[32] The best treatment model he found was the professional model provided to doctors and pilots.

Although Anne and Joan were helped through a professional program, most of the participants in this study could not afford a facility with such a wide range of services and activities.[33] Even expensive treatment did not necessarily improve outcomes. Joe's father paid thousands of dollars for experimental treatment programs that were popular but unsuccessful. However, comprehensive treatment was available to two of the poorest participants in this study. Their recovery stories provide insight into what a successful treatment program should include.

ALICIA

Alicia, introduced in chapter 3, had four children who were often in foster care while she was using drugs, in prison, or in treatment. She experienced a variety of treatment programs as she struggled to regain control over her use and custody of her children. Her last relapse was when her mother died, and she was drug free for seven years when I interviewed her. Her turning point came when she participated in a community-based program for single mothers with drug problems. Although the program required drug abstinence, it also provided for all of her social needs. They trained her *and* found her a job (rather than simply giving her a list to call). They paid for her apartment until she could afford it so her children could live with her while in recovery, and not with foster parents while she recovered. She said she stopped drugs because she was tired, but I examined what this meant.

> Alicia: I got tired. I started thinking about these kids. These kids didn't ask to come here. I'm responsible for them. I've got to do what I can for them. And if I get high, I can't do that. I try to give them the best I can ... I graduated from Journey Home [recovery house] in 2004. While I'm at Journey Home, I get in the program, because this is the program I'm living here with—The Seed Project. I've been here since 2003. I got my children back [and] I've been staying here ever since. I went back to school. I got my certificate in dental care technician. I'm working now.
>
> Miriam: Do you have a lot of help right now?
>
> Alicia: The only thing they [The Seed Project] do for me is pay my utility bills. Right now, my lease coming up to be due. They're going to want me to pay $600 and something dollars for the apartment. Right now I'm paying $475 because during the first part of the recession I lost eight hours. But then I got them back. They wanted me to pay $600 something then, but when I lost eight hours, they cut it down to $475.
>
> Miriam: So it's subsidized.
>
> Alicia: It goes by the income.
>
> Miriam: So you'll be okay?
>
> Alicia: I done come too far—I have to be dependent on them to take care of me and my family to when we got somewhere to live—when I first moved here in this program, I didn't pay but forty dollars in rent. I got government welfare checks. I got food stamps. I worked my way out of all of that.

My conversation with Alicia shows that it was not just "getting tired" that motivated Alicia to stop drugs and be reunited with her children—she needed the resources to do this. The community-based treatment program continued to target resources to her specific needs until she had enough resources or access to resources (social capital) to sustain her recovery, which made all the difference.

Elijah had been in and out of treatment programs all his life. He was almost two years drug free when I interviewed him. Elijah said he heard a "spirit" tell him to come to Atlanta, Georgia.

> I started to think I was crazy, so that Friday I paid the dope boys off and I had seventy-eight dollars left. I went to the Greyhound bus station and asked them how far will seventy-eight dollars take you? He said Atlanta, Georgia. And so I got on and came one-way, and I stepped off the Greyhound about two o'clock in the morning. I looked to the left, looked to the right. I really didn't know what was going on, so I just started walking. For the first few days here I used drugs . . . I went out camping in the road and I met someone who told me about Davidson Place being a shelter where you could stay there for a couple of months free. In order to stay there you had to take an occasional urinalysis test. But they provided a cot for you and a meal in the evening, and so I did that for a while.

> But one night there was a counselor. I was tired, and he was talking about a treatment center. So he kept on talking, and he looks at me and said, "What are you doing?" I said, "I'm trying ta get some sleep." He said, "We have a wonderful program here, and I'm not gonna let you sit here 'cuz you don't look like the type of person that wanna throw your life away." Him not knowing I'm fifty-five years old and all what I been through. But he actually cared! It's the first time somebody cared. So he said, "when the counselors come downstairs, you come by early tomorrow, make an appointment to see one of the counselors," and that's what I did. And after I saw her, she sent me to this, you know, connection with an outreach program downtown that's called Right-Up. So they said I qualify to go with that, but how it all begin is I had to remain abstinent long enough—that's what treatment did—to hear what people was saying. So that's how it began. I completed that Right-Up course, which is about twelve weeks.

Elijah was adamant that he would never relapse again. I asked him how he can be so sure. "Because the pleasure outweighs the pain," he said without hesitation. "It feels good not to use today. It feels good to have a sixty-inch TV in my room and a DVD. I receive some income, enough to pay my rent."

Elijah gave credit to a "spirit" directing him to Atlanta, but his fortunate connection with Davidson Place, a residential community-based shelter, and Right-Up, a program that paid for his apartment, was the turning point to successful recovery. A compassionate counselor and stable housing were necessary resources for the homeless like Elijah.[34] And these resources cost much less than what it would cost to keep Alicia or Elijah incarcerated.

HARRY: BETWEEN A ROCK AND A HARD PLACE

In June of 2007, Harry was sent to a residential treatment facility in Wernersville. When he left, he received a piece of paper called the "Certificate of Completion and Commitment" signed by the superintendent. He was given an "Aftercare Plan" that consisted basically of going to 12-step meetings. Harry had been through this exact same treatment program and aftercare plan twice in the last four years—in 2004 and 2007—both times graduating with a certificate and a to-do list, that included attending 12-step meetings. He would have many more to-do lists when he moved to Philadelphia, a city that widely publicized their great reentry programs. He had two basic needs: housing and employment—the programs provided neither.

After Harry participated in the mayor's reentry program and did not find employment, I came to Philadelphia to help Harry apply for college. In August of 2008, Harry was accepted at the Community College of Philadelphia (CCP) on a Pell grant. Once he started classes, he had some structure in his life. He enthusiastically participated in the work-study program, and worked as many hours as the program allowed. With his work-study pay and student loans, he could support himself, but he still needed a place to stay.

He lived temporarily with friends while looking for a room near the college. He tried the rooms advertised near the college for students to rent. Every time he called they told him to come by in person. Once the landlords saw Harry, a 56-year-old college student who looked like he had seen the harder side of life, they always had some excuse why he could not rent the room. Some were honest and told him that he just did not fit the type of person they were looking for. I started calling landlords for him, but even if they took Harry sight unseen and I cosigned his rental contract, they would have to agree to let his parole officer visit to approve the place. He never got to this point.

Harry was getting depressed about the situation and I was afraid he might slip back into problematic drug use. I knew he used alcohol and marijuana, since he could control them and still attend school and work. But a heroin habit would put him back into the criminal world looking for money for drugs. For a few weeks I paid for Harry to stay in a private halfway house managed by an enterprising recovering user. Within a few weeks Harry was asked to leave because he had alcohol on his breath. The manager told me he ran a drug and alcohol-free home. Harry went back to couch-surfing.

He finally found a place in West Philly. It was a boarding house, but a lot better than a halfway house with 12-step rules. Harry had no rules except to pay the rent. The landlord said it was not a problem for the parole officer to check out the premises—he seemed to have had parolees as boarders before. Harry said the rent was really cheap because it was a Black community. That did not bother him, and it did not bother the community that he was White.

With stable housing, Harry's mood changed. He was happy. He was excited about his studies. He loved working in the library where he talked with students and library staff all day. Finally, he could cook his own food in his own kitchen, which he said was rarely used by the other boarders. He called me while he was preparing his vegetarian meals, excited when he found some exotic root vegetable for a tasty salad he concocted. He liked to sit outside on the porch as he read his books for classes and wrote papers, listening to the children play kickball and their mothers call to them from their own porches where they sat during the balmy evenings.

When I came to Philadelphia for a visit, I saw the neighborhood was a little neglected. Vacant lots looked like lost teeth in the line of row houses. Porches sported scruffy sofas and chairs. The corner store had bars on the windows and a thick glass enclosure protecting the cashier from the clients. The basement of the house nearby held a makeshift kennel, and I could hear the dogs barking fiercely. Harry was the only White guy in the neighborhood. But this was not the Bluff. Children played on the sidewalks, mothers pushed babies in strollers, and cars cruised the streets lazily—and no one seemed to mind that Harry was here.

Harry developed a good relationship with a few of his professors. His computer professor encouraged him to work in the computer lab and continue to take computer classes, but Harry realized he was too far behind to have a career in computers. He liked his ceramics classes the best. He said he felt like he was completely absorbed when doing ceramics, and if he was stressed, it went away when he was working on a piece of clay. After taking a writing class he started work on a book. I had not seen Harry so inspired about life since he was a kid. He was on his own, but he had a safe place to live, he had a job, and he had a vision for his future. And unlike when he was in Florida, this future did not include working the graveyard shift at Denny's all-night restaurant. His work environment in the college made all the difference.

Harry had submitted a change of residence form to his parole officer and was worried about getting approval for the new place. I was worried because

I knew Harry smoked a little marijuana every day—a few puffs during the day to control stress and a few at night to go to sleep. He had been using this amount since he left treatment, never more or less. Harry always drank gallons of water the day before he was going to see his parole officer, since he believed it watered down the urine test. I told Harry that I did not think it worked, but it had always worked for him. We were hoping his change in residence address would mean a change in parole officers, since Agent Lapinsky was the parole officer from hell.

On his first visit to Agent Lapinsky's office, Harry sat in the front room and heard another parolee in the office telling Lapinsky that he was late and had to leave to get to work on time. Lapinsky barked that he did not like to be told anything and called for two other agents to come get the man and put him in lockdown. Harry sat frozen in fear as two agents went into the office, pulled the surprised parolee out of the room, and put him in a back room. Harry could hear him being locked down. The man would not be making it to work on time that day, and might never be going back to work. Harry was terrified of being put in lockdown—it meant he would miss work and school. It also meant he might be sent back to prison.[35]

A few weeks after Harry moved, he was called into the parole office by Lapinsky, where he learned his last urine test was positive for marijuana. He was put in lockdown in the other room. After a few hours he was given a treatment plan and told that if he did not do everything in the plan, he would be sent back to prison. Lapinsky's plan required him to attend an approved treatment program four days a week and 12-step group meetings every day. The required treatment program was on the other side of town, far from the college. Harry explained he would be missing two classes every week if he had to go to that particular treatment program and asked if he could go to one closer to his school. Lapinsky refused to change the plan.

We both knew Harry would not be able to pass his college courses if he missed so many classes. If he failed, he would be kicked off the work-study program too. Everything would be lost. It was a terrible situation and Harry was desperate, but he decided being out of prison was better than keeping his work-study job. "If I don't have school I have no future out here," he said with a sigh as we discussed this on the phone. "But I am not going back to prison."

I looked online for a treatment program closer to the college and found three that were approved by the city reentry programs. I called his parole officer. Lapinsky treated me no better than he treated Harry. His initial fake cordiality turned mean as soon as he found out why I had called. I explained that the treatment facility he had chosen was too far from his college and would mean that Harry missed his classes, but I had found some treatment programs near Harry's school that he could attend instead.

Lapinsky did not agree. "The program I sent Harry to is paid through his Medicaid," he said. "It is the only program Medicaid will fund." I anticipated he would say this because I suspected Lapinsky had some "special relationship" with this specific treatment program. Perhaps he got kickbacks. Whatever the reason he wanted Harry to go to only this treatment facility, I anticipated that Lapinsky would make up other excuses. So I already found which programs in the area Medicaid funded, and I had already called two that were near the school. They had room for Harry, and the administrators told me they had other students from the college. When I informed Lapinsky of the other treatment options, he became extremely annoyed. "We can't make plans around Harry's personal schedule," Lapinsky retorted. He would not budge.

But I was not going to give up yet. I had worked with a number of treatment programs during my research, and I had made a few connections (social capital building). I called my contact at a local drug court and asked for advice, since he worked in the criminal justice system. He suggested I contact Lapinsky's supervisor, which I did immediately. Time was ticking. Harry already missed a few classes going to the treatment program on Lapinsky's plan.

Lapinsky's supervisor was a Black woman. Based on my experiences, I felt that she would be more understanding about Harry's situation than Lapinsky—a White male with a macho attitude. Also as a supervisor, she was more concerned about Philadelphia's reentry statistics, and she realized that Lapinsky's plan would make Harry a recidivist—another bad statistic. She agreed with me that Harry should not miss classes to attend treatment, especially if he could attend it nearby. She told me to tell Harry to start the program nearby and she would take care of Lapinsky.

As soon as I heard this, I called Harry. He was on his way to the treatment program across town. Since he was worried that Lapinsky would be angry, he went to the treatment that night anyway, missing another class. He said he would keep going until he got approval from his parole officer before he switched programs. I crossed my fingers hoping the supervisor would follow up on what she told me.

Lapinsky called Harry the next day ordering him to come in. Harry was right. Lapinsky was furious. He yelled at Harry and called him a sissy for letting his sister defend him. He threw a phone at Harry, taunting him, "Here, call your sister, you little pussy." But since Harry was not put in lockdown, he was sure that Lapinsky was told to change programs. Lapinsky approved the new plan for the treatment program near school.

A week later, Harry was assigned a new parole officer—a saint compared to Lapinsky. The new treatment program he attended required only one meeting a week with a counselor. They allowed him to use the 12-step meetings he observed for his college addiction class as his required meetings. He did not miss any more classes.

NINE

———

Social Reconstruction and Social Recovery

THE WAR ON DRUGS HAS BEEN a civil war fought against our sons and daughters, mothers and fathers, sisters and brothers. Today, families are torn apart and children are suffering because of this war. People are afraid to go to certain parts of town. Some hide in their homes with guns ready to protect them. After 45 years of war, our society needs healing. Many have called for the end of the War on Drugs, and yet it continues.[1]

The year 2009 seemed to herald a pivotal moment in drug war history, when the US director of the White House Office of National Drug Control Policy, Gil Kerlikowske, also known as the "drug czar," called for an end to the War on Drugs.[2] At that time there was little doubt that Portugal's decriminalization policy, which ended the country's drug war, had successfully decreased drug use and crime.[3] Yet, the global drug war remained.

In 2011, the UN Global Commission on Drug Policy declared, "the global war on drugs has failed, with devastating consequences for individuals and societies around the world," and called for all nations "to end the criminalization, marginalization and stigmatization of people who use drugs ... and begin the transformation of the global drug prohibition regime."[4] The report provided 11 recommendations on how to end the War on Drugs. The commissioners of the report were international political leaders and former leaders of nations, writers, human rights activists, and public intellectuals. Their recommendations were not implemented.

The United Nations call to end the War on Drugs was reiterated in a 2014 report, *Taking Control: Pathways to Drug Policies That Work,* published in anticipation of the 2016 United Nations General Assembly Special Session (UNGASS) on drugs. Viewed by some to be the session that would end the War on Drugs, the public statement written by the members of the Global

Commission on Drugs after the April 21, 2016 meeting in New York clearly indicated that the war was not over.[5]

> The Global Commission on Drug Policy is profoundly disappointed with the adopted outcome document agreed at the UN General Assembly Special Session (UNGASS) on "the world drug problem." The document does not acknowledge the comprehensive failure of the current drug control regime to reduce drug supply and demand.
>
> Nor does the outcome document account for the damaging effects of out-dated policies on violence and corruption as well as on population health, human rights and wellbeing. By reaffirming that the three international conventions are the "cornerstone of global drug policy," the document sustains an unacceptable and outdated legal status quo.[6]

The War on Drugs will eventually end, and after the war our society will need reconstruction. A blueprint already exists for such reconstruction, but we do not need to wait to help those who have been wounded.[7] Programs and models that have worked to stem the tide of destruction caused by prohibition and punishment can be put into wider practice, and new programs based on emerging research findings can be developed. But before we can discuss solutions, we need to understand the call for a paradigm shift in how we view the problem.

PARADIGM SHIFT

Successful solutions start with forming a different definition of the situation.[8] The narratives in this book show that a major paradigm shift is required to effectively address problem drug use. The current dominant paradigm assumes that addiction is a disease, a moral breach, or a character flaw. The individual's drug use is viewed as the problem. This individual-oriented paradigm has largely failed. Instead, addiction must be understood socially as a way that large numbers of people adapt to the breakdown of an emotionally sustaining culture under the influence of an unchecked capitalist economy.[9] The social contract that held society together is broken—that is *the* problem.

I do not suggest that the War on Drugs was a conspiracy.[10] I acknowledge that some drug use stems from mental health issues and that continued use can lead to serious health issues and death. But I am arguing that drug use is usually temporary and nonproblematic, but problematic use is often the result of trauma, poverty, alienation, and loss of hope for a better life. The drug problems in contemporary society have been socially constructed by the War on Drugs.[11] To end this war, we must deconstruct the problem of drug use and start with a new paradigm.

By changing our paradigm (how we think about drugs and drug users), we can focus our efforts on the real problems present in a small fraction of drug use situations. We can distinguish people who might be in a difficult phase in their lives from those who have financial, social, or familial problems. We can ask whether drugs are being used to meet a temporary challenge in life or whether more lasting situational or societal issues exist that are impacting a specific population of problem drug users, such as poverty, a criminal record, and unemployment. We can focus on those who have more serious issues that require the attention of mental health professionals and not waste time and money treating those who are not sick.[12]

In chapter 4, I discussed the only eight people in the study who were never incarcerated, showing that they avoided involvement in the criminal justice system because they had access to resources and protective networks (social capital). Because they did not have a criminal record, they could support themselves and be contributing members of society. Those caught up in the criminal justice system were not able to do this, and they never returned to the level of socioeconomic status that they had before incarceration.

I suggested that the "maturing out" theory of drug use proposed by Charles Winick was an evidence-based social phenomenon; however, the War on Drugs did not allow baby boomer drug users to mature out.[13] Forced into prison or ineffective treatment, they were denied the normal transitions into adulthood, which provide roles and responsibilities that motivate them to control or stop drug use.[14] Living in drug-market communities created by the War on Drugs, drug users were caught up in the criminal justice system for minor nonviolent drug offenses, resulting in full immersion into a criminal culture.[15] Entire swaths of American landscapes became ghettos of despair.[16] After this prolonged civil war, society will need reconstruction to address the damage done, but only a paradigm shift in our view of the problem will provide effective solutions and guidance.

A paradigm shift in our view of the "drug problem" will involve at least three major changes in policy and program implementation: (1) disentangle treatment from law enforcement; (2) shift funding from law enforcement *back* to public housing and other social services, including comprehensive treatment; and (3) support and allow controlled moderate drug use as well as abstinence.

Disentangle Treatment from Law Enforcement

Recidivism rates of 60 to 80 percent indicate that coerced control of drug use through incarceration does not work well.[17] Formal control by treatment, whether voluntarily or as an alternative to incarceration, has its own set of problems. Treatment programs vary widely in what they provide; they often use a one-size–fits–all program, and relapse rates range from 40 to 80 percent.[18] Today, relapse has become accepted as part of the process of recovery, thus providing a steady supply of returning treatment clients.[19]

Treatment should not be a funding opportunity for police departments, jails, or treatment industries. Only by separating profit from treatment can we unlink greed as a motive for arresting and treating problem drug users. Law enforcement is not the answer to the drug use problem—the evidence from what is called the "Portugal Experiment" overwhelmingly supports decriminalizing drugs for personal use, and disentangling treatment from law enforcement.

In 2000, Portugal had one of the worst drug problems in the world. Desperate to do something different than what was being done at the time and not working—incarceration and one-size-fits-all drug treatment—the new administration adopted a drastic paradigm shift. In 2001, a new drug policy was implemented that decriminalized all drugs.[20] Decriminalization is not the same as total legalization, but it means no criminal record for drug users. Drug regulations were processed in noncriminal settings separated from the criminal justice system. Members of the newly formed Commissions for Dissuasions of Drug Addiction issued an "infraction" with a fine and a warning to people who caused problems due to their drug use, and only these local commissions decided the course of action for people with multiple infractions.[21]

The new policy was based on research showing that the setting of drug use and the mindset of the user are the most important factors when determining if drug use is problematic.[22] The Dissuasion Commissions developed very strict guidelines to help with their determinations, such as amassing evidence to ascertain if the person needed treatment *before* recommending treatment, and inquiring not only about the drug used but also the place and circumstances of drug use. Each local commission was mandated to minimize any sense of stigma and avoid making the person feel any guilt or shame due to the drug use.

Studies conducted after Portugal's decriminalization found drug use by young people in high school decreased while the number of people treated for drug use rose by 20 percent.[23] Lifetime use and prevalence decreased among all age groups for all drugs. In addition, the number of drug traffickers (a criminal offense) incarcerated decreased steadily. The number of people using substitution treatment (e.g., methadone) grew dramatically, indicating that de-stigmatizing drug use resulted in more people seeking treatment—*not* more people seeking drugs. Compared to all other countries in the European Union, Portugal's drug prevalence rates were lower than average, with the cannabis use rate being the lowest rate of all European countries.[24]

Shift Public Funding to Needed Services

We know that poverty, inequality, unemployment, inadequate housing, and childcare services are social factors that instigate and intensify drug use activities.[25] The money to increase public housing and other social services is already in the national budget, but over the past 40 years, public funding was diverted to pay for jails and prisons. As public monies toward prison building increased, funding for public housing decreased.[26] The same inverse relationship was seen as federal funding for correctional budgets increased, while funding for welfare and food stamps decreased.[27] Despite providing more funds to address each new drug epidemic and building more prisons to incarcerate people who used drug, drug use and drug trafficking increased.

Shifting money from jails and prisons to certified treatment will provide enough to cover the public costs for comprehensive treatment, as well as reduce the profit-making motives that lead to corruption.[28] Treatment should be targeted to individual needs, not the other way around. Drug treatment programs should be certified by a standardized national certification process, like other healthcare services, and based on evidence-based outcomes.[29]

Controlled Drug Use

As shown in this book, drug use is impacted by social situations that vary over time.[30] When examining the turning points from controlled use to out-of-control abuse, and from use to abstinence, the drug user life stories discussed in this book revealed long periods of controlled drug use and long periods of abstinence (also in the life of the same individual). Changing situations, such as incarceration, loss of employment, and loss of loved ones, were often the catalyst into problematic use of drugs. A stable situation often led to nonproblematic controlled use *or* abstinence. Understanding the social situation of the user is the key to effective solutions for problematic use of drugs. But a shift in how we view treatment success is needed to accept that controlled drug use, not solely abstinence, can reduce problematic drug use.

People who use drugs have learned to control drug use in specific situations under certain conditions, at different points in their drug trajectory. Moses, Alicia, and Elijah each in different situations used different strategies for their successful recovery.[31] Yet their lives and the lives of their loved ones might have been spared immense suffering if solutions other than incarceration had been offered earlier, or if controlled drug use had been an option. At various points in their drug trajectories, Omar, Jordan, and Abel stopped all drug use but marijuana, but they were still under the threat of losing their house, being discharged from treatment, or rearrested, since abstinence was required by housing authorities, treatment protocol, and probation rules.

Most of the baby boomers discussed in previous chapters learned to use drugs only in certain times or in specific places. Some controlled their use due to their social roles, such as the work of parenting, called informal social control.[32] But as long as controlled drug use is not an option, relapse will remain as part of the process of recovery. I argue that relapse does not always need to be part of recovery when controlled use is taught, learned, and supported by treatment professionals.[33] This requires that we adopt a paradigm shift in drug recovery perspectives. Until that shift happens, we can incorporate programs that focus less on the individual and more on the social environment.

CONTEMPORARY PROGRAMS THAT WORK

There is no silver bullet solution, of course. However, there are many programs that are working toward reducing drug use and alleviating the suffering caused by the drug war. I discuss only a few contemporary models that have been shown to be very effective. Until the US government endorses and implements suggestions proposed by the UN Commission on the War on Drugs, until the public embraces a paradigm shift in our response to drug users, and until policymakers change laws to ensure future generations do not live under a drug war again, we can work to address the damage.[34] We can expand programs that relieve suffering, provide basic needs for survival, and focus on social recovery.

Harm Reduction

Harm reduction was a public health response to drug use that proposed a health model to reduce harms of drug use rather than seeking to stop drug use through treatment or punishment. As a grassroots approach, it incorporates insights of experienced drug users and is often staffed *by* drugs users *for* drug users. Assumed to have started in Amsterdam, harm reduction was favored by many leading US academics in the early 1990s and viewed as a more realistic, practical, and humane approach than contemporary models.[35] But by the late 1990s, General McCaffrey, then heading the Office of National Drug Control Policy (ONDCP), signaled strong opposition to any harm reduction measure, saying it was a "slippery slope" toward legalization of drugs.[36] While harm reduction programs increased around the world, they stagnated in the United States.[37] In 1988, the US Congress banned federal funding from being spent on harm reduction strategies or harm reduction research, which President Obama lifted in 2009.[38]

As a global movement, there are no directives on how to practice harm reduction, but common principles include the acceptance that drug use is a complex issue with a wide range of behaviors, not all of which are problematic. Harm reduction emphasizes quality of life for the individual and the community. With a strong adherence to human rights tenets, harm reduction strategies strive to achieve a nonjudgmental delivery of services to those who need them. Acknowledging the power differentials inherent in race, class, gender, age, and economic realities, a harm reduction approach is sensitive to individual vulnerabilities. While respecting the rights of drug users, the approach does not minimize the danger of real harms associated with drug use behaviors.[39]

One of the harm reduction practices that caused the most controversy was the "syringe exchange program" (SEP), which has been legal in the Netherlands since the 1980s. However, it was not until the discovery that injecting drug users were a high-risk group for AIDS transmission through sharing syringes that SEPs proliferated throughout the world. Countries that implemented SEPs and other harm reduction strategies saw an immediate reduction in HIV transmission among injecting drugs users; early adopters of harm reduction had much lower rates of HIV infection than late adopters.[40] For various reasons, many of them based on unfounded moral principles that giving clean syringes to drug users encourages drug use, the United States was a late adopter of SEPs, and SEPs still operate illegally in some states.[41]

A new harm reduction strategy is the supervised injection facility (SIF) where drug users can have a safe place to inject their own drugs with clean paraphernalia (syringes, cotton, clean water). Studies show SIFs reduce the spread of infectious diseases, such as HIV / AIDS, and reduce costs to the community for medical emergency services and overdose deaths.[42] At the time of this writing, there is one long-running and successful SIF in Vancouver, Canada, but there are no SIFs in the United States.[43]

While harm reduction has expanded to include social justice and human rights as core principles, one of the criticisms of harm reduction is the failure to implement structural interventions that address poverty, inequality, and racial oppression in the community.[44] Harm reduction is a human rights approach focused on adverse health effects of drug use, but it usually does not include strategies to integrate drug users back into community life.

Methadone, a medical substitute drug for prescription opioids (heroin or prescription pain pills), is a harm reduction approach. Introduced in the late 1960s in the United States, methadone was grudgingly accepted because of the intolerable rates of heroin use at the time, but it remained a stigmatized treatment option due to the addictive properties of methadone and its diversion to illegal drug markets.[45] Buprenorphine, a pharmaceutical substitute for opioids, has become more popular in the last decade but is still addictive and can be abused.[46] Nevertheless, these two legal options for people who are physically dependent on opioids allow them to maintain their roles in society without fear of arrest or adverse events from street opioids, such as overdose. With the recent rapid increase in heroin and prescription opioid deaths, law enforcement and politicians now support these legal but formerly stigmatized harm reduction programs. However, methadone clinics are not required to offer counseling and often do not address the social situation and structural causes of addiction.

Many baby boomers in this study who were dependent on opioids were able to stop using drugs illegally by enrolling in a methadone program. Some eventually stopped methadone and other drugs, while others continued to use methadone for years, thereby maintaining control of drug-seeking behavior. Essentially, methadone, or the newer drug substitute burprenorphine, allows opioid users to be free from worry about incarceration so they are able continue to engage in legal employment and other social roles in their lives. For most other drugs, there are no medical substitutes, although marijuana is commonly used by many as a substitute for other drugs.[47]

Medical marijuana (cannabis)[48] can help reduce cravings for other drugs, and recent research suggests that cannabis is beneficial as an alternative treatment for opioid addiction.[49] Although people who are addicted to other drugs are using cannabis under a doctor's care to control or stop problematic use, many treatment providers view cannabis as having addictive properties and do not support its use for treatment, even while they support a more addictive drug like methadone. As long as marijuana is classified as a federal Schedule 1 drug, meaning it has no medical purposes, most health providers will not embrace its therapeutic uses.[50]

The state where the baby boomer study was conducted was not a state that legalized marijuana for medical purposes; nevertheless, eleven baby boomers in the study stopped using heroin, methamphetamine and / or cocaine / crack with the help of cannabis. Some secretly used cannabis while in treatment, while others used cannabis to stop hard drug use on their own. Other baby boomers said they used cannabis to lower hard drug use or reduce craving and withdrawal symptoms. The federal classification of marijuana / cannabis as a Schedule 1 drug must be changed to allow more research on cannabis as treatment for addiction. But while politicians and scientists continue debating its legal and medical status, problematic drug users are using cannabis to self-medicate or as a harm reduction strategy.

Community-Based Initiatives

Community-based initiatives are gaining popularity as evidence of their success increases.[51] As shown in the lives of Elijah and Alicia, who were helped by community-based programs that focused on reintegration into the community, these grassroots initiatives address more than drug use and health. Typically operated by staff who live in the community, they are more aware of the social, economic, and cultural problems that cause drug use than are treatment clinicians and social workers from outside the community. Their goal is more than drug abstinence. Such programs often rely fully on grants, donations, and charitable contributions, which do not provide a stable source of income. Many of the most successful community-based programs have long waiting lists, and some are forced to close for lack of funding.

Other community-based solutions include a variety of initiatives that focus on aspects of the drug user's life other than drugs, such as incorporating "art therapy" and encouraging creative expression in treatment or drug preventative programs.[52] For example, a coffee house frequented by college students and the homeless in Tacoma, Washington, was shown to decrease drug addiction simply by offering a place for social interaction.[53] These strategies are often successful, but they rely on intermittent and uncertain sources of funding. They need permanent sources of funding to continue.

Housing First

The Housing First model was started by Dr. Sam Temberis in New York City.[54] Developed for the homeless with mental health and substance abuse disorders (dual diagnosis), the founders believe that stable housing is the first and highest priority before abstinence from substance use or involvement in treatment.[55] In contrast to established models for the homeless that required treatment before housing, the Housing First model used a consumer choice and harm reduction philosophy that starts with meeting the physical needs of the homeless.[56]

This model for independent housing for homeless people with dual diagnosis was met with much resistance from the homeless provider industry, but it had significantly better outcomes than the dominant "treatment first" models practiced by virtually all housing programs at the time.[57] Although the homeless "experts" in the field said it would never work, today the Housing First model is recognized as a best evidence-based practice by the Substance Abuse and Mental Health Administration (SAMHSA). While Housing First program directors host occasional social events, such as birthday celebrations, the homeless in these programs have little incentive or opportunity to build their social capital. Social programs mimicking a Housing First model for recovery are needed.

SOCIAL RECOVERY: A PARADIGM SHIFT

Social Recovery is a model that focuses mainly on increasing social capital.[58] Social Recovery builds on two related concepts: (1) social capital and (2) recovery capital. Social capital, discussed in chapter 3, is defined as the social resources available to individuals within their communities and across social networks.[59] Social capital theory is used to explain the unequal distribution of social resources that can act as a barrier or help individuals to obtain desired goals.[60] Sociologist Robert Putnam popularized the theory by showing how engagement in social activities, such as bowling together with friends, increases social capital.[61] Conversely, as drug users lose their connection to family and friends and disengage in social activities, their social networks shrink until they are linked only to drug-using networks. Losing mainstream social capital, they become less integrated in conventional society.[62] Many are alienated when they stop drug use after leaving prison or treatment, and with few avenues to increase their social capital, they return to drug-using networks.

The concept of "recovery capital" was developed based on a correlation found between social capital and recovery from addiction.[63] Recovery capital is the sum of the resources that can be accessed through social relations and networks to sustain recovery and avoid returning to problematic drug use. Ironically, while recovery capital was originally developed as a process in "natural recovery,"[64] over time it became linked to participation in 12-step treatment.[65] However, treatment recovery networks often become insular. Introduction to new social networks is critical for sustained recovery, but treatment programs usually do not link people to new social networks beyond recovery networks. For example, a recent study focused on network dynamics of recovery capital among drug treatment participants found that while the treatment strategies were very successful at severing ties to old networks, they were not adept at fostering ties to new positive social networks in the community.[66] Their findings show the need for more effort to be placed on linking treatment participants to mainstream networks centered on meaningful activities outside the treatment environment.[67] Social Recovery focuses exclusively on the social environment with an emphasis on *new* network building.

The Social Recovery model returns to the theoretical foundation of recovery capital.[68] It places primary emphasis on increasing recovery capital by facilitating links to positive social networks that go beyond 12-step or other recovery networks. Facilitating access to new social networks is the premise of social capital building.[69] Treatment recovery groups such as 12-step can unintentionally hinder access to new social networks by providing strong social support within the recovering network and discouraging contact with others. For example, people in recovery are warned not to socialize with any network that includes drinking alcohol, which eliminates most social clubs and social activities. Without social capital at the right time and right place, people are likely to relapse when faced with the same issues that led to problematic drug use. Social Recovery goes beyond recovery capital. Whereas recovery capital refers to the combined social, physical, human, and cultural capital available to a recovering person, Social Recovery *facilitates the process of acquiring* the skills, resources, and networks that enhance people's ability to live in society without resorting to problematic substance use.[70] This means interacting in the real world.

Treatment philosophy tells the person who is dependent on drugs "you need to want to change," and many who seek treatment do succeed, but only for a short time. Once they step back into the real world, the problems that were so overwhelming are still there. As they become aware of the barriers they face and the lack of opportunities to overcome them, they become trapped in feelings of shame and despair.[71] A Social Recovery approach directs attention to the social environment with a primary focus on human interaction. It places less emphasis on individual behavioral change and more on the social and relational processes of recovery within mainstream society.

As discussed previously, diverse paths are needed for different problem issues. Some individuals require comprehensive medical or mental health treatment along with Social Recovery. Others need Social Recovery to learn to enjoy life in conventional society. A few need more substantial support.

Social Recovery can be implemented at every level of social interaction. It can be used at the individual level to help a friend or a loved one enjoy activities other than drug use. Schools, churches, clubs, or social-minded organizations can organize Social Recovery initiatives at the community level. Treatment program directors can incorporate Social Recovery as a component of their program with a greater focus on activities outside recovery groups. A Social Recovery model does not need to be approved first by politicians or doctors. Social Recovery is not a drug substitute or an alternative drug program—it's a paradigm shift in recovery that can activate a movement.[72]

HARRY DOES SOCIAL RECOVERY

Harry's life started to revolve more and more around the community college where he attended classes and worked. His new hobby in ceramics was like art therapy, healing his mind and comforting his soul.[73] I often called Harry in the evening to hear he was working with some clay on the porch while talking to mothers sitting on their porches nearby as they watched their children playing in the streets.

The community college professors seemed to like Harry and he received excellent recommendations, which helped him get the best work-study positions as a student assistant. First he took an assistantship with one of his professors in the computer lab. The job was mostly answering phones and paperwork at a desk. While he learned to use Word and Excel programs, he was alone most of the time, and having been in the hole for so many years, he wanted to be around people now. When he heard about a work-study position in the library, he applied for it and got the job.

Harry really enjoyed working in the library, but mostly he enjoyed talking with people. Often his job involved sitting at the entrance checking IDs, and he learned the names and faces of everyone who came to the library. He referred to them by name and often chatted with them pleasantly. His colleagues accepted him despite his colorful history, which he did not try to hide. The Community College of Philadelphia was full of people with problematic histories. Few students, however, were ex-felons nearing 60. However, Harry's nonjudgmental, easygoing nature made him a friend of everyone. He was thriving with the social attention, but on weekends he had nowhere to go but to Debbie's house, to visit the family of his former prison buddy, Justin.

Harry continued making good grades in all his classes, never failing a class. He began to have more faith in his abilities and took more strenuous courses. He enrolled in a course in sociology and made an A, which he said was easy because it was everything about his life. He took a course in addiction studies and became friendly with the professor, who was intimately familiar with recovery issues.

We both experienced personal grief upon learning that our mother had died. Harry was especially affected by this news because he had not seen her since his last release from prison. Although we were prepared, knowing her health was deteriorating, when she finally passed away, Harry was shaken. I expected his drug use to increase, and we talked often about controlling it. He appeared to be able to maintain control and did not miss any classes except when attending the funeral.

Our mother was buried with our father in Tennessee in the Veterans Memorial Cemetery. I sent Harry a ticket for a train. He could not take a plane since he had no license and no picture ID except for his student card, which the TSA security would not accept. Harry stayed at my house before and after the funeral. He was a perfect guest. He ate what we prepared since my husband and I were also vegetarian. Although I did not ask him to do so, he always made his bed in the morning and cleaned up after himself. I had to leave him alone all day while I worked, and he had no indicators of being intoxicated or high when I came home in the evening.

My husband brewed beer as a hobby, and we had a beer kegerator in the basement with two taps pouring homebrew. I told Harry he could get a beer whenever he wanted, knowing he would not take advantage of the situation. One evening Harry asked if I could take him to the store to get a bottle of whiskey. "But you can have anything you like in our liquor cabinet," I said. "No," he explained, "that stuff is expensive. Your husband might be saving it for company."

Harry was especially loved by my four-year-old grandson, who had more energy than most adults could handle. Harry never tired of playing with him. He drew pictures with him, read him books, listened to his stories, and taught him how to set up the chessboard pieces. I never saw my grandson sit as quietly as when Harry explained what each chess piece could do and how to move them around. Harry stayed in the room where my grandson usually stayed if he slept overnight, and when Harry left, my grandson told me, "I don't want anyone else to use my room again but Uncle Harry."

One night I suggested we go to a dance. My friend Tammy enjoyed contra dancing and asked me to join her for a local contra dancing event. Contra dancers have a particular way of dancing that neither Harry nor I could do, but it was considered good clean fun for middle-aged people who do not feel comfortable in the contemporary club scene. I thought Harry might like the social aspect of the dance. He was up to doing anything I suggested, as long as I came along. I had just arrived home from work when Tammy arrived, so I suggested Harry go with her and I could walk to the dance later.

When I arrived about an hour later, I found the community gym, where the dance was held, packed with swirling dancers in colorful clothes. But I could not find Harry. Tammy said she had not seen him for a while. Looking outside to see if Harry stepped out for a smoke, I found him leaning against the wall of the brick building, looking like a classic Clint Eastwood—a tall, thin, solitary man with a gaunt, experience-lined face—pulling a drag from his hand-rolled cigarette. He held the tiny butt in his characteristic way, between thumb and first finger, cupped in the palm of his hand. It fit his character well.

"Don't you like the dance?" I asked, coming from behind.

"Well, it's not really my thing, you know. I don't know anyone," he responded, looking genuinely happy to see me. "But now that you are here, maybe it will be better."

"Yeah, well, I don't like it either," I said. "Why don't we go around the corner to my favorite pub."

His face lit up like a child on Christmas morning getting the present he secretly desired. "Really?" he exclaimed. "Yeah, that sounds great."

We went to the Brick Store Pub, a trendy establishment that sold craft beers from micro breweries. Sitting at the bar, Harry took a German beer and I had my favorite IPA. Since we were walking home, we had a few pints. Time passed slowly, as if we had all the time in the world. The familiar, cozy atmosphere of the Brick Store Pub made me feel like everything was all right, and life would be fine in the future. The polished wood bar, shaped like a deep horseshoe, allowed me to see my friends sitting in our favorite spot at the corner of the bar. I waved and they acknowledged me back. The amiable bartender was keeping everyone happy, offering respite from a hard day of work with a smile and a chat. And Harry, my beloved brother, was here having a beer with me. A great beer in the right setting has a way of smoothing the rough edges of reality.

"I always have this sense of loneliness—alienation, or anomie as I learned they call it in sociology," Harry said, interrupting my utopian reverie. "I mean the professors at school talk with me, and the students—everyone is nice to me and seems to enjoy my company at school. But I can't imagine any of them asking me to hang out in the evening, you know. I just don't fit in."

"It'll take time," I said. "When you're done with college, we can look for a place here for you, so you can be nearer to your family." I also experienced the feeling of not fitting in for many years, but I wanted to offer hope, not despair.

Harry looked up and flashed his great smile. I was so glad he had a set of dentures, because his smile made a world of difference. It changed a brooding Clint Eastwood look into a more charming Christopher Walken.

"Don't feel bad for me," he interjected. "I go to Debbie's home most weekends, but it's outside Philly and I am not supposed to go without putting in a request to my probation officer. She always treats me like family. But, you know, I could enjoy coming here to the Brick Store Pub after work. Meet you here. Have a few beers with you and your friends over there."

"Everyone fits in at the Brick Store," I answered. "And you can join us. Once you graduate and move down here, we can enjoy a beer at this pub every evening."

Back in Philadelphia, it was time for Harry to decide on a major officially. I suggested an associate degree in culinary arts, but he reminded me that he is a vegetarian and has been for 40 years. He did not think he would be able to cut up and prepare meat very well. I agreed. Harry said he enjoyed the addiction classes. Not only was it easy for him, having been required to participate in numerous addiction programs both in prison and at every release, but also he really liked his professor. The school offered an addiction counselor certificate and he was motivated, but I was not so sure the treatment providers would accept him.

"How can you be an addiction counselor if you drink alcohol and smoke marijuana every day?" I asked him, knowing that all treatment programs in the United States push abstinence only.

"Yeah, I thought about that," he replied. "I figured it won't hurt my work."

I laughed at this because he was probably right. Recently he told me that his supervisor at the library, who liked Harry very much, told him that one of the other workers said he always smelled like whisky.

"Yes, I guess I do. You see I carry around a flask of whiskey and take a sip now and then throughout the day," he replied sincerely. "It sort of eases my mind, you know. Does it affect my work?"

"No," she answered after a thoughtful pause. "I guess it doesn't." She never mentioned it again.

I figured it would not interfere with his work as a counselor either, as long as he controlled it. And I had proof he could do this. After I interviewed Harry for the pilot study, I started taking notes on his daily drug-using habits. One day Harry surprised me by saying he cut back on his drinking. The first time was in April 2009. I wrote this in my notes, because up until this point he thought his drinking did not interfere with his working and studying. Now he thought it did.

"It sort of makes me tired in the evening," he told me, "which is not very good when I have to do homework. Drinking too much in the evening also makes me a little groggy in the morning, and I have morning classes to attend."

My notes showed he cut his daily drinking in half during this time. Typically, he drank about four or five beers and three or four shots of whiskey during the day. On weekends, he drank more beer and about the same amount of whiskey. Since he started drinking in the morning, he never became intoxicated, but alcohol is a depressant and induces sleep. Needing to stay awake to study, he cut his daily alcohol intake in half. His marijuana intake remained about two or three tokes a day regardless of the day, but he never missed a day of school or work. I call this controlled use that is not problematic.

With his graduation drawing near, I began to look for a house to rent or buy for Harry in Atlanta. He was working on his addiction counselor certificate, and we discussed starting a boarding room house where he could live with other men and women who were trying to stop problematic use of hard drugs but might not have a problem with alcohol or marijuana. It would be what is called a "wet" home where moderate drinking was allowed.[74] Based on a Housing First model, no one would be kicked out of this home for smoking marijuana or having a few drinks. If it got out of control, we would work together to bring it under control through Social Recovery strategies.

I shared my ideas about Social Recovery with Harry, and he helped refine it by applying real life situations. We talked about the different activities the men and women might enjoy, such as going to slam poetry, taking art courses, joining a running group. Harry said to put ceramics classes on the list, since it had helped him so much. Harry registered for every ceramics class he could get. For one assignment, he made a bust of himself that was displayed in the library showcase where he worked. He had an interesting face to sculpt, with pronounced cheekbones, large eyes, and a high forehead.

Harry had reached a turning point. One evening he told me something I never thought I would hear.

"I think I might be able to do this, you know, living in the real world thing," he said. "At first I was doing it because it made you happy, and I had nothing else to do anyway. I was pretty sure I would be sent back, or be killed trying to run. I could not see me living long in society. But now, I can—and I like it. And I think I might make it out here after all."

The Community College of Philadelphia had changed Harry's life. Having a responsibility in mainstream society motivated him to stop hard drug use and to use alcohol and marijuana less frequently. This was the social control mechanism that he was never allowed to have while being in prison and on parole. Now, for the first time in 40 years, he saw a place for himself in society without having to be a criminal. He now had responsibility, routine activities, and a sense of identity within society—the mechanisms of social control.[75] Now for the first time, he had a dream of "conventional routes of social achievement," something he never had before.[76]

The mortgage foreclosure crisis was just starting to hit Atlanta hard about this time. The unintended consequence of this national economic disaster, called the "Great Recession," was more affordable home prices. I thought I might have enough money for a down payment on a foreclosed home for Harry when he graduated next semester and came to Atlanta. As a drug use ethnographer working in the field, I knew several people who were looking for inexpensive housing while they were trying to control their use or maintain sobriety. I spent many evenings talking with Harry and making plans for our recovery home.

"I was walking on Market Street the other day when some guy called me over. Turns out it was someone who had been in Wernersville with me, a

Black dude they call Snap," Harry told me on the phone with a hint of anxiety in his voice. "He was surprised to see me in Philly and asked for my address."

"Who is he?" I asked, a little worried myself, having met some of the people leaving the prison recovery home in Wernersville. "A friend from the halfway house?"

"Not really. I mean everyone's your buddy in prison, but I didn't know him at Camp Hill, just when I got to Wernersville." Harry continued. "But, I wanted to tell you, that dude is in some kind of trouble. Yesterday two angry dudes barged into my place looking for him. They didn't knock—just opened the door and went through the entire house. They made no effort to hide the guns they were carrying either."

"God, that's scary," I replied, feeling a sense of apprehension. "Please, don't hang out with that guy anymore."

"I don't plan on it," Harry said, pausing as he took a long drag from his cigarette. "And I do plan to get out of town this weekend—I'm going to Debbie's house."

Despite how well Harry was doing, the fact remained that Harry lived in what is called the inner city. This was not the gentrified Old City or Center City—the tourist destinations in Philadelphia. He lived in a real inner city where the poor and marginalized and mostly minority populations lived. Harry was one of the marginalized, and this neighborhood was the only place that accepted him. Although my beliefs, what some might call values, dictated that race should not be an issue in where Harry lived, the fact remained that Harry was the only White person within ten city blocks. Would I be thinking like a racist if I wanted to get him out of this neighborhood because he was the only White? Shouldn't all the marginalized have the opportunity to live in better neighborhoods regardless of their color? Yes, they should—but they don't. I cared deeply about that, but Harry was my brother. This little incident made me start looking in nicer neighborhoods for Harry's new home in Atlanta.[77]

IN CLOSING

Although an analysis of the War on Drugs was not one of the aims of the study on which this book is based, it was impossible to ignore its influence on the lives of the people who told their stories. The War on Drugs spread to become omnipresent in every facet of social life, corrupting the fabric of society and the social contract with authority. Rarely has one policy so powerfully infiltrated the structure of society and every social institution. It changed the "maturing out" of drug use, a verified social phenomenon, into the aberrant process of maturing into problematic drug use throughout a lifetime.

Baby boomers were young when the drug war was implemented and they allowed it to continue and expand. It is now their war. Not all baby boomers supported it, but their silence was interpreted as consent. It left a bleak social landscape of desolate communities, broken families, and ruined lives. For many, the drug war transformed the American dream into the American nightmare. It sucked the humanity out of medical, health, and social services that were designed as social safety nets to stop vulnerable lives from falling into deeper poverty.

The title of this book is the motif of the stories told—baby boomer drug users are hurting. Many were hurt before they started using drugs; others were hurt by society's response to drug use. In this book I included a wide range of baby boomer drug users from different categories of race, gender, socioeconomic status, and sexual orientation, as well as different drug use trajectories. Everyone should find someone to empathize with in this book. I ask that you stretch your empathy to include more. Use compassion to do something to change this situation. If you are a baby boomer, this is your legacy!

The drug war has become normalized, and the generations after the baby boomers never knew a time when the War on Drugs did not exist. This book adds to a growing body of work calling for an end to the war, a more just response to drug use, and more humane solutions to real drug problems. It is time to end the war and start reconstruction and recovery.

> "An invasion of armies can be resisted, but not an idea whose time has come."
>
> VICTOR HUGO

Epilogue

My head cocked to one side, reacting to the sounds coming from neighbors in one of the row houses down the street. Was it a fight or just a loud but friendly squabble between a man and his partner? None of my business, I thought with a sigh. I ran a hand through my thick hair, thanking my dad for his genes—he still had a full head of hair when he died in his eighties. I returned to my textbook, taking notes for homework due tomorrow.

I liked this neighborhood. I liked that mothers napped on porch chairs while their kids played on the streets. Men sat on doorsteps, 40s in hand, flicking dice and snapping up cash. Cars cruised up and down the streets slowly, windows lowered, music blaring, guys calling out to the pretty girls. At night, however, sometimes mothers hollered when their husbands stumbled home penniless and drunk. Children cried seeing their parents fight. And occasionally a passing car blasted gunfire instead of music.

My mind wandered off my book and notebook again, falling back into distant foggy memories of my own turbulent childhood. I knew what the neighbors were experiencing. In contrast to my 30 years in prison, where life is monotonous almost beyond what a human soul can handle, my childhood was unpredictable. In prison I knew that my confined state was not a conscious choice but a monotony that is thrust upon you with the knowledge that today will be the same tomorrow, and the next day, until release by parole or death.

But before the inertia that described my life, I had a family, a large family. They lived in neighborhoods just like this one, facing the same problems. A mother more interested in praying for her alcoholic husband than leaving him, sisters I felt responsible to protect but abandoned, and a father who spent more time in bars than at work. I understood what surviving childhood in poverty was all about. I felt at home here.

I returned to my textbook, rubbing my eyes. I never expected to be at an age when I had to wear reading glasses and resisted the need to use them. Instead I squinted to read the small print, a dead give-away that I was having a hard time seeing.

I was tempted to get the last bottle of Heineken I had saved in the refrigerator and call it a day, but I had to finish this for tomorrow. It was beginning to click—I saw the light at the end of the tunnel. It probably helped that I was no longer chained to powders and pills. I lit a joint and took two tiny puffs before carefully extinguishing it with my fingertips, browned from years of saving cigs for later. I placed it in the small Altoids mints tin I kept for used joints. Weed enhanced my focus, and within twenty minutes I finished the chapter and wrote my notes for class. I headed to the kitchen for the beer.

I heard the front door squeak as I was standing in the kitchen ready to open the bottle. The kitchen was at one end of a long hallway that led to the front door. Guessing my roommate had come home early, I went to the hallway to greet him when I saw someone come through the door I did not know. Shit, I thought, I should have locked the door.

The hammering whack, whack, whack, whack, whack, whack, whack of steel plummeted into my stomach—a few bullets hit my legs. I became aware of cold numbness and wet stickiness. Looking down, I saw blood gushing from my leg, and then my knees buckled. Two men were arguing as they passed by my body but I could not see them—I did not want to see them. I was facedown on the floor and stayed motionless. I heard more gunshots; none hit me.

Time passed slowly as their voices faded and I became more attuned to my heartbeat. Thump. Whish. Thump. Whish. I realized I was lying in a pool of blood still pouring out of my gut and leg. I started thinking of my mother and what I said when she was buried in the ground a few months ago. "I'll be with you soon."

The ambulance sirens snatched me violently out of my reverie and I felt powerful pain permeating throughout my body as they turned me over. I saw from their faces that it looked bad. "Call my sister," I said as they put me on the stretcher. "404-317-2581."

SEPTEMBER 8, 2009, *PHILADELPHIA DAILY NEWS*

A man was killed yesterday and another critically injured by gunfire inside a West Philadelphia boarding home, police said. Both men were shot multiple times about 3:30 p.m. on 62nd Street near Callowhill, police said. Medics on the scene pronounced a 34-year-old man dead at 3:42 p.m. The other man was taken to the Hospital of the University of Pennsylvania, where he was in critical but stable condition last night, police said.

OCTOBER 3, 2009, *PHILADELPHIA INQUIRER*

On Saturday, Harry Williams, 58, died of wounds suffered on September 7 at his residence in the 300 block of North 62d Street in West Philadelphia. In critical condition after the shooting, he remained at Hospital of the University of Pennsylvania, where he was pronounced dead at 11:42 a.m.

DECEMBER 6, 2012, PHILADELPHIA COUNTY
COURTHOUSE

The police said it was a drug deal. I told him Harry was never involved in drug dealing. They did not believe me. I told them about the thugs Harry mentioned, but they were not interested. I found a list of phone numbers and bullet casings in Harry's room after they finished their investigation, but they said they did not need them. All they wanted was Harry's phone. I found his phone at the hospital with his personal effects and turned it in.

Three years later, I heard Snap testify in court that Harry had nothing to do with the drug deal. He said he used Harry's house for a meeting between a drug dealer and Jarvis, the other man found dead in the house, because no one knew them in the neighborhood. Snap claimed he did not kill Harry and Jarvis, and he was not even there—he only arranged the meeting. He would not tell who the dealer was because his wife and child had been threatened. The jury did not believe him. Snap got life in prison without parole. The evidence was based primarily on pings from his phone and character assassination.

I asked the DA for Snap's file. When I read his rap sheet, I realized that Snap's life was much like my brother's. Snap was younger by twenty-three years, but like Harry he started abusing substances at a young age. He had a number of traumatic incidents as a child, and he suffered from depression. He had twenty arrests as a juvenile and was committed to juvenile reform institutions. Like my brother, being in a reformatory led to a life of crime. In and out of jail as an adult, he had no record of legal employment. Snap, a

Black male, was a victim of the New Jim Crow. My brother was not Black, but his life was very similar. And when I received Harry's death certificate in the mail, his race was listed as "Black."

"Indeed, I tremble for my country when I reflect that God is just."

—THOMAS JEFFERSON
(from Harry's prison notebook of quotes)

The Older Drug User Study Methodology

THE MIXED METHODS APPROACH

Research on drug trajectories is usually based on statistical analysis of large samples, while in-depth understanding of drug trajectories set in social and historical context is largely missing. To fill this research gap, I collaborated with a mathematician / data scientist to design a study on the life history and drug use trajectories of older adults. Our combined knowledge, experience, and skills produced an innovative mixed methods design to capture complex life history data. The National Institutes of Health (NIH), with support from the American Recovery and Reinvestment Act of 2009, funded the study, called the Older Drug User Study (ODUS).[1]

Three types of data were collected: ethnographic field data, in-depth life histories, and retrospective survey data. Respondents were recruited using ethnographic field methods.[2] Interviews were conducted in private or semi-private places in the field, and respondents were read a consent document and provided verbal approval, which was recorded. Interviews lasted between three to five hours on average, and respondents were paid a $40 stipend for their time. The university Institutional Review Board (IRB) approved the methods, and the study received a certificate of confidentiality (CoC) from the National Institute of Drug Abuse, which protected our study data and staff from court subpoena.

ETHNOGRAPHIC FIELDWORK AND RECRUITMENT

Ethnographic research requires the researcher to spend many hours each day in communities where drug users live and interact to become familiar with the settings and people.[3] Fieldwork often starts in known "natural settings" of drug use; however, in this study I also incorporate "relational ethnography" with a focus on the social relations of drug users.[4] I started ethnographic fieldwork by walking streets, talking to people, sitting in bars, pool halls, and all-night restaurants, and hanging out in places where drug use or drug dealing occurs. Once I developed "street cred" and trust, people introduced me to others in their social networks. I often spent entire days with the same people for months at a time.[5]

A range of urban, suburban, and rural neighborhoods were targeted throughout the study to ensure the inclusion of respondents from wealthy, middle-class, and marginalized communities. While all the fieldwork was conducted in the greater Metropolitan Atlanta area, respondents had lived in different geographic locations during their lives, mostly in the United States.

Other than meeting face-to-face during fieldwork, respondents were recruited with what is called snowball sampling and targeted sampling techniques.[6] Snowball sampling involved asking respondents to refer others to call me. If the people they referred qualified and participated in the study, the referrer received a small fee ($10).

Targeted sampling was used to recruit respondents from different social networks. Targeted sampling provided a mechanism that adjusts to the target population to obtain systematic information when true random sampling is not feasible and convenience sampling is not rigorous enough. I often hired someone as a "community consultant" to help with targeting efforts.[7] Sometimes called "key informants" I prefer to use the term consultants for people who are members of a drug-using community, since the term "informant" arouses suspicion. Community consultants fill a number of vital roles, such as facilitating introduction to drug-using networks, adding legitimacy to the research, explaining local norms and practices, and providing feedback on the validity or gaps in data-collection processes.[8]

A strategy that aided recruitment success involved passing out fliers and leaving small informational cards about the study in different locations, such as stores, bars, restaurants, methadone clinics, homeless shelters, and the only harm reduction center in Georgia. Fliers advertised the need for current or former drug users for a paid health study and included my cell phone number.

The community-based sample consisted of 100 respondents who were age 45 to 65, and included both active and former users of heroin, cocaine, crack, and / or methamphetamine. All used at least one of these drugs in the last 10 years, which means they used the drug past age 35, when they should have matured out of hard drug use. The inclusion of former users allowed for an investigation of life events and social circumstances surrounding cessation. The final sample was diverse in terms of age, race, ethnicity, and gender as well as socioeconomic status. The full sample included 60 male respondents, 39 females, and 1 transgender. The mean age at the time of the interview was 52 years old. Among them, 52 self-identified as Black / African American, 44 White, 2 Hispanic / Latino, and 2 identified as other.[9] Nine had been diagnosed with HIV, 3 had AIDS, and 36 had been diagnosed with hepatitis C. Sixty-seven people in the sample reported to have injected drugs at some point in their life. Sixteen had less than a high school diploma, 28 had a high school diploma or GED, 47 had some college, and 9 had a college or advanced degree.

ODUS DATA COLLECTION INSTRUMENTS

There were very few examples of life history data collection models that combined both qualitative and quantitative data collected for the entire life.[10] Most mixed methods collection involved collecting quantitative and qualitative data separately and combining results in various ways during the analysis.[11] Our study produced an innovative combined data collection technique based on lessons learned during pilot interviews. We began by using a Life History Matrix (see Table 1) that helped to frame the questions for the digitally recorded life history interview, and was updated with new information as the in-depth interview was recorded. This was followed by a computer-assisted survey to collect the demographics and drug history data. I pilot-tested the first interview with my brother, Harry.

During the first part of the interview with Harry, we worked together to figure out when he first went to a reformatory, when he was in jail, when he lived at home, and other important dates in his life. Since I knew much of Harry's story, I helped him recall events and time periods based on where we moved that year or who was president. When we began the survey part of the interview, I realized I was not capturing important details about his life because only the "qualitative" part of the data collection was audio-recorded and not the quantitative part. He often told stories to elaborate on his survey responses. I tried to capture this on the paper life history matrix where I had scribbled dates and notes, but it became a mess of erased pencil markings and smudges. This experience prompted me to restructure the interview process for a more authentic and compelling life history. A timeline and a few memory tools were added to verify the data—not because people lie but because they forget exact dates. Perhaps the most significant innovation that emerged from Harry's pilot interview was the realization that one interviewer was not enough to collect a comprehensive life history.[12]

My co-investigator, the mathematician / data scientist, was conducive to innovation, but he worked with abstract numbers and had never collected data in a face-to-face interview. I invited him to come with me during an interview, and after observing the process, he redesigned the computer-assisted survey instrument to allow a more flexible data collection.[13]

Three critical data collection innovations were developed: (1) a unique computer-assisted survey of yearly data modules that could be accessed for data input or correction at any time during the interview; (2) flexibility to collect qualitative and quantitative data that follow the flow of the interview process; (3) a collaborative interviewing process comprising two trained interviewers with specific roles and responsibilities for each individual interviewer.

TABLE I Life History and Turning Points Matrix # ____

Age:____ Race:____ Sex:____

Age													
Date													
Substance													
Use													
Drug Roles													
Treatment History													
Residence													
Family Roles													
Work Roles													
Criminal Justice													
Involvement													
Partners													

QUANTITATIVE DATA

Using a computer-assisted personal interview program (CAPI) uniquely developed for the ODUS, the quantitative data were collected and stored in two data sets called the "DEMOGRAPHIC 30 DAY" data set and the "YEARLY" data set.

The demographics of the respondents (age, race, gender) were collected using the DEMOGRAPHIC 30 DAY survey, which included questions on recent (past 30-day) work, residence, income, and other variables that constitute socioeconomic status (SES). The DEMOGRAPHIC 30 DAY survey also collected past 30-day drug use and current HIV / AIDS and HCV status. The DEMOGRAPHIC 30 DAY data set included 246 variables. The unit of analysis in the DEMOGRAPHIC 30 DAY data set is the respondent, identified with a unique ID number.

Once the demographics and past 30-day data were collected, this module was closed and the respondents were asked questions on their entire life history using the YEARLY survey. This survey included as many "yearly modules" as the years in the respondent's life. Each year included the same questions on residence, family, work, relationships, health, education, criminal justice involvement, drug use by type of drug, frequency of use, route of administration, drug treatment, sexual history, and risk behaviors. Opening a new YEARLY survey for every year of the respondent's life allowed us to ask identical questions for every year. Skip patterns were programmed into the software to skip entire sections of the year if they were not relative to the year. For example, a question first asked if any drugs were used in that year, and if not, all drug use questions were automatically skipped. If something was missed or a mistake was caught later in the interview, it was easy to open that specific year to fix it. The YEARLY data set comprised 308 variables for *every year* of the respondent's life. The unit of analysis in the YEARLY data set is PERSON-YEAR.[14]

QUALITATIVE DATA

The qualitative part of the interview consisted of the life history matrix and in-depth life history. The life history matrix was used to set the stage and facilitate the recall of specific events and specific time periods regarding drug use and social context over the life course. The matrix also informed the data collection during the interview and was referred to during the survey. The semi-structured interview guide included questions on social, economic, behavioral, and health details surrounding childhood, adolescent, young adult, and adult stages in life. The semi-structured interview guide was referred to only when needed, since the questions were well known by the trained interviewers. Specific transitions and turning points identified on the matrix were discussed in more detail and embedded in social, historical, and political context during the qualitative interview. A timeline (see Table 2) was used to provide respondents with memory cues and an historical context in which to place events in their lives.[15]

INTERVIEWING AS ART

The order of the data collection did not matter as much as the flow of the process and the interaction between the interviewers and respondent. For example, if I already knew the respondent from previous communication in the field, I might start with the in-depth interview, since I had already established rapport. But if I just met the respondent, or the respondent seemed hesitant to talk about personal

TABLE 2 Timeline

1945	Atomic bomb dropped on Hiroshima
1950	1st credit card
1950	Lavender Scare—purge of gay men and women from military and government jobs supported by discriminatory Senate report
1951	1st color TV
1952	APA (American Psychological Association) lists homosexuality as a sociopathic personality disorder
1954	1st civil rights movement begins
1955	Montgomery bus boycott
1954	*Brown v. Board of Education*, desegregation of schools
1957	Sputnik 1 launched
1960	Civil Rights Act signed into law
1960	Kennedy becomes president
1961	Berlin Wall built
1962	United States enters Vietnam
1962	Supreme Court declares addiction to be a disease, not a crime
1963	President Kennedy assassinated
1964	Civil Rights Act of 1964
1964	Methadone maintenance introduced
1965	Malcolm X assassinated; Bloody Sunday

TEEN/YOUNG ADULT

1968	Civil Rights Act of 1968
1968	Robert F. Kennedy and Martin Luther King Jr. assassinated
1969	Stonewall Inn riot in Greenwich Village
1969	Federal Hate Crime Law
1969	Woodstock Festival (summer)
1969	Altamont Rock Festival (winter)

YOUNG ADULT/MIDDLE ADULT YEARS

1970	Comprehensive Drug Abuse and Control Act
1971	War on Drugs declared by President Nixon
1972	Tuskegee Study ends
1973	US leaves Vietnam
1973	APA removes homosexuality from the DSM
1973	DEA (Drug Enforcement Administration) created
1974	Nixon resigns
1976	Jimmy Carter elected president
1977	Voyager launched
1978	Jamestown suicides

1979	3 Mile Island
1980	Reagan administration introduces "Just Say No" and D. A. R. E.
1981	President Reagan breaks air traffic controllers' strike
1981	First music video shown on MTV
1981	First US AIDS case reported, called GRID (Gay-Related Immunodeficiency Disorder)
1983	Microsoft Word released; Japan Nintendo
1984	Mac APPLE invented
1984	Privatization of prisons
1984	Mandatory Federal Sentencing
1985	Reagan ramps up War on Drugs
1986	Iran-Contra, CIA using cocaine money
1986	Reagan signs Anti–Drug Abuse Act
1987	Black Monday on stock market
1989	Office of National Drug Control Policy
1990	Ryan White Care Act signed
1991	World Wide Web debut to public
1992	LA Riots—Rodney King
1993	World Trade Center bombing
1993	Don't Ask, Don't Tell policy

MIDDLE AGE/OLDER YEARS

1994	"3 Strikes and You're Out" laws begin
1994	North American Free Trade Agreement (NAFTA)
1995	World Trade Organization established
1996	President Clinton signs DOMA (Defense of Marriage Act)
1998	eBay founded, Google founded
2000	Bush defeats Gore
2000	Comprehensive Methamphetamine Control Act
2001	9/11
2002	No Child Left Behind Act signed
2003	Crash of shuttle Columbia
2004	Massachusetts recognizes gay marriage
2005	Combat Methamphetamine Epidemic Act
2008	Obama elected president

matters, I would start with the survey, which was more objective and standardized. Sometimes I would switch from one to the other when the respondent seemed to really want to talk about an event brought up in the survey.

The entire interview process was digitally recorded from the reading of the consent form. Transcribers were trained to transcribe all conversations or narratives that were not a direct response to a closed-ended survey question. For example, if the respondent described a certain kind of treatment program when answering the CAPI survey question on how many times she was in treatment that year, the description would be transcribed. The recordings were also used during quality control of the data when needed to verify or correct a response in the survey data.

COLLABORATIVE INTERVIEWING

Each interview was conducted by two highly trained interviewers; one responsible for the quantitative data and the other primarily for the qualitative data. As one interviewer collected either qualitative or quantitative data, the other filled in the matrix, checked the timeline, and took extensive notes. Typically, at least one of the two had already met the respondent and would conduct the in-depth interview, which required more trust and rapport between the interviewer and respondent than when collecting the survey data. Sometimes we matched demographics (such as a female interviewer conducting the in-depth part with a female respondent) although this could change by situation. The interviewer not responsible for conducting the in-depth interview took copious notes to help prepare for the survey collection, and the interviewer not conducting the survey would use the notes and timeline to check for any inconsistencies (or vice versa). A few times the survey and in-depth interview occurred simultaneously when the interview process took on a life of its own.[16]

The complexity of the data required a comprehensive and time-consuming interaction, but we did not want to tire our respondents or negatively impact the validity of the data by its length. We took breaks for refreshment or restroom visits and were respectful of respondents' time. However, we found that respondents seldom tired of talking about their life.

All of the data collection materials were openly shared with respondents during the interview, and they were offered copies of the matrix, timeline, and interview guide if requested. Often respondents looked at the timeline along with the matrix so they could figure out the exact year. Sometimes respondents asked for a date to be changed as they recalled events in more detail. The change was recorded and corrections made on the matrix. If changes needed to be made on the survey, the ODUS survey computer program allowed us to easily pull up the year, affirm validity, or make corrections as needed.

While collaborative ethnography has been shown to improve data collection and findings, as well as help make the time in the field safer, little has been written about collaborative interviewing.[17] Our colleagues questioned whether having two interviewers might intimidate the one respondent; however, respondents expressed gratitude that two people listened to them so intently and were determined to get every detail correct. Instead of being offended or embarrassed when an inconsistent response was caught, respondents were happy that we were so interested in their lives.

In many cases, they felt a bond to us that was unusual for such a brief acquaintance. Some told us emotionally that no one had ever paid so much attention to them or listened to their entire story without judgment. Others said they felt it was a healing process for them to merely recollect things they never told anyone, and it relieved their sense of shame as we discovered structural influences on their lives together.

QUALITY CONTROL

The entire interview process, including both the quantitative and qualitative components, was digitally recorded. Within a week after each interview, the team of researchers met in a conference room with copies of the life history matrices, interviewer notes, and transcripts for each interview conducted in the previous week. Using an overhead projector, the quantitative survey data, downloaded into an SPSS spreadsheet, was displayed on a large screen as we looked for gaps and inconsistencies across years. The SPSS data had previously been quality controlled for statistical inconsistencies, and first these inconsistencies were discussed and corrected. We also visually looked for nonstatistical inconsistencies or mistakes.

Quality control incorporated using all the data collected (ethnographic field notes, matrices interviewer notes, surveys, transcripts, memos), and cross-checking between these data sources in an iterative process. The recording was consulted if the solutions were not found in other sources. Consensual validity was reached through negotiated validity, wherein team members achieved consensus through persuasive and supported argument.[18] In some cases the respondent was consulted to help clarify the discrepancy.

DATA VISUALIZATION IMAGES

Another methodological innovation emerging from this study was the development of data visualization images (DVIs), created to see what the data were showing regarding drug trajectories. The data visualization images exhibit binary variables, such as drug use and other social variables collected on each respondent. The data is imaged as a color-coded matrix, with a column representing a given year of the respondent's life and a row representing a trajectory for a given variable over the life of the individual. For every cell, the two possible values of the binary variable are color-encoded as light (empty) or dark (shaded) cell. For example, in the case of drug use variables, a dark cell represents use and a light cell represents no use for a given year.

The point of the DVI is to be able to view as much data as possible, aligned by year. The variable values were simplified to provide a succinct image of the respondents' life over time and the potential relationships between the selected variables.

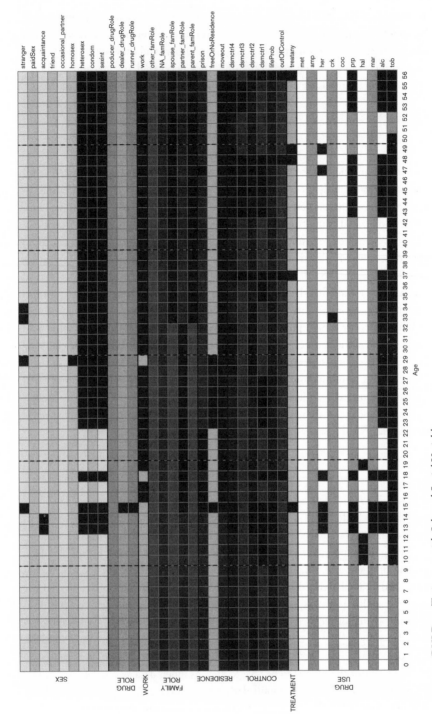

FIGURE 1. DVI Drug Trajectory with Selected Social Variables

TABLE 3 Legend for Data Visualization Images

	DVI Row label	Shaded if variable is...
SEX	stranger	'yes, a stranger'
	paidSex	'yes, paying or paid sex partner'
	acquaintance	'yes, an acquaintance'
	friend	'yes, a friend'
	occasional_ partner	'yes, occasional partner'
	homosex	If male and sextype_2='yes, male sex with male', or If male and sextype_3='yes, female sex with female'
	heterosex	'yes, heterosexual'
	condom	'Sometimes' or 'Never'
	sexint	'Yes'
DRUG ROLE	producer_ drugRole	'yes, Produce drugs'
	dealer_ drugRole	'yes, Dealer'
	runner_ drugRole	'yes, Runner'
WORK	work	If not the following: 'N/A (did not start working yet)' 'Unemployed, not seeking work' 'Looking for work' 'Disabled, not working'
FAMILY ROLE	other_ famRole	'yes, some other role'
	NA_ famRole	'yes, N/A'
	spouse_ famRole	'yes, spouse'
	partner_ famRole	'yes, partner'
	parent_ famRole	'yes, father or mother'

(continued)

TABLE 3 *(continued)*

	DVI Row label	*Shaded if variable is. . .*
RESIDENCE	prison	'Yes'
	freeOrNo-Residence	'Live in someone's home for free', 'Government paid home', 'Homeless on street', 'Shelter', or 'Prison'
	moveout	Shaded from moveout year (meaning the respondent moved out from his/her original home that year). All subsequent years will be shaded even if the respondent moved back home.
CONTROL	dsmctrl4	'Yes, had to take more drugs to get same effect'
	dsmctrl3	'Yes, often wanted to cut down on or control your drug use but couldn't'
	dsmctrl2	'Yes, used larger amounts of drugs or used drugs for a longer period of time than intended'
	dsmctrl1	'Yes, spent a great deal of time using drugs, getting drugs or getting over its effects'
	lifeProb	'Often' or 'Always'
	outOfControl	'Often' or 'Always'
TREATMENT	treatany	'Any type of 12-Step program' or 'Other'
DRUG USE	met	'yes, used methamphetamine'
	amp	'yes, used amphetamines'
	her	'yes, used heroin'
	crk	'yes, used crack'
	coc	'yes, used cocaine'
	prp	'yes, used prescription pills'
	hal	'yes, used hallucinogens/LSD/ecstasy/club drugs'
	mar	'yes, used marijuana'
	alc	'yes, used alcohol'
	tob	'yes, used tobacco'

We abridged the information provided in the quantitative data into a single binary variable for each year. For the purposes of examining life stories, the DVI offers a brief visual overview for contrasting drug use trajectories with other variables of interest over the life course. This information was useful to guide the qualitative exploration of drug use, transitions, turning points, behaviors, and social context of drug use over the life course. Any variables in the data set may be added to the DVI, but using all variables would make the image unwieldy. Figure 1 shows a DVI representing drug use and other selected variables for respondent #24.[19] Table 3 shows the legend for the DVI.

INTEGRATING DVI TRAJECTORIES WITH LIFE STORIES

The graphs produced by quantitative numerical data provided an overview of an individual's life, but they were used mainly to study drug trajectories. The DVIs showed discontinuous drug use trajectories for the majority of respondents, with large gaps between use periods. Using different social variables on the DVI for comparison, we could see what else was happening in the respondent's life that might be influencing use, cessation, or relapse. Triangulating the DVI with transcript data provided greater insight. For example, the DVI shown in Figure 1 indicates that #24 stopped using heroin and prescription pills for over 20 years, but it does not provide insights on why he used heroin for a few years in his late forties and why he is using prescription pills illegally now. The social context of his specific turning points and transitions were examined more in-depth in his life history matrix, transcript (life story), field notes, and interviewer notes. All data sources were triangulated to become familiar with the life course of every person in the study, enhancing the exploration of transitions, trajectories, and other details in their lives.

CODING

The ODUS study included 100 qualitative interview transcripts ranging from 20 to 70 pages long. Over the three years of data collection and quality control, all transcript data were read, coded, and recoded by team members.[20] Coding ODUS data consisted of three phases. First, all transcripts were coded by at least two coders. The team hand-coded the first few interviews using the constant comparison method commonly employed in grounded theory.[21] Next, transcripts were entered into a computer program, QSR NVivo, used for storing, managing, and coding the qualitative data. NVivo facilitated the coding and the development of themes identified as "nodes" in NVivo.[22]

At least two researchers coded every transcript in NVivo using a coding list of themes that included 13 main areas related to historical context, social context, personal issues, drug trajectories, criminal justice, and health. Dozens of subnodes referenced thousands of comments from respondents. These comments could be instantly retrieved for any theme and cross-referenced to compare by age, gender, race, or other variables.[23]

ANALYSIS FOR THIS BOOK

I analyzed all data for this book, which was a lonely endeavor until I became so absorbed in the baby boomers' stories it seemed as if we were living our lives together. First, I read and reread each transcript many times, and once I gave them pseudonyms, I began calling them by these names in my mind and during conversations with my research muses.

In addition to reexamining all the sources of data and reviewing all interview data coded in NVivo, I hand-coded the transcripts of the individuals discussed in this book. I started with all the interviews I had conducted or met personally. Only one transcript was a person I had not met personally but was included here because he was one of the eight respondents who had no criminal justice record (discussed in chapter 4). I then coded the 38 interview transcripts in NVivo and developed 45 new main codes and 36 subcodes, which organized the themes of the book chapters. Field notes and interview notes were included in this coding process.

With the 38 interviews as the foundation, I compared my coding with the coding conducted by the team on the full sample of 100 transcripts to be sure I was not missing any important influences on drug trajectories, historical or social context details, or personal life issues that were not represented in my coding. I found no new data to include.[24]

Quotes used in the preceding chapters are presented as spoken without editing. Three periods signify a natural pause in their talk or where a section of the quote was deleted for the sake of brevity, when it did not distract from or interfere with the intended meaning. I inserted words in brackets to define a term, explain the context, or replace a town or name to ensure confidentiality. Pauses in parentheses indicate natural long pauses. All names are pseudonyms.

The DVIs helped me to choose the respondents to focus on who best illustrated the themes in each chapter, and increased validity through cross-checking the information in the DVI trajectories with my coding. Their lives presented in this book are characteristic of other respondents who were not included in order to keep this book at a readable length. These were very difficult decisions to make, but I know that those who did not appear in this book will be discussed in future writings based on this rich life history study.

INTRODUCTION

1. The methodological details of the study's data collection and analysis are found in the Appendix.

2. Hirsch, "Confidential Informants."

3. Haney, "A Culture of Harm."

4. Ibid.

5. McCaffrey, Keynote Address, Opening Plenary Session, National Conference on Drug Abuse Prevention Research.

6. In 2014, 50 percent of federal prisoners were serving time for drug offenses; see Carson, *Prisoners in 2014*. From 1993 to 2009, nearly one-third of total state prison admissions were for drug crimes; see Rothwell, "Drug Offenders in American Prisons."

7. International agreements such as the Single Convention on Narcotic Drugs of 1961, the Convention on Psychotropic Substances of 1971, and the UN Convention against Illicit Traffic in Narcotic Drugs and Psychotropic Substances of 1988 impacted drug policy worldwide.

8. See Greenwald, "Drug Decriminalization in Portugal."

9. Although the chapters on race, gender, and age are distinct, they are viewed as "reciprocally constructing phenomena that in turn shape complex social inequalities"; see Collins, "Intersectionality's Definitional Dilemmas," 2.

10. I use capital letters for the War on Drugs since it is an officially declared war.

11. Gray, *Why Our Drug Laws Have Failed*. Some would argue that the War on Drugs succeeded in its main intent to control Black populations; see Alexander, *The New Jim Crow*.

12. According to the US Bureau of Census, the years of birth for baby boomers are 1946 to 1964, although some research uses 1945 to 1965; see Keister and Deeb-Sossa, "Are Baby Boomers Richer Than Their Parents?"

13. Charles Winick's "maturing out" thesis was based on heroin addicts; see Winick. "Maturing Out of Narcotic Addiction." When subsequent studies

confirmed Winick's thesis, it became known as the "maturing out hypothesis"; see Waldorf and Biernacki, "Natural Recovery from Heroin Addiction."

14. Winick, "Maturing Out of Narcotic Addiction"; Prins, *Maturing Out.*

15. Surveys collected annually in research funded by the Substance Abuse and Mental Health Services Administration (SAMHSA) are the primary sources of information on the extent of illicit drug, alcohol, and tobacco use in the civilian, noninstitutionalized population of the United States aged 12 years old or older. This longitudinal study was known as the *National Household Survey on Drug Abuse* (NHSDA) until 2002, when the name changed to *National Survey of Drug Use and Health* (NSDUH). Although the data collection methods changed over the years, the longitudinal data can be used to identify trends by age group over time.

16. Blow, "Substance Abuse among Baby Boomers"; Korper and Raskin, "The Impact of Substance Use and Abuse by the Elderly."

17. See trend data results reported in Substance Abuse and Mental Health Services Administration: *Summary of Findings from the 1998 National Household Survey on Drug Abuse; Summary of Findings from the 1999 National Household Survey on Drug Abuse.*

18. Substance Abuse and Mental Health Services Administration: *Results from the 2003 National Survey on Drug Use and Health; Results from the 2006 National Survey on Drug Use and Health National Findings; Results from the 2010 National Survey on Drug Use and Health: Summary of National Findings; The DASIS Report: Adults Aged 65 or Older in Substance Abuse Treatment.*

19. Boeri et al., "Reconceptualizing Early and Late Onset"; Cepeda et al., "Trajectories of Aging Long-Term Mexican American Heroin Injectors."

20. Inciardi, *The War on Drugs IV.*

21. Gray, *Why Our Drug Laws Have Failed.*

22. Alexander, *The New Jim Crow*; Duke, "Mass Imprisonment, Crime Rates, and the Drug War"; Contreras, *The Stickup Kids;* Duck, *No Way Out;* Goffman, *On the Run;* Hart, *High Price;* Pattillo et al., *Imprisoning America.*

23. Gray, *Why Our Drug Laws Have Failed;* Inciardi, *The War on Drugs IV.* "Of the 1,561,231 arrests for drug law violations in 2014, 83.1% (1,297,384) were for possession of a controlled substance." This is an increased in arrests for possession from the previous 15 years. See "Crime in the United States 2014—Arrests," *FBI Uniform Crime Report,* September 2015, Washington, DC: US Department of Justice. Retrieved from http://drugwarfacts.org/cms/?q = node/34#sthash.PwlvKYtQ.dpuf

24. Global Commission on Drug Policy, *Taking Control.*

25. National Center for Health Statistics, Centers for Disease Control and Prevention. Retrieved from www.cdc.gov/nchs/fastats/accidental-injury.htm

26. Scholars argue that the underlying motivation for the War on Drugs was to control the Black population; see Alexander, *The New Jim Crow.*

27. According to *Merriam-Webster's Dictionary*, a "civil war" is "a war between opposing groups of citizens of the same country." I refer to the War on Drugs as a "civil war" because it is a war fought by US citizens against other US citizens.

28. Smith, "Women's Perspective as a Radical Critique of Sociology."

29. See Appendix for more details of the methods, sample description, and analysis used in the study.

30. Only Harry was interviewed in Philadelphia as part of the pilot testing for this study.

31. Names as well as places and towns are changed to protect identities of respondents. If states are changed they are in the same region to account for differences in geographic trends in drug use. The location where the study took place—Atlanta, Georgia—is not changed in the narratives; however, counties are replaced for increased anonymity. Some details that might identify a person, such as profession or number of children, are modified without changing the context of the story.

32. Urban ethnographer Matthew Desmond described ethnography as "what you do when you try to understand people by allowing their lives to mold your own as fully and genuinely as possible." Desmond, "Relational Ethnography," 563.

33. For a description of ethnographic drug research, see Page and Singer, *Comprehending Drug Use.*

34. For discussions of qualitative research, see Agar, *The Professional Stranger;* Creswell, *Research Design;* Strauss and Corbin, *Basics of Qualitative Research.*

35. Atkinson, *The Life Story Interview as a Bridge in Narrative Inquiry;* Maines, "Narrative's Moment and Sociology's Phenomena."

36. See Elder, "Time, Human Agency, and Social Change." For the seminal work on how life course was used to examine the effects of policy on a generation see Elder, *Children of the Great Depression.* For a contemporary work on a life course study of older men, see Laub and Sampson, *Shared Beginnings, Divergent Lives.*

37. Sociologist C. Wright Mills was one of the first to explain the relationship between biography, history, and social structure, showing the importance of understanding how society shapes individual lives; see Mills, *The Sociological Imagination.*

38. Alexander, *The New Jim Crow.*

39. I use the term Black to be more inclusive, and it was usually the term used by respondents. However, I use African American when respondents use this term instead.

40. Austin and Irwin, *It's about Time.*

41. Boeri et al., "Conceptualizing Social Recovery."

1. THE HISTORICAL AND SOCIAL CONTEXT

1. See details of study design and instruments in the Appendix.

2. Developmental models describe an "unfolding" or evolutionary process of age-graded activity that increases over time; see Moffitt, "Adolescence-Limited and Life-Course-Persistent Antisocial Behavior." In contrast, the baby boomers in this study show disrupted and discontinuous trajectories of drug use and crime throughout their lives. For an in-depth discussion of discontinuity in life trajectories, see Laub and Sampson, *Shared Beginnings, Divergent Lives.*

3. Turning points are processes that occur over time embedded in social context, often with identifiable triggering events, as seen in Ted's story.

4. Although I did not need to verify Ted's story for the purposes of this study, I felt compelled to verify the story for readers of this book and found newspaper articles online that validated specific details of his family tragedy.

5. National Center for Health Statistics, Vital Statistics of the United States, and National Vital Statistics Reports (NVSR). Retrieved from www.cdc.gov/nchs /nvss.htm

6. For an historical overview of crime in this period, see Garland, *The Culture of Control*.

7. Ibid., 96.

8. Bourgois and Schonberg, *Righteous Dopefiend*.

9. Putnam, *Bowling Alone*.

10. Durkheim, *Suicide*.

11. Specifically, a reference to flower children converging on San Francisco's Haight-Ashbury district in 1967, "Summer of Love" also represents the values and norms of the hippie movement during the late 1960s.

12. For accounts of how the military impacts criminal trajectories, see Laub and Sampson, *Shared Beginnings, Divergent Lives;* Hart, *High Price;* Moore, *The Other Wes Moore*.

13. Ted was 19 years old in 1972; the draft ended in 1973.

14. For a description of historical cycles in US response to drug use problems; see Musto, *The American Disease*.

15. For ethnographic portraits of how the penal system replaced the educational system for young men, see Goffman, *On the Run;* Singer, *The Face of Social Suffering*.

16. Bourgois, *In Search of Respect;* Contreras, *The Stickup Kids*.

17. Chen and Kandel, "The Natural History of Drug Use from Adolescence to the Mid-Thirties in a General Population Sample."

18. Courtwright, *Forces of Habit*.

19. Foucault, *The Birth of the Clinic*.

20. For in-depth discussions of the medicalization of addiction, see Bourgois, "Disciplining Addictions"; Fraser et al., *Habits*.

21. For an in-depth examination of the social and historical context of managing addiction from the turn of the twentieth century and how control over opiate users created a tightly knit junkie subculture, see Acker, *Creating the American Junkie*. For a description of the classic era of heroin use, and historical cycles of criminal justice and medical approaches to heroin users, see Courtwright, *Forces of Habit*. For a fascinating account of how politics, culture, and powerful special interests shaped drug policy, see Musto, *The American Disease*. For a contemporary examination of the impact of drug policy and economic structural inequality, see Bourgois, *In Search of Respect*.

22. See Berger and Luckmann, *The Social Construction of Reality;* Becker, "Becoming a Marihuana User."

23. See Bob Dylan, "Walls of Red Wing."

24. See contrasting arguments in Gottfredson and Hirschi, *A General Theory of Crime;* Laub and Sampson, *Shared Beginnings, Divergent Lives.*

25. Foucault, *Discipline and Punish;* Fraser et al., *Habits.*

26. Sociologist Anthony Giddens developed conceptual tools for analyzing the intersection of agency and structure, illustrating them as two sides of the same coin; see Giddens, *The Constitution of Society.* Life-course theorists link social history with social structure to examine variation in behavior over time; see Elder, "The Life Course Paradigm." Age-grade social control theory, which focuses on the impact of social structure and situational context on human agency, is informed by life course theory; see Laub and Sampson, *Shared Beginnings, Divergent Lives.*

27. Analyzing trends in crime control, David Garland suggests that "socially situated actors reproduce (or transform) the structures that enable and constrain their actions"; however, in modern times, special interests and competing solutions to social problems eroded previous structural supports; see Garland, *The Culture of Control,* 77.

28. For the multiple factors that influence drug use behavior interact in complex ways, see Bourgois, *In Search of Respect;* Sered and Norton-Hawk, *Can't Catch a Break.*

29. Acker, *Creating the American Junkie;* Courtwright, *Forces of Habit;* Musto, *The American Disease.*

30. Heroin was first promoted as a nonaddictive substitute for morphine; see Acker, *Creating the American Junkie,* 84.

31. Ibid., 6.

32. Moral entrepreneurs define what is good or bad for society, often creating a norm or rule to enforce behaviors; see Becker, *Outsiders.*

33. The racial and ethnic prejudice fueling the propaganda campaign by Anslinger is discussed in more detail in chapter 7. Also see Inciardi, *The War on Drugs IV.*

34. The number of people who use drugs is always difficult to determine and there has been some dispute over whether drug use was as widespread in the 1960s as believed. Since the 1970s, scientific survey methods have been used to estimate the number of drug users in the general population, but the estimates have major drawbacks, and miss drug users who are homeless, institutionalized, or incarcerated. Nevertheless, they do show trends over time. For example, in 1998, an estimated 14 million people in the United States were using illegal drugs, and by 2005 this number had risen to 20 million; see Inciardi, *The War on Drugs IV.*

35. Acker, *Creating the American Junkie.*

36. Inciardi, *The War on Drugs IV.*

37. Similar to statistics on drug users, crime statistics must be viewed with healthy skepticism and are socially constructed measures; see Brownstein, *The Rise and Fall of a Violent Crime Wave.*

38. For a discussion of the how crime, control, and culture interacted during this period, see Garland, *The Culture of Control,* 90.

39. Musto, *The American Disease.*

40. Murphy et al., "An 11-year Follow-up of a Network of Cocaine Users"; Hamid, "The Developmental Cycle of a Drug Epidemic."

41. Reinarman and Levine, *Crack in America.*

42. Reinarman, *The Social Construction of Drug Scares.*

43. Boeri, *Women on Ice;* Shukla, *Methamphetamine.*

44. Durrant and Thakker, *Substance Use and Abuse.*

45. Kolodny et al., "The Prescription Opioid and Heroin Crisis."

46. Opioid is the term used when referring to synthetic opiates, although recently used for both natural and synthetic opiates. I use opiates when discussing the historical context and opioids when referring to more recent use of prescription medication.

47. Neuroscientist Carl Hart writes that "our theory about dopamine's role in reward has not been appreciably revised since it was originally proposed. . . . a growing body of evidence casts doubt on this simplistic view of reward" since different drugs have different responses on different people. He found in his own field and among his colleagues that "there is resistance when findings throw a monkey wrench in conventional wisdom about addiction" and very little research is reported about people who do not lose control when using drugs; see Hart, *High Price,* 78, 80.

48. Race, gender, class, and age are discussed in more depth in subsequent chapters.

49. The importance of relationships is discussed in more detail in chapter 3.

50. Garland, *The Culture of Control.*

51. For a full discussion of the impact of outsourcing and offshoring policies on the US economy, see Spence and Hiatshwayo, "The Evolving Structure of the American Economy and the Employment Challenge."

52. For a discussion on how globalization efforts through NAFTA have impacted US families, see Zaccone, *Has Globalization Destroyed the American Middle Class?*

53. A number of baby boomers in this study were impacted by the 2008 recession. Many lost their homes, their jobs, and even their partners when they were unable to find work, which was often a catalyst to using drugs.

54. Same-sex marriage was not recognized in all states until a Supreme Court decision in 2015.

55. Twelve-step literature is ambiguous regarding the position of leaders; however, leadership is discussed in the *Alcoholics Anonymous and Twelve Steps and Twelve Traditions* manual (the "Big Book").

56. Parole violations increased dramatically due to the War on Drugs. The number of people reincarcerated for probation and parole violations reached a peak in 2006, when it accounted for over half of admissions into jail and prison. See Carson and Golinelli, "Prisoners in 2012."

57. Therapeutic Communities (TCs) are long-term residential programs run largely by peers who have recovered; some have used controversial tactics and cult-like tactics. See Ofshe, "The Social Development of the Synanon Cult"; see also Shavelson, *Hooked.*

58. The positive recidivism reduction found in studies evaluating TCs can also be explained by the fact that TCs are residential programs that last for at least two years and often train and employ drug-free participants to stay on as counselors, giving them a sense of purpose and belonging; see Wexler et al., "Outcome Evaluation of a Prison Therapeutic Community for Substance Abuse Treatment."

59. Stable recovery is defined as at least five years of remission; see Granfield and Cloud, *Coming Clean.*

60. For a brief history of heroin in New York, see Frank, "An Overview of Heroin Trends In New York City."

61. Golub and Johnson, "Cohort Changes in Illegal Drug Use among Arrestees in Manhattan."

62. For research on the historical influences and consequences of these laws, see Reinarman and Levine, *Crack in America.*

63. The law was changed under the Obama administration but differences in sentencing and perspectives still exist between cocaine and crack; see Gotsch, "Breakthrough in US Drug Sentencing Reform."

64. More discussion of racial biases in crack arrests and its impact on minority communities is found in chapters 4 and 5. For ethnographic accounts, see Contreras, *The Stickup Kids;* Sterk, *Fast Lives.*

65. Kosmin et al., *American Religious Identification Survey 2001.*

66. Dix-Richardson and Close, "Intersections of Race, Religion, and Inmate Culture."

2. THE LIFE COURSE OF BABY BOOMERS

1. Elder, "The Life Course Paradigm."

2. Human agency encompasses the idea that a person has free will to act. This concept is central to theories of self-control. It is also central to the belief that individuals can choose to change if they want to, a premise of most drug treatment programs. For an overview of how human agency is used in life course theory, see Elder, "Time, Human Agency, and Social Change."

3. A cohort is an aggregate of individuals who experience the same events at the same time. Although often defined by age (birth cohorts), the term is used to define aggregates of people transitioning through life at the same time. The term "generation" is also used as an aggregate of individuals with a similarity of location, experiences, and thought; see Mannheim, "The Problem of Generations." Schumann and Scott suggest that Mannheim's definition of generation is more congruent with the concept of cohort; Schuman and Scott, "Generations and Collective Memories."

4. Elder, *Children of the Great Depression*; Laub and Sampson, *Shared Beginnings, Divergent Lives.*

5. Research reveals that the most influential period affecting individual behavior occurs during the time known as one's "coming of age," or the transition into young

adulthood; Brim and Wheeler, *Socialization after Childhood;* Haveren, "Historical Perspectives in the Family and Aging."

6. *Happy Days* was a popular American television sitcom depicting an idealized period during the time baby boomers were adolescents.

7. Alexander, *The New Jim Crow.*

8. Anderson and Bondi, "Exiting the Drug-Addict Role."

9. Giele and Elder, *Methods of Life Course Research.*

10. According to Carl Hart: "One of the most fundamental lessons is that a correlation between factors does not necessarily mean that one factor is the cause of another. This important principle, sadly, has rarely informed drug policy. In fact, empirical evidence is frequently ignored when drug policy is formulated." Hart, *High Price,* 18.

11. Cheal, "Relationships in Time."

12. Formal social controls of behavior, such as laws and bureaucratic rules, are distinguished from informal social controls, such as normative behavior for an employee; see Laub and Sampson, *Shared Beginnings, Divergent Lives.*

13. Moffitt, "Adolescence-Limited and Life-Course-Persistent Antisocial Behavior," 674.

14. Their life stories also exposed "situated contingencies"; see Laub and Sampson, *Shared Beginnings, Divergent Lives.*

15. Weinberg, "Out There."

16. Gottfredson and Hirschi, *A General Theory of Crime.*

17. Laub and Sampson, *Shared Beginnings, Divergent Lives.*

18. Akers, *Social Learning and Social Structure.*

19. Carl Hart's research shows that our actions are governed to a large extent by rewards (called reinforcers), which can be effective for changing addictive behavior; see Hart, *High Price.*

20. West and Prinz, "Parental Alcoholism and Childhood Psychopathology."

21. GED is the acronym for General Education Diploma, a high school equivalency certificate.

22. California and New York were the first states to introduce tough-on-crime laws that included mandatory sentencing for drug charges. Recently, California voters approved Proposition 47, which reduced simple drug possession to a nonfelony in the state.

23. Williams, *Heaven's Harlots.*

24. Since the 1990s, the UN Committee against Torture has repeatedly condemned the use of solitary confinement in the United States. In 2011, the UN special rapporteur on torture warned that solitary confinement "can amount to torture or cruel, inhuman, or degrading treatment or punishment when used as a punishment." See American Friends Service Committee, "The Role of For-profit Prison Corporation"; see also Aswadu, "A Black View of Prison."

25. Joshua Price writes that "to enter solitary confinement in the contemporary prison is to enter a remnant of the early nineteenth-century practices of incarcera-

tion"; Price, *Prison and Social Death,* 92. Also see Haney, "A Culture of Harm"; Haney and Zimbardo, "The Past and Future of US Prison Policy"; Haney et al., "Examining Jail Isolation."

26. Justin Douglas and his family claim he did not commit the murders and they were set up by FBI-motivated snitches who received lighter sentences. Their real names have been replaced.

27. Research found debilitating health effects of solitary confinement including emotional breakdown, anxiety, and headaches; see Haney and Lynch, "Regulating Prisons of the Future."

28. Boeri, "Hell, I'm an Addict, but I Ain't No Junkie."

29. Jeffrey Fagan and Ko-Lin Chin's drug developmental model included a process from initiation, escalation, and maintenance to discontinuation and renewal; see Fagan and Chin, "Social Processes of Initiation into Crack."

30. Charles Faupel modeled the drug career in four phases: (1) the occasional addict, (2) the stable addict, (3) the freewheeling addict, and (4) the street junkie. Movement between these phases is contingent on changes in the availability of drugs and the life structure of the user's current life experiences; see Faupel, *Shooting Dope.* Lawrence Kolb, a psychiatrist working with opiate addiction treatment in the early twentieth century, distinguished two types of opiate addicts based on statistical reports; however, when he sat down and talked with opiate users, he was able to distinguish six types; see Acker, *Creating the American Junkie.*

31. While categories are helpful for analytical and diagnostic purposes, Howard Becker reminds us that the categories we devise of human behavior belong to distinct systems that differ over time; see Becker, *Outsiders.*

32. *The Diagnostic and Statistical Manual of Mental Disorders (DSM),* developed by the American Psychiatric Association, is often used to diagnose if a person needs treatment, but not what type of treatment to use; American Psychiatric Association, *Diagnostic and Statistical Manual of Mental Disorders DSM-5.*

33. Elder, "The Life Course as Developmental Theory"; Faupel, *Shooting Dope.*

34. The nine phases of drug use include: (1) controlled user; (2) weekend warrior; (3) habitué; (4) marginal user; (5) problem addict; (6) using dealer / runner; (7) using hustler / sex worker; (8) junkie; (9) relapsing addict / junkie. For a discussion of the nine phases and how they can be used, see Boeri, *Women on Ice.* The labels of the phases were changed since norms regarding the use of stigmatizing terms such as "addict" and "junkie" changed.

35. Although terms such as "addict" and "junkie" are currently considered stigmatizing (see previous note), I used them because they were the words used by the people I interviewed at the time.

36. Professional programs are discussed more fully in chapter 8.

37. While it is difficult to find valid statistics on relapse rates, reports show that 40–60 percent of people relapse after treatment; see McLellan et al., "Drug Dependence, a Chronic Medical Illness."

1. In 2008 the maximum US Federal Supplemental Security Income (SSI) monthly payment was $637; the individual amount was calculated based on current living arrangements. Retrieved from www.ssa.gov/ssi/text-living-ussi.htm

2. Elder, "The Life Course as Developmental Theory."

3. The impact of earlier life events on the life trajectories is an important insight into a life course perspective; see Haveren, "Historical Perspectives in the Family and Aging."

4. Concurrent with a decline in marriages, half end in divorce and about 30 percent of children live in single-parent families due to divorce; see Edin and Kefalas, *Promises I Can Keep.*

5. The social context of life after incarceration will be discussed more in chapter 4. For ethnographic accounts, see Ross and Richards, *Behind Bars;* Sered and Norton-Hawk, *Can't Catch a Break.*

6. John Laub and Robert Sampson write that one of the troubling findings of their analysis on the life course of juvenile delinquents is the counterproductive effects of punitive sanctions over the long run of individual lives; see Laub and Sampson, *Shared Beginnings, Divergent Lives.*

7. Ibid.; Inciardi, *The War on Drugs IV.*

8. Anthropologist Claire Sterk distinguished between drug-using partners and those who were non-using partners; see Sterk, *Fast Lives.* Others distinguish marriage as a positive turning; see Laub and Sampson, *Shared Beginnings, Divergent Lives.*

9. Howard Becker emphasized the importance of "the negative case" as the key to advancing scientific knowledge. The essential argument is that finding out that your ideas are wrong is a good way to learn what is right. See Becker, *Tricks of the Trade.*

10. Examples of this are described in chapter 6.

11. Hammersley et al., "Trauma in the Childhood Stories of People Who Have Injected Drugs."

12. Senator George McGovern wrote an anguished memoir of his failed attempt using tough love as a last resort for his daughter; see McGovern, *Terry.*

13. This community is the focus of the docudrama *Snow on tha Bluff.* A review of the film describes the area as "urban wilderness, a kind of wild west set in destroyed suburbs" (www.vice.com/read/snow-on-tha-bluff). *Urban Dictionary* defines the Bluff as an area known for its "high crime rate and illegal drug activity" and says that more recently it is used as a generic term in rap songs to refer to any high-intensity drug trafficking area (www.urbandictionary.com/define.php?term = The Bluff).

14. Andrew Sullivan described the no-knock entry, killing, and cover-up by the Red Dog police in "Atlanta's Red Dog Squad," *The Atlantic,* September 22, 2009 (www.theatlantic.com/daily-dish/archive/2009/09/atlantas-red-dog-squad/196250 /). My inquiries revealed that even professors who taught in universities near the

Bluff did not know this community existed. The racial divisions that still exist in the South will be discussed more in chapter 5.

15. Elijah's and Alicia's stories of rehabilitation are discussed in Chapter 8.

16. For a detailed ethnographic discussion of supportive relationships among drug users, dealers, and their families and friends, see Duck, *No Way Out.*

17. Catan and Perez, "A Pain-Drug Champion Has Second Thoughts."

18. Laub and Sampson, *Shared Beginnings, Divergent Lives.*

19. Putnam, *Bowling Alone.*

20. Bourdieu, "The Forms of Capital"; Coleman, *Foundations of Social Theory;* Portes, "Social Capital."

21. Loïc Wacquant argues that social capital is "both relational (as opposed to substantial) and an indexical notion, and its value is defined only in relation to a specific social space or arena of action"; see Wacquant, "Negative Social Capital," 27.

22. Blackshaw and Long, "What's the Big Idea?"; Lin, "Building a Network Theory of Social Capital."

23. Some scholars distinguish between "bonding" social capital that results from relationships between individuals in the same community or network, and "bridging" social capital that results from relationships across social divisions or physical divisions; see Lockhart, "Building Bridges and Bonds"; Wuthnow, "Religious Involvement and Status-Bridging Social Capital."

24. Read more about Alicia's story in chapters 6 and 8.

25. For an in-depth discussion of the loss of social roles and social ties available after incarceration, see Price, *Prison and Social Death.*

26. Stryker and Serpe, "Identity Salience and Psychological Centrality."

27. While the 12-step movement is often called "self-help," the individual is largely dependent on help provided through the social support of other meeting members and the "sponsor." Since there is a 12-step meeting running somewhere virtually anywhere in the United States, a 12-step member is never alone; see Cheever, *My Name Is Bill;* Katz, *Self-Help in America.*

28. Hart, *High Price.*

29. See chapter 2 for more details of Harry relationship with Justin—a pseudonym.

30. See Ross and Richards, *Behind Bars,* for more insights on life in prison.

4. THE WAR ON DRUGS AND MASS INCARCERATION

1. See chapter 3 for a description of the Bluff community.

2. For an ethnographic description of "corner boys," see Duck, *No Way Out.*

3. Drug courts are an alternative to incarceration for nonviolent drug offenders that involve a closely monitored drug treatment plan, case management by drug court staff, frequent interaction with a drug court judge, and drug testing. The structure of programs and intensity of monitoring vary widely between drug courts; however, graduated phases are standard. While a minimum of two years in the

program is the goal, some stay in for more than two years, and others may opt to return to jail rather than continue. The drug court aim is to induce behavioral change, and attendance at 12-step meetings is usually required; see Nolan, *Reinventing Justice*. For critiques of drug court see Cloud et al., "Addressing Mass Incarceration"; Jensen et al., "Adult Drug Treatment Courts."

4. See chapter 8 for additional discussion of drug courts.

5. Court fees, fines, and paying for one's own jail time is a trending practice that places more burden on the poor; see Goffman, *On the Run;* Wacquant, *Punishing the Poor.*

6. Studies show prescription opioid use serves as a stepping-stone to heroin use and created an opioid epidemic among the working and middle class; see Cicero et al., "The Changing Face of Heroin Use in the United States"; Kolodny et al., "The Prescription Opioid and Heroin Crisis"; Unick et al., "Intertwined Epidemics."

7. See chapter 3 for more about the Atlanta Harm Reduction Center.

8. For people living from paycheck to paycheck, car trouble can mean the loss of a job, failing school classes, and missing appointments that may result in being cut off from food stamps or other social services.

9. Police and the media tend to define gangs liberally; see Duck, *No Way Out.* In this story, Omar used the term gang and told me the name of the gang, which I confirmed through other sources.

10. Here and elsewhere in this book, I am careful to be as transparent as possible when explaining unusual occurrences—not because I doubt what was told to me, which I do not, but because of criticism of ethnographic researchers who report the lived experiences of marginalized and disenfranchised people no one else listens to; see for example Campos, "Alice Goffman's Implausible Ethnography 'On the Run' Reveals the Flaws in How Sociology Is Sometimes Produced, Evaluated, and Rewarded"; Parry, "A Reckoning."

11. Charge stacking is when police mount the charges so that some stick, or it scares the accused into making a plea deal; see Stuntz, *The Collapse of American Criminal Justice.*

12. The racial disparities in the War on Drugs are discussed more fully in chapter 5.

13. For a discussion of deviant cases and central theses, see Becker, *Outsiders;* Becker, *Tricks of the Trade.*

14. Steve Woolgar quoted in Fraser et al., *Habits,* 238.

15. In the 1930s, Harry Anslinger led a campaign to demonize marijuana as a dangerous drug by linking marijuana use to Mexicans and urban Blacks; see Chapkis and Webb, *Dying to Get High.* President Nixon launched the War on Drugs in 1971; see Inciardi, *The War on Drugs IV,* 256.

16. Retrieved from www.dea.gov/about/history.shtml

17. Acker, *Creating the American Junkie;* Inciardi, *The War on Drugs IV.*

18. The Comprehensive Drug Abuse Prevention and Control Act was amended in 1984 to allow federal law enforcement to keep all assets of value, and state and local law enforcement to keep up to 80 percent, which substantially increased the budgets of state and local agencies; see Alexander, *The New Jim Crow.* According to

the American Civil Liberties Union (ACLU), civil asset forfeiture is a legal mechanism allowing law enforcement to take and keep property it claims is connected to illegal activity without charging the property owner with a crime, see ACLU, "Civil Asset Forfeiture: Coalition for Forfeiture Reform Member Organizations" (www .aclupa.org/issues/forfeiture/).

19. Baicker and Jacobson, "Finders Keepers"; Crawford, "Civil Asset Forfeiture in Massachusetts."

20. Alexander, *The New Jim Crow*, 81.

21. Ibid., 77.

22. Ibid., 76–78.

23. Ibid., 73–74.

24. For example, see "Tewksbury Owner Fights Feds' Attempt to Seize Alleged Drug Motel," December 29, 2011. Retrieved from http://boston.cbslocal .com/2011/12/29/owner-fights-feds-attempt-to-seize-drug-motel/

25. Retrieved from www.drugpolicy.org/new-solutions-drug-policy /brief-history-drug-war

26. Chapkis and Webb, *Dying to Get High*.

27. Retrieved from www.aclu.org/feature/fair-sentencing-act. The Trump administration is poised to roll back criminal justice reforms and civil rights legislation passed under the Obama administration.

28. Early indicators from the Trump administration forewarn of a reversal in the trend to legalize cannabis and greater federal enforcement of marijuana laws in states that have legalized it for recreational purposes.

29. Alexander, *The New Jim Crow*, 84.

30. Drug Policy Alliance, "The Federal Drug Control Budget: New Rhetoric, Same Failed Drug War," February 2015. Retrieved from www.drugpolicy.org /resource/federal-drug-control-budget

31. Office of National Drug Control Policy (ONDCP), "A Response to the Epidemic of Prescription Drug Abuse," 2011 (www.whitehouse.gov/sites/default /files/ondcp/opioids_fact_sheet.pdf). Also see Miron and Waldock, "The Budgetary Impact of Ending Drug Prohibition." See more cost analyses of the prison industrial complex in chapter 8.

32. An independent policy study conducted in 2005 found that drug use had increased tenfold since Reagan increased spending on the drug war; see Boyum and Reuter, *An Analytic Assessment of US Drug Policy*.

33. Alexander, *The New Jim Crow*.

34. Shannon and Uggen, "Visualizing Punishment." "The total correctional population consists of all offenders under the supervision of adult correctional systems, which includes offenders supervised in the community under the authority of probation or parole agencies and those held in the custody of state and federal prisons or local jails." Bureau of Justice Statistics, Key Statistics. Retrieved from www.bjs.gov

35. See Peter Wagner and Bernadette Rabuy, "Mass Incarceration: The Whole Pie 2016," *Prison Policy Initiative*, March 14, 2016. Retrieved from www.prisonpolicy .org/reports/pie2016.html

36. In 2015, the prisoner population per capita in the United States was 698 per 100,000; the next highest, the Russian Federation, was 445 per 100,000; see Walmsley, "World Prison Population List."

37. Wacquant, *Punishing the Poor.*

38. Contreras, *The Stickup Kids;* Duck, *No Way Out.*

39. Goffman, *On the Run,* 109.

40. Alexander, *The New Jim Crow;* Duck, *No Way Out;* Wacquant, *Punishing the Poor;* Philippe Bourgois, "Lumpen Abuse"; Pattillo et al., *Imprisoning America;* Price, *Prison and Social Death;* Singer, *The Face of Social Suffering.*

41. Many of Harry's views and descriptions of prison life are corroborated by the founders of "Convict Criminology," a perspective in the field of criminology founded by ex-convict academics. See Ross and Richards, *Behind Bars;* Ross and Richards, *Convict Criminology.*

42. For a description of Marion prison, see Santos, *Inside.*

43. Haney et al., "Examining Jail Isolation"; Haney, "A Culture of Harm"; Haney and Lynch, "Regulating Prisons of the Future."

44. UN Special Rapporteur on Torture Juan E. Méndez told the General Assembly's third committee, "Segregation, isolation, separation, cellular, lockdown, Supermax, the hole, Secure Housing Unit ... whatever the name, solitary confinement should be banned by States as a punishment or extortion technique" (www.un.org/apps/news/story.asp?NewsID = 40097#.V2xJS64-jRX). The human rights organization American Friends Service Committee maintains: "Prison isolation must end—for the safety of our communities, to respect our responsibility to follow international human rights law, to take a stand against torture wherever it occurs, and for the sake of our common humanity" (www.afsc.org/resource/solitary-confinement-facts). Some prisons continue to put prisoners in solitary confinement for years. See, for example, www.theguardian.com/us-news/2016/feb/19/albert-woodfox-released-louisiana-jail-43-years-solitary-confinement

45. Abuses of solitary confinement and the effects of prolonged isolation are discussed in Grassian, "Psychopathological Effects of Solitary Confinement"; Haney and Zimbardo, "The Past and Future of Us Prison Policy"; Richards, "USP Marion the First Federal Supermax."

46. Schlosser, "The Prison-Industrial Complex."

47. Wacquant, "The New 'Peculiar Institution'"; Pettit and Western, "Mass Imprisonment and the Life Course"; Pattillo et al., *Imprisoning America.*

48. Alexander, *The New Jim Crow.* The War on Drugs and race is discussed in chapter 5.

49. Lopez v. United States, 373 U.S. 427 (1963); Hirsch, "Confidential Informants."

50. Natapoff, *Snitching.*

51. Contreras, *The Stickup Kids;* Goffman, *On the Run;* Jacques and Wright, *Code of the Suburb;* Lee, "Drug Informants."

52. Kathryn Johnston, a 92-year-old woman who lived in the Bluff community in Atlanta, was shot and killed by police who raided her house looking for drugs on

false testimony from an informant, see Ted Conover, "A Snitch's Dilemma," *New York Times Magazine*, June 29, 2012. Retrieved from www.nytimes.com/2012/07/01/magazine/alex-white-professional-snitch.html?_r = 0

53. Waverly Duck tells the story of a young man who was killed on suspicion of snitching, which may have been a false suspicion. Duck, *No Way Out*, 90–91.

54. Commonwealth of Pennsylvania vs. Harry Stephen Williams. Transcript of Proceedings of Preliminary Hearing, Before Louise B. Williams, D.J., December 11, 1987 at 3:00 p.m.

55. Anne was impacted by the treatment system that was shaped by the War on Drugs, which will be discussed further in chapter 8.

56. Centers for Disease Control and Prevention. Retrieved from www.cdc.gov/drugoverdose/pdmp/

57. As discussed in chapter 3, the social capital provided by steady employment and partner relationships is a protective factor; see Laub and Sampson, *Shared Beginnings, Divergent Lives.*

5. THE RACIAL LANDSCAPE OF THE DRUG WAR

1. Although I use the term Black in this book to be inclusive of people of color from the Caribbean or other areas who are not American but live in the United States, I also use African American to emphasize the political and historical context, such as the civil rights movement.

2. Michelle Alexander argues, "far from being a worthy goal, colorblindness has proved catastrophic for African Americans. It is not an overstatement to say the systematic mass incarceration of people of color in the United States would not have been possible in the post–civil rights era if the nation had not fallen under the spell of colorblindness." See Alexander, *The New Jim Crow*, 240–41.

3. Studies show that it is not the physiological or chemical effects of crack that apparently turns users into instant addicts but other factors associated with crack users; see Reinarman and Levine, *Crack in America.*

4. In 1988, the new Anti–Drug Abuse Act made possession of crack, which is cocaine based, the only drug to have a mandatory sentence for first-time offenders; see Alexander, *The New Jim Crow*, 53–54. The Fair Sentencing Act (FSA) of 2010 lowered the disparity in sentencing between crack and cocaine but did not eliminate it. Under the Trump administration, a return to mandatory sentencing has been proposed, reestablishing the racial disparities inherent in these laws.

5. Bourgois, *In Search of Respect;* Contreras, *The Stickup Kids;* Goffman, *On the Run;* Pettit and Western, "Mass Imprisonment and the Life Course"; Wacquant, *Punishing the Poor.*

6. Alexander, *The New Jim Crow*, 12–15.

7. Drug crimes here refer to possession or intent to distribute charges and not the violent crime generated by the illegal status of drugs.

8. Substance Abuse and Mental Health Services Administration, *Comparing and Evaluating Youth Substance Use Estimates from the National Survey on Drug Use and Health and Other Surveys;* Johnston et al., *Monitoring the Future National Survey Results on Drug Use 1975–2008.*

9. McCabe et al., "Race / Ethnicity and Gender Differences in Drug Use and Abuse among College Students"; Merline et al., "Substance Use among Adults 35 Years of Age."

10. Rates of substance use are mostly equal (between 8.8 and 10.5 for most races except Asians); see Substance Abuse and Mental Health Services Administration, *Results from the 2013 National Survey on Drug Use and Health,* 26.

11. Blacks are nearly four times more likely than Whites to be arrested for marijuana possession; see Human Rights Watch, *World Report 2015.*

12. Alexander, *The New Jim Crow;* Hart, *High Price;*

13. Bruce Western estimates that contemporary Black men without a high school degree have a 60 percent chance of imprisonment during their lifetime; see Western, *Punishment and Inequality in America.*

14. In 2014, about 37 percent of imprisoned males were Black, 32 percent were White, and 22 percent were Hispanic. Black males had higher imprisonment rates across all age groups than all other races; see Carson, *Prisoners in 2014.*

15. Schuller, "Reflections on the Use of Social Capital."

16. Black men and women are also subject to racism from other minority groups; see Contreras, *The Stickup Kids.*

17. Bobo and Thompson, "Unfair by Design."

18. Price, *Prison and Social Death.*

19. Wilson, *When Work Disappears.*

20. Wacquant, *Punishing the Poor,* 15, 160.

21. Nixon aide John Ehrlichman admitted that the War on Drugs was started to disrupt African American communities and implement intense racial targeting by police; see Hilary Hanson, "Nixon Aide Reportedly Admitted Drug War Was Meant to Target Black People," *Huffington Post,* March 25, 2016 (www.huffingtonpost.com/entry/nixon-drug-war-racist_us_56f16a0ae4b03a640a6bbda1).

22. Jim Crow was the system implemented to legally discriminate and segregate African Americans after slavery was abolished in the United States; see Woodward, *The Strange Career of Jim Crow.* In 1999, Ira Glasser suggested a "new Jim Crow" was created by the War on Drugs; see Glasser, "American Drug Laws." Loïc Wacquant discussed mass incarceration and racism in reference to Jim Crow; see Wacquant, "Deadly Symbiosis When Ghetto and Prison Meet and Mesh"; Wacquant, "Race as Civic Felony." Michelle Alexander wrote, "something akin to a racial caste system currently exists in the United States"; Alexander, *The New Jim Crow,* 2 (see 2–11 for supporting evidence).

23. Ibid.

24. Wacquant, "The New 'Peculiar Institution.'"

25. Ibid., 205.

26. Ibid.

27. See chapter 3 for a description of the Bluff.

28. While early studies on drug courts showed promising results, and offering a treatment program would seem better than languishing in jail, subsequent studies were mostly critical of the strategies used by drug courts; see Tiger, *Judging Addicts;* Nolan, *Reinventing Justice;* Parsons et al., "A Natural Experiment in Reform."

29. Loïc Wacquant pointed out that while embezzlement, fraud, and other crimes committed by the privileged class were treated with leniency and much less imprisonment time, the severity of punishment for crime committed by career criminals and small-time hoodlums, whether violent or nonviolent, steadily increased over time; see Wacquant, *Punishing the Poor,* 125–26.

30. Few people in the study identified as Latino / a and instead called themselves Hispanic—the term popular at the time. I use both terms here.

31. This is one of the few people who I did not interview personally; I used the interviewer notes and talked to one of the interviewers, who had been in the military himself. He had heard similar stories from other career military men.

32. I was reminded of another time I picked Harry up when he was released from Lancaster County jail, and he asked me to drop him off at a friend's house. I was 16 years old and paralyzed with fear when I saw my brother walk in the front door as people were spilling out the back door and jumping from first-floor windows. Within minutes Harry was the only person led out of the house by uniformed and nonuniformed police and put in the back of a patrol car. The drug house was being raided just as Harry walked in.

33. Pell grants are federal government aid funds for people with very low income. Although there is a "box" on the application asking if the applicant has ever been convicted of a drug crime, the suspension of funding is sometimes lifted after the completion of a drug treatment program.

6. WOMEN DOING DRUGS

1. Becker, *Tricks of the Trade.*

2. Ingrid used many aliases, and when I first asked her age she told me she was 44. Later, in the interview, she gave me the correct birth date, indicating that her age was 56, but she told me 44 because she did not want AHRC to know her real age since she used another alias for them. I am compelled to write this to show readers the nuances of being honest when living in the rough and trying to avoid surveillance. Ingrid survived using a variety of social services and nonprofit organizations that collected data on her age, name, and other demographics. She used aliases to avoid being caught by law enforcement, who might run data from social services looking for people with warrants; see similar reports in Goffman, *On the Run.*

3. Although the benefits of using an alias to avoid detection of previous criminal records has decreased with widespread use of electronic fingerprinting by the police, a recent study shows over 80 percent of arrestees still used aliases; see DeLisi et al., "Alias."

4. Anthropologist and linguist Daniel Everett argues that humans are "hard-wired for freedom" and that our greatest evolutionary adaptation is adaptability itself, namely the "freedom to adapt to a variety of environmental and cultural contexts"; University of Chicago Press review of Everett, *Dark Matter of the Mind*, http://press.uchicago.edu/ucp/books/book/chicago/D/bo16611802.html

5. On-site drug testing kits that police officers use in the field are extremely inaccurate and should not be used as the sole basis for drug charges, see Ryan Gabrielson and Topher Sanders, "Busted," *ProPublica*, July 7, 2016 (www.propublica.org /article/common-roadside-drug-test-routinely-produces-false-positives). This was an actual peppermint candy in Ingrid's story. Police have been known to arrest on drug charges even when the drug is never tested; see Boeri, Gibson and Harbry, "Cold Cook Methods."

6. Ingrid asked for my help, which is why I inquired. See more on the difficulties of acquiring social services in chapters 8 and 9.

7. Sered and Norton-Hawk, *Can't Catch a Break*, 107–25.

8. Victoria was adamant that she did not exchange sex for crack, the worst position for women in the drug world hierarchy, but she exchanged sex for money to get crack. See also Sterk, *Fast Lives*.

9. See Tsemberis, "From Streets to Homes"; Padgett et al., "Housing First Services for People Who Are Homeless with Co-Occurring Serious Mental Illness and Substance Abuse." The Housing First model is discussed further in chapter 9.

10. Race, gender, class, and age are social demographics. The relevance of social demographics cannot be easily separated, and they are embedded in historical and social context.

11. Sex is used to refer to the biological attributes of male and female, while gender is used to refer to both biological and social aspects of being male or female and masculine and feminine identity. Often these terms are used interchangeably.

12. Bourgois et al., "The Everyday Violence of Hepatitis C among Young Women Who Inject Drugs in San Francisco"; Ettore, *Women and Substance Use;* Taylor, *Women Drug Users.*

13. Edin and Kefalas, *Promises I Can Keep;* Sterk, *Fast Lives.*

14. Boyd, *Mothers and Illicit Drugs;* Campbell, *Using Women.*

15. The literature on stigma draws primarily from the work of Erving Goffman, who conceptualized stigma as a socially constructed characteristic that discredits a person in the eyes of others. Stigma is linked to contemporary constructions of stereotypes, prejudicial attitudes, and discriminatory behaviors that help explain societal reactions to drug-using mothers; see Goffman, *The Presentation of Self in Everyday Life;* Neale et al., "Recovery from Problem Drug Use"; Radcliffe, "Motherhood, Pregnancy, and the Negotiation of Identity."

16. Campbell, *Using Women;* Knight, *Addicted. Pregnant. Poor.*

17. Murphy and Rosenbaum, *Pregnant Women on Drugs;* Sered and Norton-Hawk, *Can't Catch a Break;* Woodall and Boeri, "When You Got Friends in Low Places, You Stay Low."

18. Boeri et al., "Suburban Poverty"; Radcliffe, "Motherhood, Pregnancy, and the Negotiation of Identity;" Sered and Norton-Hawk, *Can't Catch a Break*.

19. Alexander, *The New Jim Crow;* Desmond and Kimbro, "Eviction's Fallout."

20. Goffman, *On the Run;* Duck, *No Way Out*.

21. Anderson, "Dimensions of Women's Power in the Illicit Drug Economy"; Sterk, *Fast Lives*. Randol Contreras describes how women working with young men who rob drug dealers in extremely dangerous situations take more risks than men in order to prove themselves and feel needed; see Contreras, *The Stickup Kids*.

22. Anderson and Levy, "Marginality among Older Injectors in Today's Illicit Drug Culture"; Boeri, *Women on Ice*.

23. Hemerijck, "The Self-Transformation of the European Social Model (S)"; Mahon, "Child Care."

24. Wilkinson and Marmot, *Social Determinants of Health*.

25. Ibid.; Knight, *Addicted. Pregnant. Poor*.

7. AGING IN DRUG USE

1. Blow, "Substance Abuse among Baby Boomers," 1–12; Boeri et al., "Reconceptualizing Early and Late Onset"; Levy and Anderson, "The Drug Career of the Older Injector"; Patterson and Jeste, "The Potential Impact of the Baby-Boom Generation on Substance Abuse among Elderly Persons."

2. Gfroerer et al., "Substance Abuse Treatment Need among Older Adults in 2020."

3. Blow et al., "Misuse and Abuse of Alcohol, Illicit Drugs, and Psychoactive Medication among Older People"; Conner and Rosen, "'You're Nothing but a Junkie'"; Rosen et al., "Older Adults and Substance-Related Disorders."

4. Marmot, "Social Determinants of Health Inequalities"; Palar et al., "Food Insecurity Is Associated with HIV, Sexually Transmitted Infections and Drug Use among Men in the United States."

5. Research shows that 43–67 percent of injection drug users have been infected with HCV; see Jordan et al., "Incidence and Prevalence of Hepatitis C Virus Infection among Persons Who Inject Drugs in New York City"; Bramson et al., "State Laws, Syringe Exchange, and HIV among Persons who Inject Drugs in the United States."

6. Emlet et al., "The Graying of HIV / AIDS"; Kwiatkowski and Booth, "HIV Risk Behaviors among Older American Drug Users"; Levy et al., "The Graying of the AIDS Epidemic."

7. Crystal et al., "The Diverse Older HIV-Positive Population."

8. Carson and Sabol, "Aging of the State Prison Population."

9. Wacquant, *Punishing the Poor*.

10. Chiu, "It's About Time."

11. Ibid.; Carson, *Prisoners in 2014*.

12. Decker et al., "Criminal Stigma, Race, Gender and Employment"; Pager, "Double Jeopardy"; Pager and Quillian, "Walking the Talk?"

13. United States Social Security Administration, Publication No. 05–10072, "How You Earn Credits," January 2014; Publication No. 05–10029, "Disability Benefits," January 2014.

14. 31 U.S.C. § 3123, "Payment of Obligations and Interest on the Public Debt"; United States Social Security Administration, "2014 Annual Report of the Board of Trustees of the Federal Old-Age and Survivors Insurance and Disability Insurance Trust Funds."

15. United States Social Security Administration, Office of the Chief Actuary, "Old-Age, Survivors, and Disability Insurance Trust Funds, 1957–2013." Retrieved from www.ssa.gov/oact/STATS/table4a3.html

16. United States Social Security Administration, "Social Security: What Prisoners Need to Know."

17. John is referring to a popular book at the time; see Berne, *Games People Play*.

18. Akers, "Addiction"; Alexander, "Addiction"; Boshears et al., "Addiction and Sociality."

19. Alfred Lindesmith, who studied opiate users in 1938, argued that if the opiate user "fails to realize the connection between distress and the opiate, he escapes addiction; whereas if he attributes withdrawal discomfort to opiate and thereafter uses the opiate to alleviate it he invariably becomes addicted." Lindesmith, "A Sociological Theory of Drug Addiction," 593.

20. Morgan and Zimmer, "The Social Pharmacology of Smokeable Cocaine"; Weil, *The Natural Mind;* Weinberg, "Out There"; Weinberg, "Post-Humanism, Addiction and the Loss of Self-Control."

21. American Psychiatric Association, *Diagnostic and Statistical Manual of Mental Disorders DSM-5.*

22. For a full discussion of the *DSM* changes over the years, see Fraser et al., *Habits.*

23. Wise, "Addiction Becomes a Brain Disease."

24. Leshner, "Addiction Is a Brain Disease"; Courtwright, "The NIDA Brain Disease Paradigm"; Reinarman and Granfield, "Addiction Is Not Just a Brain Disease."

25. Hart, *High Price,* 287.

26. Ibid., 90–91.

27. Winick, "Maturing Out of Narcotic Addiction."

28. Laub and Sampson, *Shared Beginnings, Divergent Lives.*

8. THE CULTURE OF CONTROL EXPANDS

1. Narconon, a program once used in prisons and in high school curriculum, has been exposed as a cult-like treatment model developed by Scientology; see Ofshe, "The Social Development of the Synanon Cult"; Tewksbury, "Scientology and the

State"; Lennox and Cecchini, "The Narconon™ Drug Education Curriculum for High School Students."

2. Using heroin on purpose to qualify to participate in a methadone program was mentioned by other participants in the study.

3. Garland, *The Culture of Control.*

4. Davies, *Myth of Addiction;* Fraser et al., *Habits;* Levine, "The Discovery of Addiction."

5. For more discussion of the historical and cultural development of drug control and the growth of vested interest groups seeking to keep drugs illegal, see Acker, *Creating the American Junkie;* Courtwright, *Forces of Habit;* Musto, *The American Disease.*

6. Davis, "Masked Racism."

7. Schlosser, "The Prison-Industrial Complex," 56.

8. Wacquant, "Four Strategies to Curb Carceral Costs."

9. Kearney et al., "Ten Economic Facts about Crime and Incarceration in the United States."

10. Vera Institute of Justice researchers found that the total taxpayer cost of prisons in the their 40-state study was 13.9 percent higher than the cost reflected in those states' combined corrections budgets. Henrichson and Delaney, "The Price of Prisons."

11. Wacquant, *Punishing the Poor.*

12. Ibid., 29.

13. American Civil Liberties Union, "Banking on Bondage."

14. American Friends Service Committee, "The Role of For-profit Prison Corporation."

15. Ibid.

16. Brownstein, *The Rise and Fall of a Violent Crime Wave;* Lyons and Rittner, "The Construction of the Crack Babies Phenomenon as a Social Problem"; Parsons, *Meth Mania.*

17. Aiello, "'We Incarcerate to Set Free'"; Haney et al., "Examining Jail Isolation"; Haney and Zimbardo, "The Past and Future of US Prison Policy": Richards, "USP Marion the First Federal Supermax"; Ross and Richards, *Convict Criminology.*

18. See Abel's description of solitary confinement in chapter 4. The mental and physical health consequences of solitary confinement include anxiety, panic, paranoia, hallucinations, self-mutilations, suicidal ideation and behavior—symptoms analogous to those of torture victims; see Haney and Lynch, "Regulating Prisons of the Future," 477.

19. Jordan did not have a sex change; she used the term transsexual and transgender interchangeably.

20. The civil forfeiture allowance in the Comprehensive Crime Control Act was discussed in chapter 4; see Baicker and Jacobson, "Finders Keepers."

21. Okie, "A Flood of Opioids, a Rising Tide of Deaths."

22. Drug treatment courts are therapeutic programs typically involving daily 12-step group meetings, drug addiction counseling, weekly court appearances before

a drug court judge, random drug testing, and, in some cases, life skills training. They are designed to last two years, but since judges can send "clients" back to jail for short periods of time while in the program, the actual time needed to "graduate" can be more. Some participants decide to leave drug court and serve out their sentences in jail. The programs vary widely across the country depending on the judge and resources. Although some studies show drug courts are successful, other studies are highly critical of some drug court tactics; see Nolan, *Reinventing Justice;* Tiger, *Judging Addicts.*

23. Caroline Isaacs defines "Treatment Industrial Complex" (TIC) as the movement of the for-profit prison industry into correctional medical care, mental health treatment, and 'community corrections." TIC includes a variety of treatment services for those in prison or on probation or parole; see Isaacs, "Treatment Industrial Complex."

24. Although Garland does not use the term treatment industrial complex, the industries are part of what Garland calls the "third sector" of the new culture of control, which include prevention, harm reduction, and risk management; see Garland, *Culture of Control,* 171.

25. Due to rising opioid overdose deaths, treatment programs began collaborating with police departments across the country to treat people before they were even arrested through "treatment not jail" programs like one initiated in Gloucester, Massachusetts. Instead of arresting "opioid addicts," the police chief of Gloucester said he would provide treatment. He was hailed as a hero by news media and law enforcement agencies. A closer inspection of his program revealed troubling issues. First, people with opioid addiction were required to come to the police station and turn over their drugs and all drug paraphernalia. This raised concerns that the person going to the police station for help might be asked to "snitch" according to community sources. Second, the treatment costs were paid for by drug forfeiture dollars and private donations with vague oversight of finances. Third, the police chief contracted with specific treatment programs, which heightened the potential for graft; see Boeri, "Hero or Heel."

26. Ellement, "Gloucester Chief Receives White House Reward." A year after receiving a White House award for his treatment program, this police chief was put on "administrative leave" for professional conduct review and retired rather than be fired for improper behavior involving women under his control (www.bostonglobe. com/metro/2016/09/20/gloucester-mayor-hires-two-firms-audit-city-police-chief-and-sergeant/EzIXLpTjZYtyoU2vNczCeO/story.html).

27. For an in-depth discussion on constructing a disease see Fraser et al., *Habits.*

28. The social environment has been shown to be a primary influence on the biological craving for drugs. The scientists conducting a study on addiction using monkeys as subjects concluded: "these data demonstrate that alterations in an organism's environment can produce profound biological changes that have important behavioral associations, including vulnerability to cocaine addiction." Morgan et al., "Social Dominance in Monkeys"; Czoty et al., "Assessment of the Relative Reinforcing Strength of Cocaine in Socially Housed Monkeys Using a Choice Procedure." See also Alexander et al., "Rat Park Chronicle."

29. The directors of the National Institute of Drug Abuse (NIDA) and the National Institute of Alcohol Abuse and Alcoholism (NIAAA) responded to criticism of the brain disease model by highlighting the impact of the environment—writing that the environment predicts the variance found in addiction more than genetics or brain abnormalities, particularly stressful environments such as disadvantaged neighborhoods, underachieving schools, juvenile detention centers, and prisons. Volkow et al., "Neurobiologic Advances from the Brain Disease Model of Addiction."

30. Thomas McLellan was featured in a 2014 NBC News series, *Hooked: America's Heroin Epidemic,* in which he described his evaluation study of treatment programs; see Dokoupil, "How to Fix Rehab."

31. Ibid.

32. Ibid.

33. For example, see treatment services for medical professionals at the Talbott Recovery Campus in Atlanta. Retrieved from https://talbottcampus.com/index.php/addiction-rehab-programs/treatment-elements/

34. Tsemberis, "From Streets to Homes"; Tsemberis et al., "Housing First, Consumer Choice, and Harm Reduction for Homeless."

35. In my research on Philadelphia reentry programs, I found a lawsuit had been won against the Pennsylvania Parole Board that prohibited lockdown measures in the parole office, which had become a common tactic used by parole officers and caused many parolees to lose their jobs. Nevertheless, the practice continued.

9. SOCIAL RECONSTRUCTION AND SOCIAL RECOVERY

1. Criminologist James Inciardi wrote his first edition of *The War on Drugs* in 1986. The fourth edition of his book was written in 2008, with an update on how to end the War on Drugs; see Inciardi, *The War on Drugs IV.* Inciardi died before he could witness the end of the war. More recent calls to end the drug war include Alexander, *The New Jim Crow;* Gray, *Why Our Drug Laws Have Failed;* Goffman, *On the Run;* Hart, *High Price;* Shukla, *Methamphetamine.*

2. Gary Fields, "White House Czar Calls for End to 'War on Drugs,'" *Wall Street Journal,* May 14, 2009. Retrieved from www.wsj.com/articles/SB124225891527617397

3. Greenwald, "Drug Decriminalization in Portugal."

4. United Nations Global Commission on Drug Policy, "Report of the Global Commission on Drug Policy," 2, 3.

5. Stuart Rodger, "The War on Drugs Could Finally Come to an End at This UN Summit," *Vice.com,* March 24, 2016. Retrieved from www.vice.com/read/end-of-war-on-drugs-ungass

6. Global Commission on Drug Policy, "Public Statement by the Global Commission on Drug Policy on UNGASS 2016," April, 21, 2016. Retrieved from www.globalcommissionondrugs.org/wp-content/uploads/2016/04/publicstatement-forGCDP.pdf

7. The Transform Drug Policy Foundation produced a blueprint for how to legalize and regulate drugs; see Rolles, "After the War on Drugs."

8. The Thomas Theorem states: "If men define situations as real, they are real in their consequences"; see Merton, "The Self-Fulfilling Prophecy."

9. This new paradigm is based on the social thinking of Karl Polanyi and other social scientists; see Alexander, "Addiction."

10. David Garland warns not to put the blame on the wrong culprit; see Garland, *The Culture of Control*.

11. Inciardi, *The War on Drugs IV*.

12. In 2014, the London School of Economics issued a report criticizing overly punitive responses to drug problems, citing its failure to treat many preexisting mental health problems, and highlighting the need to distinguishing the real problem of drug use, adding, "not all drug use is problematic"; see Collins, "Ending the Drug Wars."

13. Winick, "Maturing Out of Narcotic Addiction."

14. Similarly, the Gluecks—researchers discussed in Laub and Sampson, *Shared Beginnings, Divergent Lives*—found "delayed maturation" among juvenile delinquents who had been incarcerated in their study.

15. Wacquant, *Punishing the Poor*.

16. Boeri, *Women on Ice;* Duck, *No Way Out;* Goffman, *On the Run*.

17. Durose et al., "Recidivism of Prisoners Released in 30 States in 2005."

18. O'Brien and McLellan, "Myths about the Treatment of Addiction."

19. White, "Addiction Recovery."

20. Glen Greenwald notes that the Portuguese government could not legalize drugs due to international treaties that imposed drug prohibition; see Greenwald, "Drug Decriminalization in Portugal."

21. Ibid. Decriminalization applied only to personal use and not to traffickers or anyone who gave drugs to a minor. Traffickers were still processed through the criminal justice system.

22. This research has been around for decades; see Zinberg, *Drug, Set, and Setting*.

23. Refers to drugs for which there was prior use data; see Greenwald, *Drug Decriminalization in Portugal*.

24. Ibid.

25. Yury Fedotov, executive director of the UN Office on Drugs and Crime, wrote: "The evidence is clear: illicit drug cultivation and manufacturing can be eradicated only if policies are aimed at the overall social, economic and environmental development of communities . . . excessive incarceration is ineffective in reducing drug use and crime"; see United Nations Office on Drugs and Crime, *World Drug Report 2016*.

26. In 1980, $27.4 billion of the federal budget went toward public housing while $6.9 billion went to establishing correctional facilities; by 1990 $26.1 billion went to correctional facilities and only $10.6 billion for public housing. Statistics from the

Committee on Ways and Means, *Green Book 1996, Washington DC Government Printing Office, 1997,* cited in Wacquant, *Punishing the Poor,* 160.

27. Ibid., 159.

28. Inciardi, *The War on Drugs IV.*

29. Volkow and McLellan, "Opioid Abuse in Chronic Pain."

30. For a better understanding of the impact of situations from a sociological perspective, see Becker, *Outsiders;* Akers, *Social Learning and Social Structure.*

31. Treatment programs do not always result in successful recovery, but quality programs are more likely to produce better results. According to addiction expert Thomas McLellan: "Quality programs begin with quality employees, including mental health specialists, family therapists, and medical professionals. They tailor treatment based on the patient's needs, not rigid program dictates. They prescribe medicine, attend to physical health and educational hurdles, and they prepare the patient for a long-term recovery, including monitoring and support." Dokoupil, "How to Fix Rehab."

32. Social control theories refer to controlling behavior due to social roles and social bonding, see Hirschi, *Causes of Delinquency;* Laub and Sampson, *Shared Beginnings, Divergent Lives.*

33. Boshears et al., "Addiction and Sociality."

34. United Nations Global Commission on Drug Policy, "Report of the Global Commission on Drug Policy."

35. Marlatt, "Harm Reduction."

36. Inciardi, *The War on Drugs IV,* 304.

37. United Nations Global Commission on Drug Policy, "Report of the Global Commission on Drug Policy."

38. Congress reinstated the ban in 2011 and lifted the ban again in 2016. Retrieved from www.slate.com/blogs/xx_factor/2016/02/17/with_federal_funding_ban_lifted_needle_exchanges_open_to_address_heroin.html

39. Boeri, *Women on Ice;* Des Jarlais, "Harm Reduction"; Marlatt et al., "Help-Seeking by Substance Abusers."

40. United Nations Global Commission on Drug Policy, "Report of the Global Commission on Drug Policy," 6.

41. Bassler, "The History of Needle Exchange Programs in the United States"; Des Jarlais, "Harm Reduction." Some US cities are attempting to open SIFs using models that are more like in-house SEPs, but full SIFs are likely to be shut down by federal agents.

42. Kerr et al., "Safer Injection Facility Use and Syringe Sharing in Injection Drug Users"; Pinkerton, "Is Vancouver Canada's Supervised Injection Facility Cost-Saving?" Some US cities with epidemic opioid overdose deaths are beginning to consider SIFs.

43. Broadhead et al., "Safer Injection Facilities in North America."

44. Friedman and Touze, "Policy Bereft of Research or Theory."

45. Acker, *Creating the American Junkie.*

46. Agar et al., "Buprenorphine." Suboxone (buprenorphine with naloxone, an opioid antagonist) is prescribed by a physician but has become a sought-after drug in the illegal market.

47. Reiman, "Cannabis as a Substitute for Alcohol and Other Drugs."

48. Researchers often use the medical term "cannabis" instead of "marijuana," which has a derogatory status as an illegal drug.

49. As marijuana policy shifted, new epidemiological studies found significantly lower state-level opioid overdose mortality rates in states with legal marijuana—a relationship that strengthened over time and by proximity to marijuana dispensaries; see Bachhuber et al., "Medical Cannabis Laws and Opioid Analgesic Overdose Mortality in the United States, 1999–2010"; Powell, "Do Medical Marijuana Laws Reduce Addictions and Deaths Related to Pain Killers?" See also Lucas, "Cannabis as an Adjunct to or Substitute for Opiates in the Treatment of Chronic Pain."

50. The scientific debate over the harms and benefits of marijuana resulted in confusion that hampered federal policymakers from moving forward on marijuana legislation reform; see Bostwick, "Blurred Boundaries."

51. Agencies in the National Institutes of Health are funding more community-based participatory research (CBPR), particularly for drug-related interventions, see Aguirre-Molina and Gorman, "Community-Based Approaches for the Prevention of Alcohol, Tobacco, and Other Drug Use."

52. Using art and music as a therapeutic strategy in treatment has been around for decades and is reappearing in recent years; see Aletraris et al., "The Use of Art and Music Therapy in Substance Abuse Treatment Programs"; Horay, "Moving towards Gray"; Johnson, "Introduction to the Special Issue on Creative Arts Therapies in the Treatment of Substance Abuse."

53. The founder of the Parkland Community Change Center, a healthcare center for the socially marginalized, reopened the coffee house as a nonprofit when she saw increased drug addiction in her clinic after the coffee house closed; see Maddie Bernard, "The Coffee Effect," *Lute Times,* February 23, 2016. Retrieved from https://lutetimes.com/2016/02/23/the-coffee-effect/

54. Tsemberis, "From Streets to Homes."

55. Padgett et al., "Housing First Services for People Who Are Homeless with Co-Occurring Serious Mental Illness and Substance Abuse."

56. Tsemberis et al., "Housing First, Consumer Choice, and Harm Reduction for Homeless Individuals with a Dual Diagnosis."

57. A number of studies found that Housing First participants were placed in permanent housing at higher rates than the traditional treatment-as-usual (TAU) group, and while utilization of substance abuse treatment was significantly higher for the TAU group, no differences were found in substance use between the two groups at the end of the study; see Stefancic and Tsemberis, "Housing First for Long-Term Shelter Dwellers with Psychiatric Disabilities in a Suburban County"; Tsemberis et al., "Measuring Homelessness and Residential Stability."

58. Boeri et al., "Conceptualizing Social Recovery."

59. Bourdieu, *Distinction*; Coleman, *Foundations of Social Theory;* Portes, *Social Capital.*

60. Lin, "Building a Network Theory of Social Capital."

61. Putnam, *Bowling Alone.*

62. A lack of social integration is one of the social determinants of health inequalities; see Marmot, "Social Determinants of Health Inequalities."

63. Cloud and Granfield, "Conceptualizing Recovery Capital"; Granfield and Cloud, *Coming Clean.*

64. Granfield and Cloud, "The Elephant That No One Sees"; Granfield and Cloud, "Social Context and 'Natural Recovery'."

65. Laudet et al., "The Role of Social Supports."

66. Zschau et al., "The Hidden Challenge."

67. Ibid. The authors suggest more effort is needed on reconstructing positive social networks while in treatment by linking participants to networks centered on meaningful activities and developing stronger relationships with existing community partners, who can provide social learning through conventional healthy living activities (e.g., hiking groups, poetry clubs, etc.).

68. Granfield and Cloud, "Social Context and 'Natural Recovery'"; Waldorf and Biernacki, "Natural Recovery from Heroin Addiction."

69. Lockhart, "Building Bridges and Bonds"; Zschau et al., "The Hidden Challenge."

70. Boeri et al., "Conceptualizing Social Recovery"; Boeri et al., "Social Recovery, Social Capital, and Drug Courts"; Boeri et al., "'I Don't Know What Fun Is'"; Boshears et al., "Addiction and Sociality."

71. Sociologist C. Wright Mills' discussed the plight of working-class men and women who see their private lives "as a series of traps" from which they cannot escape; yet they do not see the social, political, and historical forces shaping their everyday existence, see Mills, *The Sociological Imagination.*

72. Please see this book's website for more details on how to implement Social Recovery at different structural levels and in different social contexts,

73. Aletraris et al., "The Use of Art and Music Therapy in Substance Abuse Treatment Programs"; Horay, "Moving towards Gray."

74. Wet homeless shelters are becoming more popular; see www.wethouse .com/

75. Laub and Sampson, *Shared Beginnings, Divergent Lives,* 47.

76. Medical anthropologist Merrill Singer writes about Tony, another Philadelphia man, who returned to his old neighborhood after being in prison—"a place where he never dreamed the dreams of middle-class accomplishments," and where the difficulties of existence "sap him of confidence he would ever come to dream such dreams"; see Singer, *The Face of Social Suffering,* 36.

77. Ibid. The importance of neighborhood factors is supported by studies among adolescents, but there is less research on the influence of neighborhoods on older adult drug use; see Friedman et al., "Social Capital or Networks, Negotiations, and Norms?"

1. The quantitative data collected in this study is archived and available at www. icpsr.umich.edu/icpsrweb/NAHDAP/studies/34296

2. Page and Singer, *Comprehending Drug Use.*

3. Ibid.

4. Desmond, "Relational Ethnography."

5. Although my research assistants helped with recruitment and interviews, in this book I focus on my research experiences, and I used transcripts primarily from respondents I met, recruited, and / or interviewed. Every researcher in this study has their own meaningful story to tell about ethnographic experiences.

6. Agar, *The Professional Stranger;* Watters and Biernacki, "Targeted Sampling."

7. For more description of targeting and community consultants, see Boeri, *Women on Ice.*

8. Shaw, "Research with Participants in Problem Experience."

9. The high numbers of African Americans / Blacks in this study reflect the population of the study location, Atlanta, Georgia.

10. See Laub and Sampson, *Shared Beginnings, Divergent Lives.*

11. Creswell, *Research Design.*

12. Using two interviewers for one face-to-face interview was virtually unheard of in research protocol, and I received disapproving comments from the audience when I presented the study findings, which is why I make an extra effort here to illustrate the utility of this innovation.

13. For more details and data collection instruments, please see the "user guide" on the Inter-university Consortium for Political and Social Research (ICPSR) website where the quantitative data is archived at www.icpsr.umich.edu/icpsrweb /NAHDAP/studies/34296. Some missing statistical data required eliminating eight respondents from the quantitative data set used for statistical analysis, but the data from all 100 respondents were used for the analysis in this book.

14. Longitudinal data such as ODUS existing in long format is also known as person period data and often used for event history analysis.

15. Sobell et al., "Reliability of a Timeline Method."

16. It is very difficult to describe this process succinctly, but in poetic terms, the interaction between three people intent on portraying the most valid life history possible, one of whom knows this information intimately and wants to share it, the other two who are highly trained in interviewing skills, is like composing a piece of art.

17. Bourgois and Schonberg, *Righteous Dopefiend.*

18. Belgrave and Smith, "Negotiated Validity in Collaborative Ethnography."

19. Numbers were used to link DVIs and other respondent interview material to protect their anonymity.

20. The research team members changed over the course of the data collection and analysis, with a core group of five, mentioned by name in the acknowledgments.

21. Strauss and Corbin, *Basics of Qualitative Research.*

22. Ibid. See other qualitative methods books for more description of coding qualitative data, such as Charmaz, *Constructing Grounded Theory;* Copes and Miller, *The Routledge Handbook of Qualitative Criminology;* Creswell, *Research Design.*

23. For examples of how the coding was used to disseminate findings, see Boeri and Tyndall, "A Contextual Comparison of Risk Behaviors among Older Adult Drug Users and Harm Reduction in Suburban Versus Inner-City Social Environments"; Boeri et al., "'I Don't Know What Fun Is.'"

24. Numerous studies find that "saturation" (the point at which no new data is found) occurs at about 20 to 30 interviews; see Strauss and Corbin, *Basics of Qualitative Research.*

REFERENCES

Acker, Caroline J. *Creating the American Junkie: Addiction Research in the Classic Era of Narcotic Control.* Baltimore: Johns Hopkins University Press, 2002.

Agar, Michael. *The Professional Stranger.* New York: Academic Press, 1980.

————, Philippe Bourgois, John French, and Owen Murdoch. "Buprenorphine: 'Field Trials' of a New Drug." *Qualitative Health Research* 11, no. 1 (2001): 69–84.

Aguirre-Molina, Marilyn, and Dennis M. Gorman. "Community-Based Approaches for the Prevention of Alcohol, Tobacco, and Other Drug Use." *Annual Review of Public Health* 17, no. 1 (1996): 337–58.

Aiello, Brittnie L. " 'We Incarcerate to Set Free': Negotiating Punishment and Rehabilitation in Jail." *Journal of Qualitative Criminal Justice & Criminology* 1, no. 2 (2013): 292.

Akers, Ronald L. "Addiction: The Troublesome Concept." *Journal of Drug Issues* 21, no. 4 (1991): 777–93.

————. *Social Learning and Social Structure: A General Theory of Crime and Deviance.* Piscataway, NY: Transaction, 2011.

Aletraris, Lydia, Maria Paino, Mary Bond Edmond, Paul M. Roman, and Brian E. Bride. "The Use of Art and Music Therapy in Substance Abuse Treatment Programs." *Journal of Addictions Nursing* 25, no. 4 (2014): 190.

Alexander, Bruce K. "Addiction: The Urgent Need for a Paradigm Shift." *Substance Use & Misuse* 47, nos. 13–14 (2012): 1475–82.

————, Patricia Hadaway, and Robert Coambs. "Rat Park Chronicle." *British Columbia Medical Journal* 22, no. 2 (1980): 32–45.

Alexander, Michelle. *The New Jim Crow: Mass Incarceration in the Age of Colorblindness.* New York: New Press, 2012.

American Civil Liberties Union. "Banking on Bondage: Private Prisons and Mass Incarceration." November 2011. Retrieved from www.aclu.org/banking-bondage-private-prisons-and-mass-incarceration

American Friends Service Committee. "The Role of For-profit Prison Corporation: Governing under the Influence." December 2015. Retrieved from www.afsc.org/document/how-profit-prison-corporations-shape-detention-deportation-policies

American Psychiatric Association. *Diagnostic and Statistical Manual of Mental Disorders DSM-5*. Washington, DC: American Psychiatric Press, 2000.

Anderson, Tammy L. "Dimensions of Women's Power in the Illicit Drug Economy." *Theoretical Criminology* 9, no. 4 (2005): 371–400.

——— and Lynn Bondi. "Exiting the Drug-Addict Role: Variations by Race and Gender." *Symbolic Interaction* 21, no. 2 (1998): 155–74.

——— and Judith A. Levy. "Marginality among Older Injectors in Today's Illicit Drug Culture: Assessing the Impact of Ageing." *Addiction* 98, no. 6 (2003): 761–70.

Aswadu, Ahmad A. "A Black View of Prison." *Black Scholar* (April–May 1971). Retrieved from www.usprisonculture.com/blog/2011/07/18/a-prisoners-words-describing-the-hole/

Atkinson, Robert. *The Life Story Interview as a Bridge in Narrative Inquiry*. Thousand Oaks, CA: Sage, 2007.

Austin, James, and John Irwin. *It's about Time: America's Imprisonment Binge*. Boston: Cengage Learning, 2011.

Bachhuber, Marcus A., Brendan Saloner, Chinazo O. Cunningham, and Colleen L. Barry. "Medical Cannabis Laws and Opioid Analgesic Overdose Mortality in the United States, 1999–2010." *JAMA Internal Medicine* 174, no. 10 (2014): 1668–73.

Baicker, Katherine, and Mireille Jacobson. "Finders Keepers: Forfeiture Laws, Policing Incentives, and Local Budgets." *Journal of Public Economics* 91, no. 11 (2007): 2113–36.

Baker, Timothy B., Megan E. Piper, Danielle E. McCarthy, Matthew R. Majeskie, and Michael C. Fiore. "Addiction Motivation Reformulated: An Affective Processing Model of Negative Reinforcement." *Psychological Review* 111, no. 1 (2004): 33.

Bassler, Sara Elizabeth. "The History of Needle Exchange Programs in the United States." In Master's and Doctoral Projects, University of Toledo, 2007.

Becker, Howard S. "Becoming a Marihuana User." *American Journal of Sociology* 59 (1953): 235–42.

———. *Outsiders: Studies in the Sociology of Deviance*. New York: Simon and Schuster, 1963.

———. *Tricks of the Trade: How to Think about Your Research While You're Doing It*. Chicago: University of Chicago Press, 2008.

Belgrave, Linda Liska, and Keruleth J. Smith. "Negotiated Validity in Collaborative Ethnography." *Qualitative Inquiry* 1, no. 1 (1995): 69–86.

Berger, Peter, and Thomas Luckmann. *The Social Construction of Reality: A Treatise in the Sociology of Knowledge*. New York: Anchor, 1967.

Berne, Eric. *Games People Play: The Psychology of Human Relationships*. London: Penguin, 1968.

Blackshaw, Tony, and Jonathan Long. "What's the Big Idea? A Critical Exploration of the Concept of Social Capital and Its Incorporation into Leisure Policy Discourse." *Leisure Studies* 24, no. 3 (2005): 239–58.

Blow, Frederick, C. "Substance Abuse among Baby Boomers: An Invisible Epidemic." In *Substance Abuse among Baby Boomers,* edited by F. C. Blow. DHHS Publication No. SMA 98–3179 (2000).

———, David W. Oslin, and Kristen L. Barry. "Misuse and Abuse of Alcohol, Illicit Drugs, and Psychoactive Medication among Older People." *Generations* 26, no. 1 (2002): 50–54.

Bobo, Lawrence D., and Victor Thompson. "Unfair by Design: The War on Drugs, Race, and the Legitimacy of the Criminal Justice System." *Social Research* 73, no. 2 (2006): 445–72.

Boeri, Miriam W. "'Hell, I'm an Addict, but I Ain't no Junkie': An Ethnographic Analysis of Aging Heroin Users." *Human Organization* 63, no. 2 (2004): 236–45.

———. *Women on Ice: Methamphetamine Use among Suburban Women.* New Brunswick, NJ: Rutgers University Press, 2013.

———. "Hero or Heel? An Ethnographic Investigation of a Police Chief's 'Angel Program' for Opioid Addicts." Paper presented at the Society for Applied Anthropology Annual Meeting in Vancouver, Canada, 2016.

——— and Benjamin D. Tyndall. "A Contextual Comparison of Risk Behaviors among Older Adult Drug Users and Harm Reduction in Suburban Versus Inner-City Social Environments." *Journal of Applied Social Science* 6, no. 1 (2012): 72–91.

———, Megan Gardner, Erin Gerken, Melissa Ross, and Jack Wheeler. "'I Don't Know What Fun Is': Examining the Intersection of Social Capital, Social Networks, and Social Recovery." *Drugs and Alcohol Today* 16, no. 1 (2016): 95–105.

———, David Gibson, and Paul Boshears. "Conceptualizing Social Recovery: Recovery Routes of Methamphetamine Users." *Journal of Qualitative Criminal Justice & Criminology* 2, no. 1 (2014): 5–38.

———, David Gibson, and Liam Harbry. "Cold Cook Methods: An Ethnographic Exploration on the Myths of Methamphetamine Production and Policy Implications." *International Journal of Drug Policy* 20, no. 5 (2009): 438–43.

———, Aukje K. Lamonica, and Liam Harbry. "Social Recovery, Social Capital, and Drug Courts." *Practicing Anthropology* 33, no. 1 (2011): 8–13.

———, Claire E. Sterk, and Kirk W. Elifson. "Baby Boomer Drug Users: Career Phases, Social Control, and Social Learning Theory." *Sociological Inquiry* 76, no. 2 (2006): 264–91.

———, Claire E. Sterk, and Kirk W. Elifson. "Reconceptualizing Early and Late Onset: A Life Course Analysis of Older Heroin Users." *Gerontologist* 48, no. 5 (2008): 637–45.

———, Benjamin D. Tyndall, and Denise R. Woodall. "Suburban Poverty: Barriers to Services and Injury Prevention among Marginalized Women Who Use Methamphetamine." *Western Journal of Emergency Medicine* 12, no. 3 (2011): 274–83.

Boshears, Paul, Miriam Boeri, and Liam Harbry. "Addiction and Sociality: Perspectives from Methamphetamine Users in Suburban USA." *Addiction Research & Theory* 19, no. 4 (2011): 289–301.

Bostwick, J. M. "Blurred Boundaries: The Therapeutics and Politics of Medical Marijuana." *Mayo Clinic Proceedings* 87, no. 2 (February 2012): 172–86.

Bourdieu, Pierre. *Distinction: A Social Critique of the Judgment of Taste.* London: Routledge. 1984.

———. "The Forms of Capital." In *Handbook of Theory and Research for the Sociology of Education,* edited by John G. Richardson, 241–58. New York: Greenwood Press, 1986.

Bourgois, Philippe. "Disciplining Addictions: The Bio-politics of Methadone and Heroin in the United States." *Culture, Medicine and Psychiatry* 24, no. 2 (2000): 165–95.

———. *In Search of Respect: Selling Crack in El Barrio.* New York: Cambridge University Press, 2003.

———. "Lumpen Abuse: The Human Cost of Righteous Neoliberalism." *City & Society* 23, no. 1 (2011): 2–12.

——— and Jeffrey Schonberg. *Righteous Dopefiend.* Los Angeles: University of California Press, 2009.

———, Bridget Prince, and Andrew Moss. "The Everyday Violence of Hepatitis C among Young Women Who Inject Drugs in San Francisco." *Human Organization* 63, no. 3 (2004): 253–64.

Boyd, Susan C. *Mothers and Illicit Drugs: Transcending the Myths.* Toronto: University of Toronto Press, 1999.

Boyum, David, and Peter Reuter. *An Analytic Assessment of U. S. Drug Policy.* Washington, DC: AEI Press, 2005.

Bramson, Heidi, Don C. Des Jarlais, Kamyar Arasteh, Ann Nugent, Vivian Guardino, Jonathan Feelemyer, and Derek Hodel. "State Laws, Syringe Exchange, and HIV among Persons Who Inject Drugs in the United States: History and Effectiveness." *Journal of Public Health Policy* 36, no. 2 (2015): 212–30.

Brim, Orville G., and Stanton Wheeler. *Socialization after Childhood: Two Essays,* New York: Wiley, 1966.

Broadhead, Robert S., Thomas H. Kerr, Jean-Paul C. Grund, and Frederick L. Altice. "Safer Injection Facilities in North America: Their Place in Public Policy and Health Initiatives." *Journal of Drug Issues* 32, no. 1 (2002): 329–55.

Brownstein, Henry H. *The Rise and Fall of a Violent Crime Wave: Crack Cocaine and the Social Construction of a Crime Problem.* Guilderland, NY: Harrow and Heston, 1996.

Campbell, Nancy. *Using Women: Gender, Drug Policy, and Social Justice.* London: Psychology Press, 2000.

Campos, Paul. "Alice Goffman's Implausible Ethnography 'On the Run' Reveals the Flaws in How Sociology Is Sometimes Produced, Evaluated, and Rewarded." *Chronicle of Higher Education,* August 21, 2015.

Carson, E. Ann. *Prisoners in 2014.* Washington, DC: US Department of Justice, Bureau of Justice Statistics, NCJ248955, 17. September 2015. Retrieved from www.bjs.gov

———— and Daniela Golinelli. "Prisoners in 2012." *Bureau of Justice Statistics,* December 2013.

———— and William J. Sabol. "Aging of the State Prison Population, 1993–2013." Washington, DC: US Department of Justice, Bureau of Justice Statistics, May 2016.

Catan, Thomas, and Evan Perez. "A Pain-Drug Champion Has Second Thoughts." *Wall Street Journal,* December 17, 2012. Retrieved from www.wsj.com/articles/SB10001424127887324478304578173342657044604

Cepeda, Alice, Kathryn Nowotny, and Avelardo Valdez. "Trajectories of Aging Long-Term Mexican American Heroin Injectors: The 'Maturing Out' Paradox." *Journal of Aging and Health* 28, no. 1 (2016): 19–39.

Chapkis, Wendy, and Richard J. Webb. *Dying to Get High: Marijuana as Medicine.* New York: New York University Press, 2008.

Charmaz, Kathy. *Constructing Grounded Theory.* Thousands Oaks, CA: Sage, 2014.

Chaudoir, Stephenie R., Valerie A. Earnshaw, and Stephanie Andel. " 'Discredited' Versus 'Discreditable': Understanding How Shared and Unique Stigma Mechanisms Affect Psychological and Physical Health Disparities." *Basic and Applied Social Psychology* 35, no. 1 (2013): 75–87.

Cheal, David. "Relationships in Time: Ritual, Social Structure, and the Life Course." *Studies in Symbolic Interaction* 9 (1988): 83–109.

Cheever, Susan. *My Name Is Bill: Bill Wilson—His Life and the Creation of Alcoholics Anonymous.* New York: Simon and Schuster, 2015.

Chen, Kevin, and Denise Kandel. "The Natural History of Drug Use from Adolescence to the Mid-Thirties in a General Population Sample." *American Journal of Public Health* 85, no. 1 (1995): 41–47.

Chiu, Tina. "It's about Time: Aging Prisoners, Increasing Costs and Geriatric Release." Vera Institute of Justice, New York, NY, 2010, 5. Retrieved from www.vera.org/

Cicero, Theodore J., Matthew S. Ellis, Hilary L. Surratt, and Steven P. Kurtz. "The Changing Face of Heroin Use in the United States: A Retrospective Analysis of the Past 50 Years." *JAMA Psychiatry* 71, no. 7 (2014): 821–26.

Cloud, David H., Jim Parsons, and Ayesha Delany-Brumsey. "Addressing Mass Incarceration: A Clarion Call for Public Health." *American Journal of Public Health* 104, no. 3 (2014): 389–91.

Cloud, William, and Robert Granfield. "Conceptualizing Recovery Capital: Expansion of a Theoretical Construct." *Substance Use & Misuse* 43, nos. 12–13 (2008): 1971–86.

Coleman, James S. *Foundations of Social Theory.* Cambridge, MA: Harvard University Press, 1994.

Collins, John. "Ending the Drug Wars: Report of the LSE Expert Group on the Economics of Drug Policy." *London School of Economics and Political Science* (2014): 71. Retrieved from lse.ac.uk/IDEAS/Projects/IDPP/The-Expert-Group-on-the-Economics-of-Drug-Policy.aspx

Collins, Patricia Hill. "Intersectionality's Definitional Dilemmas." *Annual Review of Sociology* 41 (2015): 1–20.

Conner, Kyaien O., and Daniel Rosen. "'You're Nothing but a Junkie': Multiple Experiences of Stigma in an Aging Methadone Maintenance Population." *Journal of Social Work Practice in the Addictions* 8, no. 2 (2008): 244–64.

Contreras, Randol. *The Stickup Kids: Race, Drugs, Violence, and the American Dream.* Los Angeles: University of California Press, 2012.

Copes, Heith, and J. Mitchell Miller. *The Routledge Handbook of Qualitative Criminology.* New York: Routledge, 2015.

Courtwright, David. *Forces of Habit: Drugs and the Making of the Modern World.* Cambridge, MA: Harvard University Press, 2009.

———. "The Nida Brain Disease Paradigm: History, Resistance and Spinoffs." *BioSocieties* 5, no. 1 (2010): 137–47.

Crawford, Andrew. "Civil Asset Forfeiture in Massachusetts: A Flawed Incentive Structure and Its Impact on Indigent Property Owners." *Boston College Journal of Law and Social Justice* 35 (2015): 257–319.

Creswell, John. *Research Design: Qualitative, Quantitative and Mixed Methods Approaches.* Thousand Oaks, CA: Sage, 2003.

Crystal, Stephen, Ayse Akineigil, Usha Sambamoorthi, Neil Wenger, John A. Fleishman, David S. Zingmond, Ron D. Hays, Samuel A. Bozzette, and Martin F. Shapiro. "The Diverse Older HIV-Positive Population: A National Profile of Economic Circumstances, Social Support, and Quality of Life." *Journal of Acquired Immune Deficiency Syndromes* 33, no. 2 (2003): S76–83.

Czoty, Paul, Ciara McCabe, and Michael Nader. "Assessment of the Relative Reinforcing Strength of Cocaine in Socially Housed Monkeys Using a Choice Procedure." *Journal of Pharmacology and Experimental Therapeutics* 312, no. 1 (2005): 96–102.

Davis, Angela. "Masked Racism: Reflections on the Prison Industrial Complex." *Color Lines* 1, no. 2 (1998): 11–13.

Davies, John Booth. *Myth of Addiction.* New York: Routledge, 2013.

Decker, S. H., C. Spohn, N. R. Ortiz, and E. Hedberg. "Criminal Stigma, Race, Gender and Employment: An Expanded Assessment of the Consequences of Imprisonment for Employment." Department of Justice, 2014. Retrieved from www. ncjrs. gov/pdffiles1/nij/grants/244756

DeLisi, Matt, Alan Drury, Monic Behnken, Michael G. Vaughn, Jonathan W. Caudill, and Chad R. Trulson. "Alias: Lying to the Police and Pathological Criminal Behavior." *Journal of Forensic and Legal Medicine* 20, no. 5 (2013): 508–12.

Desmond, Matthew. "Relational Ethnography." *Theory and Society* 43 no. 5 (2014): 547–79.

——— and Rachel Tolbert Kimbro. "Eviction's Fallout: Housing, Hardship, and Health." *Social Forces* 94, no. 1 (2015): 295–324.

Des Jarlais, Don C. "Harm Reduction: A Framework for Incorporating Science into Drug Policy." *American Journal of Public Health* 85, no. 1 (1995): 10–12.

DiClemente, Carlo C. "Motivation for Change: Implications for Substance Abuse Treatment." *Psychological Science* 10, no. 3 (1999): 209–13.

Dix-Richardson, Felecia, and Billy R. Close, "Intersections of Race, Religion, and Inmate Culture: The Historical Development of Islam in American Corrections." *Journal of Offender Rehabilitation* 35, nos. 3–4 (2002): 87–106.

Dokoupil, T. "How to Fix Rehab: Expert Who Lost Son to Addiction Has a Plan." *NBC News,* April 7, 2015. Retrieved from www.nbcnews.com/storyline/americas-heroin-epidemic/how-fix-rehab-expert-who-lost-son-addiction-has-plan-n67946

Duck, Waverly. *No Way Out: Precarious Living in the Shadow of Poverty and Drug Dealing.* Chicago: University of Chicago Press, 2015.

Duke, Steven. "Mass Imprisonment, Crime Rates, and the Drug War: A Penological and Humanitarian Disgrace." *Connecticut Public Interest Law Journal* 9 (2009): 17.

Durkheim, Emile. *Suicide: A Study in Sociology.* Translated by J. A. Spaulding and G. Simpson. Glencoe, IL: Free Press, [1897] 1951.

Durose, Matthew R., Alexia D. Cooper, and Howard N. Snyder. "Recidivism of Prisoners Released in 30 States in 2005: Patterns from 2005 to 2010." Bureau of Justice Statistics Special Report, April 2014. Retrieved from www.nij.gov/topics/corrections/recidivism/pages/welcome.aspx

Durrant, Russil, and Jo Thakker. *Substance Use and Abuse: Cultural and Historical Perspectives.* Beverly Hills, CA: Sage, 2003.

Edin, Katherine, and Maria Kefalas, *Promises I Can Keep: Why Poor Women Put Motherhood before Marriage.* Berkeley: University of California Press. 2011.

Elder Jr., Glen H. "Time, Human Agency, and Social Change: Perspectives on the Life Course." *Social Psychology Quarterly* 57, no. 1 (1994): 4–15.

———. "The Life Course Paradigm: Social Change and Individual Development." In *Examining Lives in Context: Perspectives on the Ecology of Human Development,* edited by Glen H. Elder, Phyllis Moen, Jr., and Kurt Lüscher, 101–39. Washington, DC: APA Press, 1995.

———. "The Life Course as Developmental Theory." *Child Development* 69, no. 1 (1998): 1–12.

———. *Children of the Great Depression: Social Change in Life Experience.* Boulder, CO: Westview Press, 1999.

Ellement, J. R. "Gloucester Chief Receives White House Reward." *Boston Globe,* April 29, 2016. Retrieved from www.bostonglobe.com/metro/2016/04/29/gloucester-top-cop-receive-white-house-award/B5MS4By1tCJAyQyNK-WKM6I/story.html

Emlet, Charles A., Amanda Gerkin, and Nancy Orel. "The Graying of HIV / AIDS: Preparedness and Needs of the Aging Network in a Changing Epidemic." *Journal of Gerontological Social Work* 52, no. 8 (2009): 803–14.

Ettore, Elizabeth. *Women and Substance Use.* New Brunswick, NJ: Rutgers University Press, 1992.

Everett, Daniel L. *Dark Matter of the Mind: The Culturally Articulated Unconscious.* Chicago: University of Chicago Press, 2016

Fagan, Jeffrey, and Ko-Lin Chin. "Social Processes of Initiation into Crack." *Journal of Drug Issues* 21, no. 2 (1991): 313–43.

Faupel, Charles E. *Shooting Dope: Career Patterns of Hard-core Heroin Users.* Gainesville: University Press of Florida, 1991.

Frank, Blanche. "An Overview Of Heroin Trends In New York City: Past, Present And Future." *Mount Sinai Journal of Medicine* 67, nos. 5–6 (1999): 340–46.

Fraser, Suzanne, David Moore, and Helen Keane. *Habits: Remaking Addiction.* New York: Palgrave Macmillan, 2014.

Friedman, Samuel R., and Graciela Touze. "Policy Bereft of Research or Theory: A Failure of Harm Reduction Science." *International Journal of Drug Policy* 17, no. 2 (2006): 133–35.

Friedman, Samuel R., Pedro Mateu-Gelabert, Richard Curtis, Carey Maslow, Melissa Bolyard, Milagros Sandoval, and Peter L Flom. "Social Capital or Networks, Negotiations, and Norms? A Neighborhood Case Study." *American Journal of Preventive Medicine* 32, no. 6 (2007): S160–70.

Foucault, Michel. *Discipline and Punish: The Birth of the Prison.* New York: Vintage, 1977.

———. *The Birth of the Clinic.* New York: Routledge, 2012.

Garland, David. *The Culture of Control: Crime and Social Order in Contemporary Society.* Chicago: University of Chicago Press, 2009.

Gfroerer, Joseph, Michael Penne, Michael Pemberton, and Ralph Folsom. "Substance Abuse Treatment Need among Older Adults in 2020: The Impact of the Aging Baby-Boom Cohort." *Drug and Alcohol Dependence* 69, no. 2 (2003): 127–35.

Giddens, Anthony. *The Constitution of Society: Outline of the Theory of Structuration.* Berkeley: University of California Press, 1984.

Giele, Janet Z., and Glen H. Elder, Jr. *Methods of Life Course Research: Qualitative and Quantitative Approaches.* Thousands Oaks, CA: Sage, 1998.

Glasser, Ira. "American Drug Laws: The New Jim Crow." *Albany Law Review* 63 (1999): 703.

Global Commission on Drug Policy. *Taking Control: Pathways to Drug Policy That Works,* September 2014. United Nations Publication.

Goffman, Alice. *On The Run: Fugitive Life in an American City.* Chicago: University of Chicago Press, 2015.

Goffman, Erving. *The Presentation of Self in Everyday Life.* New York: Random House, 1959.

Golub, Andrew, and Bruce Johnson. "Cohort Changes in Illegal Drug Use among Arrestees in Manhattan: From the Heroin Injection Generation to the Blunts Generation." *Substance Use & Misuse* 34, no. 13 (1999): 1733–63.

Gotsch, Kara. "Breakthrough in U. S. Drug Sentencing Reform: The Fair Sentencing Act and the Unfinished Reform Agenda." Washington, DC: Washington Office on Latin America (WOLA), 2011.

Gottfredson, Michael R., and Travis Hirschi. *A General Theory of Crime.* Palo Alto, CA: Stanford University Press, 1990.

Granfield, Robert, and William Cloud. "The Elephant That No One Sees: Natural Recovery among Middle-Class Addicts." *Journal of Drug Issues* 26, no. 1 (1996): 45–61.

————. *Coming Clean: Overcoming Addiction without Treatment.* New York: New York University Press, 1999.

————. "Social Context and 'Natural Recovery': The Role of Social Capital in the Resolution of Drug-Associated Problems." *Substance Use & Misuse* 36, no. 11 (2001): 1543–70.

Grassian, Stuart. "Psychopathological Effects of Solitary Confinement." *American Journal of Psychiatry* 140, no. 11 (1983): 1450–54.

Gray, James. *Why Our Drug Laws Have Failed: A Judicial Indictment of War on Drugs.* Philadelphia: Temple University Press, 2010.

Greenwald, Glenn. "Drug Decriminalization in Portugal: Lessons for Creating Fair and Successful Drug Policies," April 2, 2009. Available at SSRN 1543991: Cato Institute Whitepaper Series.

Hamid, Ansley. "The Developmental Cycle of a Drug Epidemic: The Cocaine Smoking Epidemic of 1981–1991." *Journal of Psychoactive Drugs* 24, no. 4 (1992): 337–48.

Hammersley, Richard, and Marie Reid. "Why the Pervasive Addiction Myth Is Still Believed." *Addiction Research & Theory* 10, no. 1 (2002): 7–30.

Hammersley, Richard, Phil Dalgarno, Sean McCollum, Maria Reid, . . . David Liddell. "Trauma in the Childhood Stories of People Who Have Injected Drugs." *Addiction Research & Theory,* 24 (2015): 1–17.

Haney, Craig. "A Culture of Harm: Taming the Dynamics of Cruelty in Supermax Prisons." *Criminal Justice and Behavior* 35, no. 8 (2008): 956–84.

———— and Mona Lynch, "Regulating Prisons of the Future: A Psychological Analysis of Supermax and Solitary Confinement." *NYU Review of Law & Social Change* 23 (1997): 477–528.

———— and Philip Zimbardo. "The Past and Future of US Prison Policy: Twenty-Five Years after the Stanford Prison Experiment." *American Psychologist* 53, no. 7 (1998): 709.

————, Joanna Weill, Shirin Bakhshay, and Tiffany Lockett. "Examining Jail Isolation: What We Don't Know Can Be Profoundly Harmful." *Prison Journal* 96, no. 1 (2016): 126–52.

Hart, Carl. *High Price: A Neuroscientist's Journey of Self-discovery That Challenges Everything You Know about Drugs and Society.* New York: HarperCollins, 2013.

Haveren, Tamara K. "Historical Perspectives in the Family and Aging." In *Handbook on Aging and the Family,* edited by Rosemary Blieszner and Victoria Hilkevitch, 113–33. Westport, CT: Praeger, 1995.

Hemerijck, Anton. "The Self-Transformation of the European Social Model (S)." *Internationale Politik und Gesellschaft,* no. 4 (2002): 39–67.

Henrichson, Christian, and Ruth Delaney. "The Price of Prisons What Incarceration Costs Taxpayers." New York: Vera Institute, 2012. Retrieved from http://archive.vera.org/sites/default/files/resources/downloads/price-of-prisons-updated-version-021914.pdf

Hirsch, Milton. "Confidential Informants: When Crime Pays." *University of Miami Law Review* 39 (1984): 131.

Hirschi, Travis. *Causes of Delinquency*. New York: Routledge, [1969] 2001.

Horay, Brian J. "Moving towards Gray: Art Therapy and Ambivalence in Substance Abuse Treatment." *Art Therapy* 23, no. 1 (2006): 14–22.

Human Rights Watch. *World Report 2015: Events of 2014*. Retrieved from www.hrw .org

Inciardi, James. *The War on Drugs IV: The Continuing Saga of the Mysteries and Miseries Of Intoxication, Addiction, Crime, and Public Policy*. Boston: Pearson / Allyn and Bacon, 2008.

Isaacs, Caroline. "Treatment Industrial Complex: How For-Profit Prison Corporations Are Undermining Efforts to Treat and Rehabilitate for Corporate Gain." American Friends Service Committee, 2014. Retrieved from www.afsc.org /document/treatment-industrial-complex-how-profit-prison-corporations-are-undermining-efforts

Jacques, Scott, and Richard Wright. *Code of the Suburb: Inside the World of Young Middle-Class Drug Dealers*. Chicago: University of Chicago Press, 2015.

Jensen, Eric L., Nicholas L. Parsons, and Clayton J. Mosher. "Adult Drug Treatment Courts: A Review." *Sociology Compass* 1, no. 2 (2007): 552–71.

Johnson, David Read. "Introduction to the Special Issue on Creative Arts Therapies in the Treatment of Substance Abuse." *Arts in Psychotherapy* 17, no. 4 (1990): 295–98.

Johnston, Lloyd D., Patrick O'Malley, Jerald Bachman, and John E. Schulenberg. *Monitoring the Future National Survey Results on Drug Use 1975–2008*, Volume II, College Students and Adults Ages 19–50 (NIH Publication No. 09–7403). Bethesda, MD: National Institute on Drug Abuse, 2009.

Jordan, Ashly E., Don C. Des Jarlais, Kamyar Arasteh, Courtney McKnight, Denis Nash, and David C. Perlman. "Incidence and Prevalence of Hepatitis C Virus Infection among Persons Who Inject Drugs in New York City: 2006–2013." *Drug and Alcohol Dependence* 152 (2015): 194–200.

Katz, Alfred Hyman. *Self-Help in America: A Social Movement Perspective*. Woodbridge, CT: Twayne, 1993.

Kearney, M. S. et al. "Ten Economic Facts about Crime and Incarceration in the United States." *Hamilton Project*. Washington, DC: Brookings Institution, 2014.

Keister, Lisa A., and Natalia Deeb-Sossa. "Are Baby Boomers Richer Than Their Parents? Intergenerational Patterns of Wealth Ownership in the United States." *Journal of Marriage and Family* 63, no. 2 (2001): 569–79.

Kerr, Thomas, Mark Tyndall, Kathy Li, Julio Montaner, and Evan Wood. "Safer Injection Facility Use and Syringe Sharing in Injection Drug Users." *Lancet* 366, no. 9482 (2005): 316–18.

Knight, Kelly Ray. *Addicted. Pregnant. Poor*. Durham, NC: Duke University Press, 2015.

Kolodny, Andrew, David T. Courtwright, Catherine S. Hwang, Peter Kreiner, John L. Eadie, Thomas W. Clark, and G. Caleb Alexander. "The Prescription Opioid and Heroin Crisis: A Public Health Approach to an Epidemic of Addiction." *Annual Review of Public Health* 36 (2015): 559–74.

Korper, Samuel P., and Ira E. Raskin. "The Impact of Substance Use and Abuse by the Elderly: The Next 20 to 30 Years." In *Substance Use by Baby Boomers: Estimates of Future Impact on the Treatment System,* edited by Samuel P. Korper and Carol L. Council. DHHS Publication No. SMA 03–3763, Analytic Series A-21. Rockville, MD: Substance Abuse and Mental Health Services Administration, Office of Applied Studies, 2002.

Kosmin, Barry, Egon Mayer, and Ariela Keysar. *American Religious Identification Survey 2001.* Graduate Center of the City University of New York, 2001.

Kwiatkowski, Carol F., and Robert E. Booth. "HIV Risk Behaviors among Older American Drug Users." *JAIDS: Journal of Acquired Immune Deficiency Syndromes* 33 (2003): S131–37.

Kyckelhahn, Tracey. "State Corrections Expenditures, FY 1982–2010." US Department of Justice, Office of Justice Programs, Bureau of Justice Statistics, 2012. Retrieved from www.bjs.gov/index.cfm?ty = pbdetail&iid = 4556

Laub, John H., and Robert J. Sampson. *Shared Beginnings, Divergent Lives: Delinquent Boys to Age 70.* Cambridge, MA: Harvard University Press, 2003.

Laudet, Alexander B., and William L. White. "Recovery Capital as Prospective Predictor of Sustained Recovery, Life Satisfaction, and Stress among Former Poly-Substance Users." *Substance Use & Misuse* 43 (2008): 27–54.

Laudet, Alexandre B., Keith Morgen, and William L. White. "The Role of Social Supports, Spirituality, Religiousness, Life Meaning and Affiliation with 12-Step Fellowships in Quality of Life Satisfaction among Individuals in Recovery from Alcohol and Drug Problems." *Alcoholism Treatment Quarterly* 24, nos. 1–2 (2006): 33–73.

Lee, Gregory D. "Drug Informants: Motives, Methods and Management." *FBI Law Enforcement Bulletin* 62, no. 9 (1993): 10–15.

Lennox, Richard D., and Marie A. Cecchini. "The Narconon™ Drug Education Curriculum for High School Students: A Non-Randomized, Controlled Prevention Trial." *Substance Abuse Treatment, Prevention, and Policy* 3, no. 1 (2008): 1.

Leshner, Alan I. "Addiction Is a Brain Disease." *Issues in Science and Technology* 17, no. 3 (2001): 75–80.

Levine, Harry G. "The Discovery of Addiction: Changing Conceptions of Habitual Drunkenness in America." *Journal of Studies on Alcohol* 39, no. 1 (1978): 143–74.

Levy, Judith A., and Tammy Anderson. "The Drug Career of the Older Injector." *Addiction Research & Theory* 13, no. 3 (2005): 245–58.

Levy, Judith A., M. G. Ory, and S. Crystal. "The Graying of the Aids Epidemic: HIV / AIDS and People Age 50 and Older." *JAIDS: Journal of Acquired Immune Deficiency Syndromes* 33 (2003): 257.

Lin, Nan. "Building a Network Theory of Social Capital." *Connections* 22, no. 1 (1999): 28–51.

Lindesmith, Alfred R. "A Sociological Theory of Drug Addiction." *American Journal of Sociology* (1938): 593–613.

Lockhart, William H. "Building Bridges and Bonds: Generating Social Capital in Secular and Faith-Based Poverty-to-Work Programs." *Sociology of Religion* 66, no. 1 (2005): 45–60.

Lucas, Philippe. "Cannabis as an Adjunct to or Substitute for Opiates in the Treatment of Chronic Pain." *Journal of Psychoactive Drugs* 44, no. 2 (2012): 125–33.

Lyons, Peter, and Barbara Rittner. "The Construction of the Crack Babies Phenomenon as a Social Problem." *American Journal of Orthopsychiatry* 68, no. 2 (1998): 313.

Mahon, Rianne. "Child Care: Toward What Kind of 'Social Europe'?" *Social Politics: International Studies in Gender, State & Society* 9, no. 3 (2002): 343–79.

Maines, David. "Narrative's Moment and Sociology's Phenomena: Toward a Narrative Sociology." *Sociological Quarterly* 34, no. 1 (1993): 17–38.

Mannheim, Karl. "The Problem of Generations." *Psychoanalytic Review* 57, no. 3 (1970): 378.

Marlatt, G. Alan. "Harm Reduction: Come as You Are." *Addictive Behaviors* 21, no. 6 (1996): 779–88.

———, Jalie A. Tucker, Dennis M. Donovan, and Rudy E. Vuchinich. "Help-Seeking by Substance Abusers: The Role of Harm Reduction and Behavioral-Economic Approaches to Facilitate Treatment Entry and Retention." *NIDA Research Monograph* 165 (1997): 44–84.

Marmot, Michael. "Social Determinants of Health Inequalities." *Lancet* 365, no. 9464 (2005): 1099–104.

McCabe, Sean Esteban, Michele Morales, James A. Cranford, Jorge Delva, Melnee D. McPherson, and Carol J. Boyd. "Race / Ethnicity and Gender Differences in Drug Use and Abuse among College Students." *Journal of Ethnicity in Substance Abuse* 6, no. 2 (2007): 75–95.

McCaffrey, General Barry R., Director, ONDCP, Keynote Address, Opening Plenary Session, National Conference on Drug Abuse Prevention Research, National Institute on Drug Abuse, September 19, 1996, Washington, DC. Retrieved from http://archives.drugabuse.gov/meetings/CODA/Keynote2.html

McGovern, George. *Terry: My Daughter's Life-and-Death Struggle with Alcoholism.* New York: Villard, 2013.

McLellan, A. Thomas, David C. Lewis, Charles P. O'Brien, and Herbert D. Kleber. "Drug Dependence, a Chronic Medical Illness: Implications for Treatment, Insurance, and Outcomes Evaluation." *JAMA* 284, no. 13 (2000): 1689–95.

Merline, Alicia C., Patrick M. O'Malley, John E. Schulenberg, Jerald G. Bachman, and Lloyd D. Johnston. "Substance Use among Adults 35 Years of Age: Prevalence, Adulthood Predictors, and Impact of Adolescent Substance Use." *American Journal of Public Health* 94, no. 1 (2004): 96–102.

Merton, Robert K. "The Self-Fulfilling Prophecy." *Antioch Review* 8, no. 2 (1948): 193–210.

Mills, C. Wright. *The Sociological Imagination.* New York: Oxford University Press, 2000.

Miron, Jeffrey A., and Katherine Waldock. "The Budgetary Impact of Ending Drug Prohibition." SSRN Working Paper Series. Washington, DC: Cato Institute, 2010.

Moffitt, Terrie E. "Adolescence-Limited and Life-Course-Persistent Antisocial Behavior: A Developmental Taxonomy." *Psychological Review* 100, no. 4 (1993): 674.

Moore, Wes. *The Other Wes Moore: One Name, Two Fates.* New York: Random House, 2011.

Morgan, Drake, K. A. Grant, H. D. Gage, R. H. Mach, J. R. Kaplan, O. Prioleau, . . . M. A. Nader. "Social Dominance in Monkeys: Dopamine D2 Receptors and Cocaine Self-administration." *Nature Neuroscience* 5, no. 2 (2002): 169–74.

Morgan, John P., and Lynn Zimmer. "The Social Pharmacology of Smokeable Cocaine: Not All It's Cracked Up to Be." In *Crack in America: Demon Drugs and Social Justice,* ed. Craig Reinarman and Harry G. Levine, 131–70. Berkeley: University of California Press, 1997.

Murphy, Sheigla, and Marsha Rosenbaum. *Pregnant Women on Drugs: Combating Stereotypes and Stigma.* New Brunswick, NJ: Rutgers University Press, 1999.

Murphy, Sheigla B., Craig Reinarman, and Dan Waldorf. "An 11-year Follow-up of a Network of Cocaine Users." *British Journal of Addiction* 84, no. 4 (1989): 427–36.

Musto, David. F. *The American Disease: Origins of Narcotic Control.* New York: Oxford University Press, 1999.

Natapoff, Alexandra. *Snitching: Criminal Informants and the Erosion of American Justice.* New York: New York University Press, 2009.

Neale, J., S. Nettleton, and L. Pickering. "Recovery from Problem Drug Use: What Can We Learn from the Sociologist Erving Goffman?" *Drugs: Education, Prevention and Policy* 18, no. 1 (2011): 3–9.

Nolan, James L. *Reinventing Justice: The American Drug Court Movement.* Princeton, NJ: Princeton University Press, 2009.

O'Brien, Charles P., and A. Thomas McLellan. "Myths about the Treatment of Addiction." *Lancet* 347 (1996): 237–40.

Ofshe, Richard. "The Social Development of the Synanon Cult: The Managerial Strategy of Organizational Transformation." *Sociology of Religion* 41, no. 2 (1980): 109–27.

Okie, Susan. "A Flood of Opioids, a Rising Tide of Deaths." *New England Journal of Medicine* 363, no. 21 (2010): 1981–85.

Padgett, Deborah K., Leyla Gulcur, and Sam Tsemberis. "Housing First Services for People Who Are Homeless with Co-Occurring Serious Mental Illness and Substance Abuse." *Research on Social Work Practice* 16, no. 1 (2006): 74–83.

Page, J. Bryan, and Merrill Singer. *Comprehending Drug Use: Ethnographic Research at the Social Margins.* New Brunswick, NJ: Rutgers University Press, 2010.

Pager, Devah. "Double Jeopardy: Race, Crime, and Getting a Job." *Wisconsin Law Review* 2 (2005): 617.

——— and Lincoln Quillian. "Walking the Talk? What Employers Say Versus What They Do." *American Sociological Review* 70, no. 3 (2005): 355–80.

Palar, Kartika, Barbara Laraia, Alexander C. Tsai, Mallory O. Johnson, and Sheri D. Weiser. "Food Insecurity Is Associated with HIV, Sexually Transmitted Infections and Drug Use among Men in the United States." *AIDS* 30, no. 9 (2016): 1457–65.

Parry, Marc. "A Reckoning: Colonial Atrocities and Academic Reputations on Trial in a British Courtroom." *Chronicle of Higher Education,* June 1, 2016.

Parsons, Jim, Qing Wei, Joshua Rinaldi, Christian Henrichson, Talia Sandwick, Travis Wendel, Ernest Drucker, et al. "A Natural Experiment in Reform: Analyzing Drug Policy Change in New York City." Vera Institute of Justice, 2014.

Parsons, Nicholas L. *Meth Mania: A History of Methamphetamine.* Boulder, CO: Lynne Rienner, 2014.

Patterson, Thomas L., and Dilip V. Jeste. "The Potential Impact of the Baby-Boom Generation on Substance Abuse among Elderly Persons." *Psychiatric Services* 50, no. 9 (2014): 1184–88.

Pattillo, Mary, Bruce Western, and David Weiman. *Imprisoning America: The Social Effects of Mass Incarceration.* Troy, NY: Russell Sage Foundation, 2004.

Pettit, Becky, and Bruce Western. "Mass Imprisonment and the Life Course: Race and Class Inequality in US Incarceration." *American Sociological Review* 69, no. 2 (2004): 151–69.

Pinkerton, Steven D. "Is Vancouver Canada's Supervised Injection Facility Cost-Saving?" *Addiction* 105, no. 8 (2010): 1429–36.

Portes, Alejandro. "Social Capital: Its Origins and Applications in Modern Sociology." In *Knowledge and Social Capital,* edited by Eric L. Lesser. Boston: Butterworth-Heinemann, 2000.

Powell, David. "Do Medical Marijuana Laws Reduce Addictions and Deaths Related to Pain Killers?" Paper presented at Health and Healthcare in America: From Economics to Policy, ASHEcon (American Society of Health Economics conference), June 22–25, 2014, Los Angeles, CA.

Price, Joshua M. *Prison and Social Death.* New Brunswick, NJ: Rutgers University Press, 2015.

Prins, Engel H. *Maturing Out: An Empirical Study of Personal Histories and Processes in Hard-Drug Addiction.* Rotterdam: Erasmus University, 1995.

Putnam, Robert, D. *Bowling Alone: The Collapse and Revival of American Community.* New York: Simon and Schuster, 2000.

Radcliffe, Polly. "Motherhood, Pregnancy, and the Negotiation of Identity: The Moral Career of Drug Treatment." *Social Science & Medicine* 72, no. 6 (2011): 984–91.

——— and Alex Stevens. "Are Drug Treatment Services Only for 'Thieving Junkie Scumbags'? Drug Users and the Management of Stigmatised Identities." *Social Science & Medicine* 67, no. 7 (2008): 1065–73.

Reiman, Amanda. "Cannabis as a Substitute for Alcohol and Other Drugs." *Harm Reduction Journal* 6, no. 1 (2009): 35–40.

Reiman, Jeffrey, and Paul Leighton. *The Rich Get Richer and the Poor Get Prison: Ideology, Class, and Criminal Justice.* New York: Routledge, 2015.

Reinarman, Craig, ed. *The Social Construction of Drug Scares, Fourth Edition.* Belmont, CA: Wadsworth, 2003.

——— and Robert Granfield. "Addiction Is Not Just a Brain Disease: Critical Studies of Addiction." In *Expanding Addiction: Critical Essays,* edited by C. Reinarman and R. Granfield. New York: Routledge, 2014.

——— and Harry G. Levine, *Crack in America: Demon Drugs and Social Justice.* Berkeley: University of California Press, 1997.

Reith, Gerda. "Consumption and Its Discontents: Addiction, Identity and the Problems of Freedom." *British Journal of Sociology* 55, no. 2 (2004): 283–300.

Richards, Stephen C. "USP Marion the First Federal Supermax." *Prison Journal* 88, no. 1 (2008): 6–22.

Rolles, Steve. "After the War on Drugs: Blueprint for Regulation." Bristol, UK: Transform Drug Policy Foundation, 2009.

Rosen, Daniel, Emily Heberlein, and Rafael J Engel. "Older Adults and Substance-Related Disorders: Trends and Associated Costs." *ISRN Addiction* (2013).

Ross, Jeffrey Ian, and Stephen C. Richards. *Behind Bars: Surviving Prison.* New York: Penguin, 2002.

———. *Convict Criminology: Longterm Solitary Confinement and the Supermax Movement.* Belmont, CA: Wadsworth, 2003.

———. *Beyond Bars: Rejoining Society after Prison.* New York: Penguin, 2009.

Rothwell, Jonathan. "Drug Offenders in American Prisons: The Critical Distinction between Stock and Flow." Washington, DC: Brookings Institution, November 25, 2015. Retrieved from www.brookings.edu/2015/11/25/drug-offenders-in-american-prisons-the-critical-distinction-between-stock-and-flow/

Santos, Michael G. *Inside: Life behind Bars in America.* New York: Macmillan, 2007.

Schlosser, Eric. "The Prison-Industrial Complex." *Atlantic Monthly* 282, no. 6 (1998): 51–77.

Schuller, Tom. "Reflections on the Use of Social Capital." *Review of Social Economy* 65, no. 1 (2007): 11–28.

Schuman, Howard, and Scott, Jacqueline. "Generations and Collective Memories." *American Sociological Review* 54, no. 3 (1989): 359–81.

Sered, Susan Starr, and Maureen Norton-Hawk. *Can't Catch a Break: Gender, Jail, Drugs, and the Limits of Personal Responsibility.* Los Angeles: University of California Press, 2014.

Shannon, Sarah, and Chris Uggen. "Visualizing Punishment." In *Crime and the Punished,* edited by Douglas Hartmann and Christopher Uggen. New York: Norton, 2013.

Shavelson, Lonny. *Hooked: Five Addicts Challenge Our Misguided Drug Rehab System.* New York: New Press, 2002.

Shaw, Victor N. "Research with Participants in Problem Experience: Challenges and Strategies." *Qualitative Health Research* 15, no. 6 (2005): 841–54.

Shukla, Rashi. K. *Methamphetamine: A Love Story.* Oakland: University of California Press, 2016.

Singer, Merrill. *The Face of Social Suffering: The Life History of a Street Drug Addict.* Long Grove, IL: Waveland Press, 2005.

Smith, Dorothy E. "Women's Perspective as a Radical Critique of Sociology." *Sociological Inquiry* 44, no. 1 (1974): 7–13.

Sobell, Linda C., Mark B. Sobell, Gloria I. Leo, and Anthony Cancilla. "Reliability of a Timeline Method: Assessing Normal Drinkers' Reports of Recent Drinking and a Comparative Evaluation across Several Populations." *British Journal of Addiction* 83, no. 4 (1988): 393–402.

Spence, Michael, and Sandile Hiatshwayo. "The Evolving Structure of the American Economy and the Employment Challenge." *Comparative Economic Studies* 54, no. 4 (2012): 703–38.

Stefancic, Ana, and Sam Tsemberis. "Housing First for Long-Term Shelter Dwellers with Psychiatric Disabilities in a Suburban County: A Four-Year Study of Housing Access and Retention." *Journal of Primary Prevention* 28, nos. 3–4 (2007): 265–79.

Sterk, Claire. *Fast Lives: Women Who Use Crack Cocaine.* Philadelphia: Temple University Press, 2011.

Strauss, Anselm, and Juliet Corbin. *Basics of Qualitative Research.* Newbury Park, CA: Sage, 1990.

Stryker, Sheldon, and Richard T. Serpe. "Identity Salience and Psychological Centrality: Equivalent, Overlapping, or Complementary Concepts?" *Social Psychology Quarterly* (1994): 16–35.

Stuntz, William J. *The Collapse of American Criminal Justice.* Cambridge, MA: Harvard University Press, 2011.

Substance Abuse and Mental Health Services Administration (SAMHSA). *Summary of Findings from the 1998 National Household Survey on Drug Abuse.* DHHS Publication No. SMA 99–3328. Rockville, MD, 1999.

———. *National Household Survey on Drug Abuse Main Findings 1998.* DHHS Publication No. SMA 00–3381. Rockville, MD, 1999.

———. *Summary of Findings from the 1999 National Household Survey on Drug Abuse.* DHHS Publication No. SMA 00–3466. Rockville, MD, 2000.

———. *Results from the 2003 National Survey on Drug Use and Health.* National Findings Office of Applied Studies, NSDUH Series H-25, DHHS Publication No. SMA 04–3964. Rockville, MD, 2004.

———. *Results from the 2006 National Survey on Drug Use and Health. National Findings,* Office of Applied Studies, NSDUH Series H-32, DHHS Publication No. SMA 07–4293. Rockville, MD, 2007.

———. *The DASIS Report: Adults Aged 65 or Older in Substance Abuse Treatment: 2005.* Office of Applied Studies. Rockville, MD, 2007.

———. *Results from the 2010 National Survey on Drug Use and Health: Summary of National Findings,* NSDUH Series H-41, DHHS Publication No. SMA 11–4658. Rockville, MD, 2011.

———. *Comparing and Evaluating Youth Substance Use Estimates from the National Survey on Drug Use and Health and Other Surveys,* HHS Publication No. SMA 12–4727, Methodology Series M-9. Rockville, MD, 2012.

———. *Results from the 2013 National Survey on Drug Use and Health: Summary of National Findings,* NSDUH Series H-48, HHS Publication No. SMA 14–4863. Rockville, MD: Substance Abuse and Mental Health Services Administration, 2014.

Taylor, Avril. *Women Drug Users: An Ethnography of a Female Injecting Community.* Oxford: Oxford University Press, 1993.

Tewksbury, D. "Scientology and the State: Narconon's Influence in the Prison System." Masters in Journalism thesis, University of Southern California, 2008.

Tiger, Rebecca. *Judging Addicts: Drug Courts and Coercion in the Justice System.* New York: NYU Press, 2012.

Tsemberis, Sam. "From Streets to Homes: An Innovative Approach to Supported Housing for Homeless Adults with Psychiatric Disabilities." *Journal of Community Psychology* 27, no. 2 (1999): 225–41.

———, Leyla Gulcur, and Maria Nakae. "Housing First, Consumer Choice, and Harm Reduction for Homeless Individuals with a Dual Diagnosis." *American Journal of Public Health* 94, no. 4 (2004): 651–56.

———, Gregory McHugo, Valerie Williams, Patricia Hanrahan, and Ana Stefancic. "Measuring Homelessness and Residential Stability: The Residential Time-Line Follow-Back Inventory." *Journal of Community Psychology* 35, no. 1 (2007): 29–42.

Unick, George Jay, Daniel Rosenblum, Sarah Mars, and Daniel Ciccarone. "Intertwined Epidemics: National Demographic Trends in Hospitalizations for Heroin-and Opioid-Related Overdoses, 1993–2009." *PLoS One* 8, no. 2 (2013): e54496.

United Nations Global Commission on Drug Policy. "Report of the Global Commission on Drug Policy." 2011. Retrieved from www.globalcommissionondrugs.org/wp-content/themes/gcdp_v1/pdf/Global_Commission_Report_English.pdf

United Nations Office on Drugs and Crime. *World Drug Report 2016* (United Nations Publication, Sales No. E.16.XI.7). Retrieved from www.unodc.org/doc/wdr2016/WORLD_DRUG_REPORT_2016_web.pdf

United States Social Security Administration. Publication No. 05-10072: "How You Earn Credits." January 2014. Retrieved from www.ssa.gov/pubs/EN-05-10072.pdf

———. Publication No. 05-10029: "Disability Benefits." Retrieved from www.socialsecurity.gov/pubs/EN-05-10029.pdf

———. "2014 Annual Report of the Board of Trustees of the Federal Old-Age and Survivors Insurance and Disability Insurance Trust Funds." Retrieved from www.ssa.gov/oact/tr/2014/tr2014.pdf

———. "Social Security: What Prisoners Need to Know." Retrieved from www.ssa.gov/pubs/10133.html

———, Office of the Chief Actuary. "Old-Age, Survivors, and Disability Insurance Trust Funds, 1957–2013." Retrieved from www.ssa.gov/oact/STATS/table4a3.html

Volkow, Nora D., and A. Thomas McLellan. "Opioid Abuse in Chronic Pain: Misconceptions and Mitigation Strategies." *New England Journal of Medicine* 374, no. 13 (2016): 1253–63.

Volkow, Nora D., George F. Koob, and A. Thomas McLellan. "Neurobiologic Advances from the Brain Disease Model of Addiction." *New England Journal of Medicine* 374, no. 4 (2016): 363–71.

Wacquant, Loïc. "Negative Social Capital: State Breakdown and Social Destitution in America's Urban Core." *Netherlands Journal of Housing and the Built Environment* 13, no. 1 (1998): 25–40.

———. "The New 'Peculiar Institution': On the Prison as Surrogate Ghetto." *Theoretical Criminology* 4, no. 3 (2000): 377–89.

———. "Deadly Symbiosis When Ghetto and Prison Meet and Mesh." *Punishment & Society* 3, no. 1 (2001): 95–133.

———. "Four Strategies to Curb Carceral Costs: On Managing Mass Imprisonment in the United States." *Studies in Political Economy* 69, no. 1 (2002): 19–30.

———. "Race as Civic Felony." *International Social Science Journal* 57, no. 183 (2005): 127–42.

———. *Punishing the Poor: The Neoliberal Government of Social Insecurity.* Durham, NC: Duke University Press, 2009.

Waldorf, Dan, and Patrick Biernacki. "Natural Recovery from Heroin Addiction: A Review of the Incidence Literature." *Journal of Drug Issues* 9, no. 2 (1979): 281–89.

Walmsley, Roy. "World Prison Population List." London: Institute for Criminal Policy Research, 2015.

Watters, John K., and Patrick Biernacki. "Targeted Sampling: Options for the Study of Hidden Populations." *Social Problems* 36, no. 4 (1989): 416–30.

Weil, Andrew. *The Natural Mind: An Investigation of Drugs and the Higher Consciousness.* Boston: Houghton Mifflin Harcourt, 1998

Weinberg, Darin. "'Out There': The Ecology of Addiction in Drug Abuse Treatment Discourse." *Social Problems* 47, no. 4 (2000): 606–21.

———. "Post-Humanism, Addiction and the Loss of Self-Control: Reflections on the Missing Core in Addiction Science." *International Journal of Drug Policy* 24, no. 3 (2013): 173–81.

West, Melissa O., and Ronald J. Prinz. "Parental Alcoholism and Childhood Psychopathology." *Psychological Bulletin* 102, no. 2 (1987): 204–18.

Western, Bruce. *Punishment and Inequality in America.* New York: Russell Sage Foundation, 2006.

Wexler, Harry K., Gregory P. Falkinand, and Douglas S. Lipton. "Outcome Evaluation of a Prison Therapeutic Community for Substance Abuse Treatment." *Criminal Justice and Behavior* 17, no. 1 (1990): 71–92.

White, William L. "Addiction Recovery: Its Definition and Conceptual Boundaries." *Journal of Substance Abuse Treatment* 33, no. 3 (2007): 229–41.

Williams, Miriam. *Heaven's Harlots: My Fifteen Years as a Sacred Prostitute in the Children of God Cult.* New York: William Morrow 1998.

Wilkinson, Richard G., and Michael Gideon Marmot. *Social Determinants of Health: The Solid Facts.* World Health Organization, 2003.

Wilson, William Julius. *When Work Disappears: The World of the New Urban Poor.* New York: Alfred A. Knopf, 1996.

Winick, Charles. "Maturing Out of Narcotic Addiction." *Bulletin on Narcotics* 14, no. 1 (1962): 1–7.

Wise, Roy A. "Addiction Becomes a Brain Disease." *Neuron* 26, no. 1 (2000): 27–33.

Woodall, Denise, and Miriam Boeri. "'When You Got Friends in Low Places, You Stay Low': Social Networks and Access to Resources for Female Methamphetamine Users in Low-Income Suburban Communities." *Journal of Drug Issues* 44, no. 3 (2013): 321–39.

Woodward, Comer Vann. *The Strange Career of Jim Crow*. New York: Oxford University Press, 1955.

Wuthnow, Robert. "Religious Involvement and Status-Bridging Social Capital." *Journal for the Scientific Study of Religion* 41, no. 4 (2002): 669–84.

Zaccone, June. *Has Globalization Destroyed the American Middle Class*. Lynbrook, NY: National Jobs for All Coalition, 2012.

Zinberg, Norman E. *Drug, Set, and Setting: The Basis for Controlled Intoxicant Use*. New Haven, CT: Yale University Press, 1986.

Zschau, Toralf, Codey Collins, Hosuk Lee, and Daniel L. Hatch. "The Hidden Challenge: Limited Recovery Capital of Drug Court Participants' Support Networks." *Journal of Applied Social Science* 10, no. 1 (2016): 22–43.

INDEX

abstinence: abstinence-only treatment models, 9, 16; abstinence philosophy, 43; addiction vs. unease of, 88; community-based initiatives and, 164, 180; controlled drug use vs., 176–77; intermittent abstinence, 54; shifting view of, 174; social capital and, 70; stable housing as precursor for, 181; 12-step programs and, 57, 71

addiction: community-based initiatives, 64, 180–81; definitions, 151–53; *DSM* for diagnosing, 152. *See also* treatment programs

adolescents: baby boomer drug use data, 16, 20–21; drug policies impact on, 8, 20; historical influences on, 25, 41, 148–49; incarceration and, 30, 71; risk factors for substance abuse, 45; social environments influence on, 29, 45, 58, 68; turning point examples, 78, 79

African Americans: colorblindness's impact on, 223n2; Jehovah's Witnesses and, 32–33; ODUS data, 196; War on Drugs and, 224n21. *See also* Blacks

aging, 8, 135–53; employment challenges, 138–46; financial concerns, 142–43, 147, 149; gender-related impact of, 140; "Graying of the AIDS Epidemic" phenomenon, 138; living conditions, housing issues and, 139, 140, 142; of prison populations, 138; reentry work-training programs, 143; Social Security programs

issues, 139, 144–46. *See also* health challenges of aging drug users

alcohol: abstaining from, 22, 44, 57; drugs vs., 1, 35; Eighteenth Amendment and, 19; Twenty-first Amendment and, 20. *See also* alcoholism

Alcoholics Anonymous (AA), 132, 150, 164

alcoholism: functional alcoholism, 50, 146; Housing First recovery model, 126, 181, 187–88, 234n57; loss of children due to, 132; marriage, divorce, and, 75; of parents, 16, 18, 35, 39, 40, 45, 50, 53, 61, 71, 75, 94; Social Recovery Model, 182; "wet" home recovery model, 187. *See also* 12-step programs

Alexander, Michelle, 100–101

American Friends Service Committee, 162

American Recovery and Reinvestment Act, 195

Anslinger, Harry J., 20, 84, 156

Atlanta Harm Reduction Center (AHRC), 78, 116, 117, 119, 120, 225n2

baby boomers: criminal theory and, 19; defined, 3–4; drug users/maturing out thesis and, 3–4, 8, 137, 153, 174, 190, 209–10n13; historical context of, 3–5, 7, 19–21, 40–41, 49, 195, 207; impact of racism on, 8, 106–11; life course theory and, 40–44; social context of, 3, 4–5, 7, 49, 195, 199, 207, 212n21

Bennett, William J., 85

Black Lives Matter (BLM) movement, 100–101

Blacks: civil rights movement and, 98; cocaine/crack use, 8, 32, 103, 114; comparative drug use, 101; disproportionate arrests of, 98, 101, 144; economic disparities of, 107; Jehovah's Witnesses and, 32–33; mass incarceration in communities, 101–2; ODUS data, 196; stereotyping of, 105; War on Drugs and, 93. *See also* African Americans

buprenorphine (Suboxone), 179, 234n46

Bush, George H. W., 85

Camp Hill state penitentiary, solitary confinement program, 48

cell restriction policy, xv

childhood: "Happy Days" version of, 41; *Ozzie and Harriet* version of, 64–65; self-control development in, 44; social context of, 16–19; trauma's impact on, 60, 61

children: abandonment by parents, 60–61; consequences of teaching colorblindness to, 106; crime theory, self-control, and, 18–19; drug-addicted births of, 122; emotional support of, 60; foster care and, 164; functional drug use and raising, 22, 105; impact of War on Drugs on, 172; influence of global macro events on, 41; loss of custody of, 11, 52, 62, 93, 122, 123–24, 128, 132, 164; mothers as primary caregivers for, 127; Social Security and, 144; transitional programs for, 126; treatment as inducement for reuniting with, 165

Christianity, 74, 148

Civil Rights Act (1964), 27

civil rights movement (U.S.): colorblindness and, 97–98, 106, 223n2; failure to end discrimination, 98; King, Jr. and, 97, 98; 1954 origins, 200*t*; political, historical context, 223n1

Clinton, Bill, 27, 85, 201*t*

club drugs, 32, 206*t*

cocaine/crack use, 103, 109, 110, 136; African Americans, historical context, 32; counteracting effect on heroin, 36; Fair

Sentencing Act and, 85; Florida epidemic, 22; freebasing method of smoking, 21, 62; incarceration for possession, 118, 119; later in life use of, 79; out-of-control addiction, 147; reasons for using, 67, 78–79, 107; as rebellion, 27; social use of, 22; socioeconomics of users, 1, 67; trends in usage, 21, 66; use in jail, 56; US Sentencing Commission recommendations, 85

cold turkey withdrawal, 1, 161

colorblindness, 97–98, 106, 223n2

Combat Methamphetamine Epidemic Act (2005), 201*t*

Commissions for Dissuasions of Drug Addiction (Portugal), 175

Comprehensive Crime Control Act (1984), 161

Comprehensive Drug Abuse Prevention and Control Act (1970), 84, 220–21n18

Comprehensive Methamphetamine Control Act (2000), 201*t*

confidential informants (CIs; snitches), 2, 7–8, 46–47, 64, 86, 89–92, 128, 133, 222n52

controlled drug use: as option in reducing drug use, 176–77; uncontrolled vs., 49, 153

crime, general theory of, 18–19

criminal justice system: budget of, 157; "class advantage" and, 107; consequences of being caught in, 174; corruption in, 162; discriminatory ways of, 100–102; entrapment tactics of, 92; funding of, 156; halfway houses run by, 111; harsh actions by, 159; incorporation of treatment solutions, 162; selective harassment by judges, 104–5; tactics used by, 2–3. *See also* confidential informants; solitary confinement

data visualization images (DVIs): coding of, 207–8; description, 203–4, 207; DVI Drug Trajectory with Selected Social Variables, 204*f*; integration with life stories, 207, 236n19; legend, 205–6*t*

Davis, Angela, 156–57

Defense of Marriage Act (DOMA), 27, 201*t*

Diagnostic and Statistical Manual (DSM), 152

Dilaudid, 36, 135, 160

divorce, 80, 95, 132; alcoholism and, 75; drug use and, 7, 75, 94, 107, 111, 131, 146; 1950–late 1960s rates, 14; as turning point, 34

dopamine hypothesis (Hart), 152

drinking. *See* alcohol; alcoholism

drug courts. *See* drug treatment courts

drug czar. *See* Kerlikowske, Gil

Drug Enforcement Agency (DEA), 21, 84, 85

drug regulation history (U.S.), 19–21

drug trajectories: challenges in predicting, 43; continuousness of, 55–56; discontinuous/stop and start, 1; diversity of, 83, 177; drug popularity and, 21; DVIs of data, 203; family influences, 76; individual circumstances in, 83, 190; influence of relationships on, 8, 59–60; life course analysis and, 7, 42; mixed method research approach to, 195; ODUS assessment tool, 9, 195–208; phases vs. stages in, 48–49; self-control and, 44; social/historical context of, 3, 24; spirituality's influence on, 32; trends of baby boomers, 21; turning points in, 7, 42, 53–54

drug treatment courts: advisory role of, 170; description, 229–30n22; as incarceration alternative, 8, 77–78, 103–4, 125, 219–20n3; mixed study results on, 225n28; success of, 140, 156; 12-step programs and, 219–20n3; varied quality of, 104

drug war: adverse influences of, 83, 95–96; baby boomers and, 4; escalation of, 2; incarcerations in, 41, 78, 85, 89; negative impact on poverty, 190; policies of, 4; racial components of, 97–114. *See also* War on Drugs

DVI Drug Trajectory with Selected Social Variables, 204*f*

DVIs. *See* data visualization images

ecstasy, 206*t*

Eighteenth Amendment (Volstead Act) (1919), 19

employment: admittance to homeless shelter with, 34; aging out of work, 141–44; challenges in finding, keeping, 25–26, 46, 56, 77, 86, 138–46; gender identity, racial discrimination, and, 41–42; incarceration, families, and, 7; parole and, 113; Philadelphia work-training program, 141, 143; post-incarceration reentry work-training programs, 143; as sex worker, 27–29, 36, 39, 54, 70, 115, 116; social capital and, 70, 77; social control and, 70; Social Security, SSI, SSDI, and, 144–46; treatment programs and, 64, 110, 179; unstable social situations and, 49; War on Drugs and, 59, 102, 145–46

ethnographic research, description, 5–6, 195–97. *See also* Older Drug User Study

European Union, 176

Fair Sentencing Act, 85

families: Al-Anon 12-step program for, 61; drug use destruction of, 9, 14; globalization's impact on, 214n52; Housing First recovery model and, 126; incarceration's impact on, 86; influence on drug trajectory, 150; *Leave It to Beaver* model of, 64–65; loss of jobs impact on, 25; maturing out thesis and, 3; *Ozzie and Harriet* version of, 64–65; parental abandonment of children, 60–61; social capital and, 94; Social Security program and, 144; tough love efforts by, 61, 62, 141, 218n12; War on Drugs impact on, 4, 58, 172, 190. *See also* children; divorce

Federal Bureau of Investigation (FBI), 85

Federal Bureau of Narcotics (FBN), 20, 84

gangs, 15, 47, 80, 96, 161, 220n9

Garland, David, 14

gay persons, 27, 28, 115, 200*t*. *See also* lesbian, gay, bisexual, and transgender (LGBT) persons; same-sex relationships; sexual orientation; transgender persons

Gay Related Immunodeficiency Disorder (GRID), 28, 210*t*

gender: culture of drug use and, 127–28;
identity issues, 27; impact of aging, 140;
interaction with age, race, social class,
41, 127. *See also* men; women
Georgia Bureau of Investigations (GBI), 92
"Graying of the AIDS Epidemic" phenomenon, 138
guard-organized sexual assault, 159–60

halfway houses, 38, 39, 53, 54, 111, 142, 157,
162, 167–68, 189
hallucinogens, 22, 206t
hard drugs. *See* cocaine/crack; heroin;
methamphetamine; opioids
harm reduction programs: Atlanta Harm
Reduction Center, xi, 78, 116, 117, 119,
120, 225n2; controlled drug use strategy,
43–44; description, 178–80; HIV,
hepatitis C, and, 137–38; medical marijuana (cannabis) use, 44, 179–80;
methadone programs, 179; origins of,
178; supervised injection facilities
(SIFs), 179; syringe exchange programs
(SEPs), 64, 117, 178. *See also* methadone
programs
Harrison Act (1914), 19
Hart, Carl, 152
health challenges of aging drug users:
hepatitis C, 28–29, 37, 56, 137–39,
196–97; incarceration-related expenses,
138; Medicaid insurance eligibility, 145;
mental health, 13, 21, 25, 127, 173; public
health programs, 53; SSI disability
programs, 136, 139, 147. *See also* HIV/
AIDS
hepatitis C: in aging drug-using population, 138; community-based sample
data, 196–97; needle-sharing and, 37,
137–38
heroin (heroin use): as 1990s crack replacement, 21; African Americans and, 32;
cannabis as aid for stopping, 180; controlled use of, 147; cultural influences,
14; diverse background of users, 1; DVI
data, 206f, 207; hepatitis C and, 37;
impact on families, 11; later in life use
of, 79; maturing out thesis and, 209–
10n13; methadone programs for, 20, 57,

93, 95, 110–11, 147–48, 179; opioid use as
stepping stone, 220n6; overcoming
addiction to, 153; Schedule I classification, 21; social context for using, 93;
socioeconomics of users, 1; spread of use
in the U.S., 21; stopping cold turkey, 1,
150; treatment programs, 13; use of
cannabis discontinuation study, 180;
Vietnam War and, 21; withdrawal in
jail, 20, 56, 152
High Intensity Drug Trafficking Areas
(HIDTA) program, 155
hippie era (1960s), 40, 45, 46, 212n11
Hispanics/Latinos: comparative drug rates,
101; crack use, 32, 114; disproportionate
arrests of, 144; economic disparities of,
107; ODUS data, 196; War on Drugs
and, 93
historical context of baby boomers, 11–33;
drug trajectories, 3, 49, 195; influence on
social context, 24; life course theory
and, 7, 40–44; ODUS data, 199, 207–8.
See also social context of baby boomers
HIV/AIDS: in aging drug-using population, 138; community-based sample
data, 196–97; DEMOGRAPHIC 30
DAY survey data, 198–99; SEPs success
in reducing, 178; SIFs success in reducing, 179; syringe sharing and, 137–38
homelessness, 5–6, 75, 99–100, 139, 157,
234n57
homosexuality, 27, 28, 115, 200t. *See also*
lesbian, gay, bisexual, and transgender
(LGBT) persons; sexual orientation
Horn, Martin, xv
hospital detox programs, 38
Housing First recovery model, 126, 181,
187–88, 234n57

incarceration: addiction treatment vs., 8–9,
43, 78, 95, 120, 125; adolescents and, 30,
71; aging of prison population, 8, 138;
confidential informants in, 2, 7–8,
46–47, 64, 86, 89–92; corruption levels,
157, 158; drug treatment courts alternative, 8, 77–78, 103–4, 125, 219–20n3;
drug use in prisons, 161–62; global rates,
86; guard-organized sexual assault,